Fisher Investments
on Energy

FISHER INVESTMENTS PRESS

Fisher Investments Press brings the research, analysis, and market intelligence of Fisher Investments' research team, headed by CEO and *New York Times* best-selling author Ken Fisher, to all investors. The Press will cover a range of investing and market-related topics for a wide audience—from novices to enthusiasts to professionals.

Books by Ken Fisher
The Ten Roads to Riches
The Only Three Questions That Count
100 Minds That Made the Market
The Wall Street Waltz
Super Stocks

Fisher Investments Series
Own the World
Aaron Anderson

Fisher Investments On Series
Fisher Investments on Energy
Fisher Investments on Materials

FISHER
INVESTMENTS
PRESS

Fisher Investments on Energy

Fisher Investments
with
Aaron M. Azelton and
Andrew S. Teufel

WILEY

John Wiley & Sons, Inc.

Library of Congress Cataloging-in-Publication Data:

Azelton, Aaron M.
    Fisher investments on energy/with Aaron M. Azelton, Andrew S. Teufel.
      p. cm.
    Includes bibliographical references and index.
    ISBN 978-0-470-28543-5 (pbk.)
      1. Energy industries.   2. Investments.   I. Teufel, Andrew S.   II. Title.
  HD9502.A2A98   2009
  332.67'22—dc22

                                                 2008032180

Printed in the United States of America

10 9 8 7 6 5 4 3 2 1

Contents

Foreword

I'm delighted to introduce the first in a series of investing guides from Fisher Investments Press—the first imprint ever from a money management firm. My firm has a heavy focus on client education, and I hope to bring investing education to a much broader audience with this series.

This particular guide focuses on Energy, one of ten investing sectors. And we'll cover them all—encompassing the entire universe of stocks! We'll also tackle regions and other categories of stocks vital to better understanding how global capital markets work.

This isn't a shortcut to finding hot stocks that only go up. Such a thing doesn't exist. Claims otherwise are fiction. Instead, this focuses on providing the basics of the Energy sector any investor—from the hobbyist to the new professional—should know. It also describes the global Energy landscape and discusses issues unique to Energy stocks: Should you focus on alternative energy? Is peak oil a real concern? What about geopolitics? Most important, it provides an analysis framework that works for this and any sector (or region or other class of securities).

In fact, the methodology and framework presented here are the same we use at my firm as part of our process to make investing decisions. This framework isn't a magic formula telling you which stocks we think are best this or any year. No matter what someone tries to sell you, investing analysis isn't about following a craft or obeying a set of rules. That won't work. Can't work! Investing success is about knowing what others don't. To do that, you need a scientific method—a query method for discovering what you can know that others can't. That's what we give you here—a method and tools to use to help increase your investing success for the entirety of your investing lifetime.

Enjoy!

Ken Fisher
CEO of Fisher Investments
Author of *New York Times* best seller, *The Only Three Questions That Count*

Preface

The *Fisher Investments On* series is designed to provide individual investors, students, and aspiring investment professionals the tools necessary to understand and analyze investment opportunities, primarily for investing in global stocks.

Within the framework of a *top-down* investment method (more on that in Chapter 7), each guide is an easily accessible primer to economic sectors, regions, or other components of the global stock market. While this guide is specifically on Energy, the basic investment methodology is applicable for analyzing any global sector, regardless of the current macroeconomic environment.

Why a top-down method? Vast evidence shows high-level, or *macro*, investment decisions are ultimately more important portfolio performance drivers than individual stocks. In other words, before picking stocks, investors can benefit greatly by first deciding if stocks are the best investment relative to other assets (like bonds or cash), and then choosing categories of stocks most likely to perform best on a forward-looking basis.

For example, a Technology sector stock picker in 1998 and 1999 probably saw his picks soar as investors cheered the so-called "New Economy." However, from 2000 to 2002, he probably lost his shirt. Was he just smarter in 1998 and 1999? Did his analysis turn bad somehow? Unlikely. What mattered most was stocks in general (and especially US technology stocks) did great in the late 1990s and poorly entering the new century. In other words, a top-down perspective on the broader economy was key to navigating markets—stock picking just wasn't as important.

Fisher Investments on Energy will help guide you in making top-down investment decisions specifically for the Energy sector. It shows how to determine better times to invest in Energy, what Energy sub-industries are likelier to do best, and how individual stocks can benefit in various environments. The global Energy sector is complex, covering multiple sub-industries and countries, each with unique characteristics. Using our framework, you should be better-equipped to identify their differences, spot opportunities, and avoid major pitfalls.

This book takes a global approach to Energy investing. Most US investors typically invest the majority of their assets in domestic securities; they forget America is less than half of the world market by weight—over 50 percent of investment opportunities are outside our borders. This is especially true in Energy. Many of the world's largest Energy firms are domiciled in foreign nations, including several in emerging markets. Since the vast majority of the world's oil reserves are in the hands of state-owned national oil companies, it's vital to have a global perspective when investing in Energy today.

USING YOUR ENERGY GUIDE

This guide is arranged into three sections. The first, "Getting Started in Energy," discusses vital sector basics and Energy's high-level drivers. Here we'll discuss Energy's main drivers—oil and natural gas prices—and all the supply and demand components for each. We'll also discuss additional drivers affecting the sector that ultimately drive Energy stock prices.

The second section, "Next Steps: Energy Details," walks through the next step of sector analysis. We'll take you through the global Energy sector investment universe and its diverse components. With so much focus on higher gas prices in recent years, it's easy to forget Energy isn't just about oil wells and gas pumps—though that's certainly a major component. There are currently seven sub-industries within the global Energy sector. We take you through each in detail, including how they operate within the sector and what drives each sub-industry specifically, so you can analyze the current operating environment to choose which sub-industry will most likely underperform or outperform looking forward.

The section also details where to find and how to interpret publicly available industry data to assist in your decision-making process. It's possible to get the necessary data for making educated bets on oil and natural gas prices, sub-industries, and individual stocks using just a few helpful websites and publications. You'll learn how to critically look at a sector: What to look for, what resources you can use, what the challenges are. And though it's not a part of the Energy sector, we also cover alternative energy and its composition and drivers.

The final section, "Thinking Like a Portfolio Manager," delves into a top-down investment methodology and individual security analysis. You'll learn to ask important questions like: What are the most important elements to consider when analyzing oil and gas firms? What are the greatest risks and red flags? This book gives you a five-step process to help differentiate firms so you can identify ones with the greater probability of outperforming. We'll also discuss a few investment strategies to help determine when and how to overweight specific sub-industries within the sector.

Note: We've specifically kept the strategies presented here high level so you can return to the book for guidance no matter the market conditions. But we also can't possibly address every market scenario and how markets may change over time. And many additional considerations should be taken into account when crafting a portfolio strategy, including your own investing goals, your time horizon, and other factors unique to you. Therefore, you shouldn't rely solely on the strategies and pointers addressed here since they won't always apply. Rather, this book is intended to provide general guidance and help you begin thinking critically not only the about the Energy sector, but investing in general.

Further, *Fisher Investments on Energy* won't give you a "silver bullet" for picking the right energy stocks. The fact is the "right" energy stocks will be different in different times and situations. Instead, this guide provides a framework for understanding the sector and its industries so that you can be dynamic and find information the market hasn't yet priced in. There won't be any stock recommendations, target prices, or even a suggestion whether now is a good time to be invested in the Energy sector. The goal is to provide you with tools to make these decisions for yourself, now and in the future. Ultimately, our aim is to give you the framework for repeated, successful investing. Enjoy.

Acknowledgments

No book is ever the product of just one or two people. A number of colleagues, friends, and business partners contributed to this book. First and foremost, we extend our sincere gratitude to Ken Fisher for giving us the opportunity to write this book. We suspect Ken knew this all along: Not only is writing a book a great professional opportunity, but it's tremendous fun as well.

Beginning with our Fisher Investments colleagues, we would like to thank the entire Fisher Investments Research staff. In particular, Joseph Hall deserves ample credit for creating virtually every graph and table in this book, with additional help from Jennifer Chou. Tom Holmes particularly assisted Aaron Azelton in helping carry out his full-time research responsibilities while he was working on this book. Outside of our most excellent Research colleagues, we'd like to thank Michael Hanson and Lara Hoffmans, whose editing contributions were instrumental in this book's completion. We would also like to thank Dina Ezzat and Evelyn Chea for their editing contributions, and Leila Amiri for her guidance on layout, graphics, and images. Marc Haberman, Molly Lienesch, and Fabrizio Ornani were also instrumental in making not only this, but the entire Fisher Investments Press imprint, a reality. And this book would be very short and not very helpful to you at all without our data vendors, so we owe a big debt of gratitude to Thomson Datastream, Thomson Reuters, and Global Financial Data in particular for their permissions. Finally, we'd like to thank our team at Wiley, who provided endless encouragement and support throughout this project, most notably David Pugh and Kelly O'Connor.

1

GETTING STARTED
IN ENERGY

1

ENERGY BASICS

Switch on a light. Heat your home. Drive to work. Power on your computer. Unless you live your entire life in a handcrafted tent in the wilderness, you can't escape using some Energy sector by-product. Just living your everyday life benefits the firms who explore, find, extract, refine, and deliver energy in all its forms to homes and businesses. And naturally, you also benefit from consuming energy on demand. So how can your portfolio benefit too?

In the first part of this book, we hope to provide all the basics necessary to understand how the Energy sector operates, what types of firms make up the sector, and the driving forces behind the sector—oil and natural gas prices. Successfully investing in Energy companies does not require a PhD in geology. What is important is a firm grasp of the laws of supply and demand, and understanding what drives the earnings and stock prices of Energy companies.

This chapter covers the basics of the Energy sector, including a primer on how oil and natural gas are found and extracted, some basic definitions, and some commonly used (but esoteric nonetheless!) terms. Don't worry if some things appear murky to start. On its face, Energy seems like a highly intricate and complex sector. And make no mistake: It can be! But the basics are really quite simple. It comes down to exploring for and extracting raw energy materials from the earth, transporting them around the world, refining them into usable petroleum or other products, and selling them for mass consumption. Some companies do just one or two of those things, while others do them all.

OIL & GAS INDUSTRY

The easiest way to think about the Energy sector is by breaking it into its two main industries: Oil, Gas & Consumable Fuels and Energy Equipment & Services. The former is what most people think of as Energy—the Exxons, Chevrons, and other megasize firms that explore for and produce oil and natural gas. The Equipment & Services industry assists the Oil & Gas industry with this process. Let's start with the Oil & Gas industry and its main function—the *integrated process*.

The Integrated Process

Companies engaging in the exploration, production, delivery, refining, and marketing of petroleum products to consumers are all part of the integrated process. Its three main segments are *upstream, midstream*, and *downstream*:

- **Upstream**: exploration—searching for hydrocarbons like oil and natural gas; and production—actually taking the resources out of the ground and selling them. Companies like Devon Energy, Anadarko Petroleum, and Apache search the globe for oil and gas reserves.
- **Midstream**: processing, storage, and transportation of hydrocarbons. This includes transporting raw energy materials around the globe via ships, pipes, and other methods. Companies like TransCanada, Williams Companies, and Enbridge own large networks of pipelines that ship a variety of petroleum products.

- **Downstream**: refining oil and natural gas into usable petroleum products for sale to consumers. Companies like Valero
  Energy, Sunoco, and Tesoro refine crude oil into gasoline and
  jet fuel.

Well-known giants like Exxon Mobil and Chevron, engaged in all
three segments of the energy business, are known as *Integrated Oil &
Gas* firms. However, for most integrated oil firms, the upstream part
of the business dominates the company's focus and resources because
it's typically the most profitable.

And though the *upstream* segment is where the vast majority of
profits are made in the Energy sector, with big profits come bigger
risks. Therefore, pure upstream firms (also known as *exploration and
production*, or E&P) are among the most risk loving in the biz. They
spend billions each year on risky explorations and speculative drilling, hoping to find new, big reservoirs of underground energy. More
often than not, they come up empty-handed—an undeniable boom-
or-bust mentality. E&Ps do business the world over, negotiating
with unpredictable (and sometimes unstable) foreign governments.
But the risks are worth it—it can mean big revenues for years to
come if an E&P firm discovers and develops a huge new petroleum
deposit.

The *midstream* segment concentrates on transporting and storing oil, natural gas, and petroleum products. Midstream firms seem
boring but are a very necessary part of the integrated process. These
firms spend their time moving raw energy materials to the regions of
the world where they're needed. This is most often done via pipelines
or ships.

The *downstream* segment (also known as *refining and marketing*, or R&M) focuses on the final stage of the integrated process.
Refining is the process of converting crude oil into usable petroleum
products—such as gasoline and diesel—while *marketing* is selling
the products to the consumer. Companies operating exclusively in the
downstream segment are called *independent refiners*. While most of
the major Integrated Oil & Gas firms have branded retail gasoline

stations (e.g., Shell, Exxon, Chevron), downstream operations are often the least profitable part of the business. As we'll explain later, the profit margins for refining and selling petroleum products are usually much, much slimmer than the profit margins for the exploration and production of oil and natural gas.

Together, the upstream, midstream, and downstream segments make up the majority of the Oil & Gas industry, so it's worth exploring each in a bit more detail.

Upstream Basics

An oil rig pumps oil from the Montana ground.
Source: © Getty Images, Inc.

Upstream activities—or E&P—can be the most profitable, but are the most risky and capital-intensive part of the Energy sector. Huge investments can be lost entirely. Conversely, large discoveries of oil deposits can generate revenues for decades to come. Let's review some upstream basics.

Geology, History, and a Bit of Etymology   The word *petroleum* is derived from the Latin *petra* (rock) and *oleum* (oil). It's generally believed oil and natural gas formed from plants and animals that died millions of years ago. These remains were driven deep into the earth over time by layers of silt and sand. This process generated an enormous amount of heat and pressure, converting the organic matter (mainly carbon and hydrogen atoms) into hydrocarbons (oil and natural gas).

Oil is found in sedimentary rock, trapped between layers of nonporous rock. Oil and natural gas deposits are found in a variety of locations around the world—from the flattest, driest deserts to the roughest, coldest mountain terrain to the deepest oceans. In nearly all cases—whether land or sea—it's necessary to drill wells through hundreds or thousands of feet of sand and silt rock.

If a reservoir is found through traditional oil and gas drilling methods, it's considered a *conventional* source. Conventional oil is the least costly to obtain and requires the least effort. Currently, the world is estimated to contain 1.3 trillion barrels of conventional oil reserves and 6,182 trillion cubic feet of natural gas.[1] However, as will be covered more in Chapter 4, this is subject to interpretation.

The first commercial oil wells were drilled in North America in the mid-1800s.[2] The US was considered to have one of the world's largest oil reserves at the time and even exported oil to foreign lands.[3] As recently as the mid-1900s, conventional sources of oil and gas were found in abundance and required relatively little effort and cost to extract.

The main difference between *unconventional* and conventional reserves is the way oil and gas are extracted. Examples of unconventional hydrocarbons include oil shale, oil sands, tight gas, and coal bed methane. While conventional reserves are trapped *between* layers of rock and can be extracted using ground pressure, unconventional reserves like oil sands and shale are trapped *within* rock and sand and are extracted through a mining process requiring enormous amounts of heat and pressure.

Nowadays, many believe the largest, most easily accessible conventional oil and gas deposits in the world are already tapped. As a result, companies must search for oil and gas in increasingly harsh environments like deep offshore or rugged, remote terrains. The advancement of technology has enabled firms to tap into increasingly remote areas and at greater depths. Moreover, technology and high oil and gas prices may also make it economically viable to tap unconventional hydrocarbons, which were previously too expensive to recover profitably.

Despite the difficult extraction process, unconventional reserves are tremendous: Canadian tar sands are estimated to contain 173 billion barrels of oil,[4] making Canada the second-largest holder of oil reserves behind Saudi Arabia. The oil shale in North America is estimated to contain over 2.6 trillion barrels of oil.[5]

Although tremendous reserves exist within unconventional sources, it remains extremely costly and technically difficult to get them. And while current high oil prices have made unconventional sources more economically viable to extract, it will still be years before they contribute meaningfully to world production. (This issue will be further explored in Chapter 4.)

Extracting Oil and Gas in Six Steps   Extracting oil and gas from the ground doesn't happen overnight. Before oil and gas production begins, there are a number of required steps in the upstream process:

1. Acquire the rights to explore for and develop oil and gas from the reserve holder. (A reserve holder is typically the owner[s] of the land a company wants to drill on.)
2. Conduct geological, geophysical, and seismic surveys to find oil and gas deposits.
3. Perform exploration drilling to test for deposits.
4. Conduct appraisal and development drilling to determine if the field contains commercially viable deposits.
5. Begin oil and gas production (or abandon the well if no commercial deposits are found).
6. Ensure payment to compensate reserve holders via royalties and/or *production sharing agreements* (PSAs).

As with most things in life, the lawyers and regulators need their say before anything can happen. A company must first acquire rights to explore for and develop oil and gas reserves from the reserve holder before it can do anything else. This is usually accomplished through the execution of a lease with the landowner.

Leases may differ in terms of duration, royalty payments, and drilling commitments. In some cases, landowners are private individuals, like a farmer with many acres of land. But often, leases are acquired from governments through auctions. For example, the US regularly holds auctions for leases in the Gulf of Mexico—an area known to have tremendous reserves of oil and gas. The highest bidder gets the right to drill.

To find conventional and unconventional oil and gas deposits, geologists use data surveys like seismic imaging and gravitational and magnetic surveys. Seismic imaging technology uses sound waves that bounce off underground rock structures and reveal possible oil and gas formations. The waves locate structural traps where faults or folds in the underground rock have created zones where oil could be trapped. Keep in mind these tests calculate the *probability* of deposits only. An exploratory well is drilled to confirm.

Once a well is confirmed to contain deposits, additional appraisal and development wells are drilled to determine its commercial viability since not all oil and gas deposits will prove to have large enough reserves or sufficient pressure for effective extraction. If a company's analysis shows the deposit does not contain sufficient reserves and pressure, it will abandon the well and try again somewhere else. But if the analysis shows an adequate amount of reserves, the company will install production equipment and start extracting resources. At this point, the focus shifts to reservoir management to assure maximum production over the reservoir's life.

Once production begins, the company typically compensates reserve holders with a share of the revenues. Depending on the region the resources are extracted, this is done via royalties or PSAs.

Royalties and Production Sharing Agreements

Royalties are payments usually calculated as a percentage of revenue from the oil and gas produced on the property. Royalty agreements vary widely depending on the country and whether the property is privately or publicly owned, but they can range between 10 to 50 percent of revenues. Oil and gas royalties are a substantial revenue source for many host governments. For the US, royalty revenues as a percentage of the economy are small (only generating about $10 billion in 2006),[*] but resource-rich regions like Alberta, Canada, rely on oil and gas royalties for a significant portion of government income.

Production sharing agreements (PSAs) determine the share a private oil and gas company will receive of natural resources extracted from a particular country. An example of a PSA is one requiring a firm to share a portion of net profits after its startup costs have been recouped, but the physical oil and natural gas reserves remain the property of the host government. Others may require joint ventures between the company and the host government's national oil company. Often, the private firm will bear most or all of the risk and cost of exploration and development. This is why it's common for firms to form joint ventures when conducting E&P activities in other countries—it's a way to share the risk and high costs of exploration.

---

[*]Minerals Management Service, Minerals Revenue Management, "All Reported Royalty Revenues" (Fiscal Year 2006), (accessed April 9, 2008).

Midstream Basics

Once production begins, companies must somehow transport oil and gas from the field to refineries that process crude oil into petroleum products. This is where the midstream segment comes into play.

The midstream process involves storage and transportation of hydrocarbons. It's essentially the "middle man" between producers and end users. Midstream assets include pipelines and crude tankers delivering oil, natural gas, and petroleum products from their origins to refiners. They also include storage terminals, where natural gas and oil are held until they're ready to be consumed or transported.

The Trans-Alaskan pipeline.
Source: © Getty Images, Inc.

Transportation methods vary depending on hydrocarbon type. Crude oil and most other petroleum products are easily shipped through tankers, pipelines, rail, trucks, or even airplanes. Natural gas poses some transportation problems and is mainly shipped through pipelines. In order to transport it via ships, natural gas must be cooled into a liquid form called *liquefied natural gas* (LNG) and requires special terminals and ships.

Mainstream investors don't typically hear much about this part of the business because it's a relatively small component of the overall Energy sector. While many Integrated Oil & Gas firms own their own midstream assets, there are also many other companies that focus specifically on this part of the business.

Downstream Basics

An oil refinery in operation.
Source: © Getty Images, Inc.

The downstream process includes refining and processing crude oil into petroleum products and managing the retail sale of those products. Crude oil by itself has few direct uses and must be refined to be usable. Refining is the process of breaking crude oil down into its various components, which are then selectively reconfigured into new products like gasoline, diesel, heating oil, propane, and jet fuel. While the majority of petroleum products are for transportation use (cars, airplanes, etc.), other petroleum products are used for industrial activities and everyday items like ink, tires, and even deodorant.

Refineries produce petroleum products based on location and demand. For instance, in California and Texas—two states with high auto usage—refineries mostly make gasoline and diesel. In Hawaii, a chain of islands with a tourism-driven economy, the majority of refineries produce jet fuel. In some developing nations, refineries may produce mainly chemicals for use in industrial activities.

Refineries also vary in the degree of complexity and types of crude they can process and are typically built to process the crude most

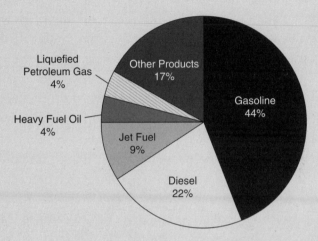

What's in a Barrel?

Oil doesn't just fuel your car. Though 75 percent of a typical barrel of oil in the US is used for gasoline, diesel, and jet fuel, oil is refined into many different products.

Figure 1.1   Products Made from a Barrel of Crude Oil
Source: Energy Information Administration.

readily available in the region. But since many countries are increasingly reliant on crude oil imports from foreign locations to meet demand, it's becoming vital for refineries to be versatile and process various types of crude.

Differences in Crude Oil   Not all crude oil is created equal, and one barrel of crude can differ vastly from another. The differences determine how easily it can be refined. Differences in crude oil are based on density and sulfur content. Common terms used to describe oil include *light, heavy, sour,* and *sweet.*

- **Light versus heavy crude** refers to the density, or weight per volume, of oil, measured as American Petroleum Institute gravity (API gravity), expressed in degrees. The higher the API gravity, the greater the density. For example, the industry defines *light* *crude* as having an API gravity higher than 38 degrees, while *heavy crude* has an API gravity below 22 degrees—medium oil is in between.[6] Light crude is more valuable than heavy because it's less expensive to refine and has higher energy content.

- **Sweet versus sour crude** refers to the sulfur content of oil. *Sweet crude* contains relatively little sulfur, while *sour crude* has substantial sulfur. Sweet crude is more valuable than sour because it's easier and less costly to refine.

Combining the two gives us the common descriptions of a barrel of oil: *light sweet* and *heavy sour*. An example of light sweet crude is the popular benchmark West Texas Intermediate (WTI) crude. By contrast, Arab Heavy oil from Saudi Arabia is heavy sour crude.

Marketing & Distribution   *Marketing and distribution* refers to the selling of petroleum products to end users (i.e., consumers). The most common and recognizable examples are the thousands of retail gasoline stations across the US and the world selling gasoline and diesel fuel for cars. Many of these stations are independently owned and operated, oftentimes licensing the names of the major oil companies. Others are owned directly by the integrated oil companies or independent refiners.

Gas stations operate by purchasing gasoline from refineries and selling it at a markup to consumers. The retail price of gasoline reflects the entire integrated process: the refiners' cost of crude oil, refinery processing costs, marketing and distribution costs, and finally, the retail station's costs and taxes.

ENERGY EQUIPMENT & SERVICES INDUSTRY

We've covered the basics of the three major segments of the integrated process—the Oil & Gas side of the Energy sector. But Energy has another big component, so let's turn our attention to the firms that assist in getting oil out of the ground.

Energy Equipment & Services firms assist oil and gas firms with exploring, drilling, and producing reserves, but they generally don't

What Makes Up the Price of a US Gallon of Gas?

Ever wonder where your money goes when you fill up your gas tank? With gasoline prices rising steadily in recent years, all those gas station owners must be raking in huge profits, right? Wrong. Most people don't realize gas stations usually make more profit selling chips and sodas than gas to road trippers.

Figure 1.2 breaks down the price of an average gallon of gas in the US. For every dollar of gasoline sold, 71 cents covers crude oil costs, 13 cents goes to taxes, 8 cents covers refining costs, and the remaining 8 cents goes to distribution and marketing (i.e., the gas station). Suddenly, selling gas doesn't appear so profitable.

Think you have it bad? In Europe, taxes generally make up over 50 percent of gasoline costs. This is why Europeans pay so much more for gas than Americans—oftentimes, more than twice as much! Such high taxes leave little petty cash for cupcakes and candy at the mini-mart. What a shame.

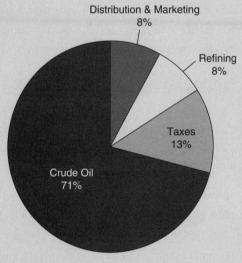

Figure 1.2   What We Pay For in a Gallon of Regular Gasoline

Source: Energy Information Administration.

own oil and gas deposits directly. These firms are hired by pure upstream oil and gas producers and integrated firms like Exxon Mobil to assist in getting hydrocarbons out of the ground. There are two main types: Oil & Gas Drilling and Energy Equipment & Services.

Oil & Gas Drilling

Drilling firms, like Transocean, Diamond Offshore Drilling, and Noble Corp., own the rigs used to explore for and produce hydrocarbon deposits. They rent their rigs to other firms, typically under a short- or long-term contract—usually charging by the day.

Why do upstream firms rent rigs? Due to the cyclical nature of the industry, owning rigs is great during up cycles—but they become extremely expensive pieces of equipment to sit idle during down cycles. Therefore, many producers find it more cost effective to contract drilling companies than to own rigs outright.

There are many different types of rigs, ranging from small service rigs mounted on trucks to enormous rigs installed on ships or offshore platforms. Rigs are mainly classified as either land or offshore rigs. (Drilling rigs are one of the most fascinating parts of the Energy sector and discussed further in Chapter 3.) As a general rule of thumb, the bigger the rig, the deeper it can drill. Rigs can also differ by:

- The commodity it drills for—oil or natural gas
- Its drilling trajectory— vertical, horizontal, or directional
- The type of well it drills—exploration, development, or infill

Oil & Gas Equipment & Services

Oil & Gas Equipment & Services firms like Schlumberger, Halliburton, and Baker Hughes provide all the equipment, services, and expertise required for oil field exploration, development, and production. They range from firms with specialized expertise in particular niches of the industry to total solution providers. While the products and services provided are too numerous to list, some key examples are:

- Drilling equipment: Equipment used for oil and gas drilling, such as drill bits, drilling fluids, mud pumps, drill pipes, and wellhead equipment.
- Pressure pumping services: Services include well cementing and stimulation, used to enhance production from wells.

- Wireline services: Data recording using electronic instruments lowered into wells.
- Directional drilling and measurement: Tools and services assisting in directional drilling and data recording.
- Seismic imaging and analysis: Data and analysis detecting the presence of oil and gas deposits using sound waves.
- Engineering and construction services: Designing, building, and operating massive oil and gas infrastructure such as refineries, LNG plants, rigs, and offshore platforms.
- Helicopters and boats: Transportation services like ferrying workers and equipment to and from offshore rigs.

In short, oil firms rely on Energy Equipment & Services companies in every aspect of the energy cycle.

Chapter Recap

Energy sector basics are fairly straightforward. The majority of firms engage in one (or more) of the three segments of the integrated process (upstream, midstream, or downstream), or they assist the companies in the integrated process. You don't need to be a geologist to understand what drives the earnings and stock prices of the Energy sector—you just need to know what those drivers are (covered in detail in Chapter 2) and have a firm grasp of the laws of supply and demand.

- The Energy Sector consists of the Oil & Gas industry and the Energy Equipment & Services industry.
- The Oil & Gas industry is broken down into upstream, midstream, and downstream segments. Together, they are known as the *integrated process*.
- Upstream is exploration and production, midstream is transportation and storage, and downstream is refining and marketing.
- The Energy Equipment & Services industry provides the Oil & Gas industry with the tools and services to explore for and produce hydrocarbons.
- The Energy Equipment & Services industry is broken down into Oil & Gas Drilling and Oil & Gas Equipment & Services.

WHAT MAKES ENERGY BURN

Key Drivers of the Energy Sector

Not all economic sectors are created equal. Each has a set of economic, political, and sentiment factors, or *drivers*, making it unique to the broader economy. Properly understanding those drivers is a key to investing success in any sector, particularly the Energy sector.

Economic and stock market drivers evolve and change in relative importance over time—what's vital in 2008 may not be in 2010 and beyond. Nevertheless, drivers discussed in this chapter are a good starting point for any Energy analysis, regardless of the investing environment.

Understanding high-level sector drivers is essential in any sector analysis. You can't understand a company or its strategy without understanding what makes the industry tick (known as *top-down* analysis, which is covered more in depth in Chapter 7). Unless you've got a firm hold on fundamental drivers, it's a near hopeless task to make portfolio allocation decisions about industries and sub-industries, let alone choose the right individual stocks. High-level sector drivers often have equal, if not greater, influence on individual stock performance than unique company-specific fundamentals. So accurately identifying drivers is a must.

While by no means comprehensive, a list of important Energy drivers includes:

- Commodity prices
- Oil and gas production growth
- Finding and development costs
- Exploration and production capital expenditures
- Refining margins
- Share buybacks and mergers and acquisitions (M&A) activity
- Sentiment
- Taxes, politics, and regulations

It seems obvious, but it's worth the emphasis: Absolute and relative oil and natural gas prices are probably the most influential factors on Energy company earnings and stock market performance. Commodity prices are ultimately determined by good-old supply and demand. Long-term energy supply and demand is difficult to predict and thus unhelpful when making investment decisions for the short to medium term. So it's a good bet to focus on the near-term supply and demand outlook, typically the next 12 to 18 months (as you should be doing for stocks in general anyway).

A note of caution: Oil and natural gas are very different commodities with their own unique supply and demand characteristics. For instance, because crude oil is more easily transported, its price is determined by global forces more than natural gas prices, which are predominantly regional. Let's look at each separately.

OIL DEMAND DRIVERS

Crude oil demand is driven by *global economic growth*. Oil is the life-blood of world economies—the basic fuel for transportation of all kinds and the power source for countless industries.

Changes in real GDP have a direct effect on oil demand. Figure 2.1 shows a simple regression of real world GDP growth and world oil demand since 1971. The chart shows a consistent positive correlation

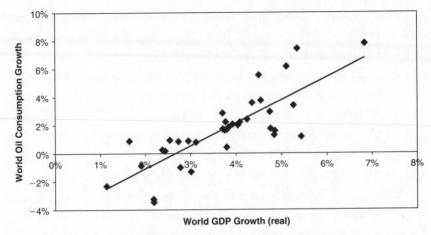

Figure 2.1   World GDP Growth vs. Oil Demand

Source: International Monetary Fund, Energy Information Administration.

between real annual world GDP growth and world oil consumption growth. In other words, higher GDP growth has historically coincided with higher oil consumption growth.

As a result, growth in world oil demand has followed world GDP growth fairly consistently, typically rising 1 to 2 percent annually. Figure 2.2 shows world oil demand has grown at an average annualized rate of 1.7 percent since 1970.

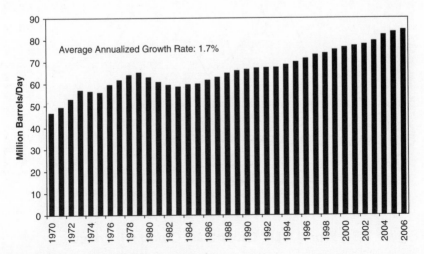

Figure 2.2   World Oil Demand

Source: Energy Information Administration.

Since oil supply is relatively fixed in the short term (it takes a long time to bring new supply online because finding and drilling a new oil well is no trivial matter), oil demand, driven by economic activity, has a large effect on oil prices in the short and medium term. Figure 2.3 shows how world GDP growth plays a major role in oil price increases. The chart represents year-over-year percentage growth of world GDP and oil prices. When economic growth began surging in 2003, it led to a corresponding surge in oil prices. Continued strong world GDP growth since then has kept oil in a positive growth trajectory.

Strong GDP growth historically leads to a corresponding increase in oil demand, thus increasing prices (when holding supply constant). Recessionary periods generally reduce oil demand, or at least slow the rate of growth in demand, sending oil prices lower.

Many energy analysts believe ever higher energy prices will eventually lead to *demand destruction*, because at some point, oil is just too expensive and we'll collectively curtail our consumption. This is no doubt true, but determining exactly at what price it will happen is exceedingly difficult. There is little to no evidence that prices over $100 per barrel have had much effect on aggregate global oil demand,

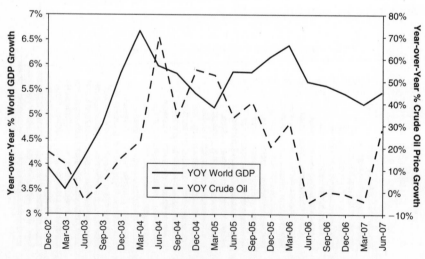

Figure 2.3   World GDP Growth vs. Crude Oil Prices
Source: Global Financial Data, Thomson Datastream.

except possibly tempering growth in consumption. Even at elevated levels, global oil demand appears to remain highly inelastic to prices.

There's little reason to believe the relationship between economic growth and oil demand will end anytime soon. Despite enthusiastic media coverage of hybrid vehicles, electric cars, and alternative fuels, the likelihood of alternatives replacing a meaningful amount of oil demand is many years, if not decades, away. Alternatives' percentage of the whole is miniscule and would require growth of many magnitudes before becoming a real marketplace force. Therefore, possible substitution effects of oil will be excluded in our analysis for now since they are so small.

Another way to see oil's economic sensitivity is to compare its movement to that of defensive economic sectors. In periods of strong economic growth (or perceived strength), economically sensitive sectors tend to outperform while defensive sectors underperform. Likewise, periods of falling economic growth are characterized by defensive sector outperformance and economically sensitive sectors' underperformance.

The effect is made visible by comparing performance differences between crude oil prices and a defensive industry like pharmaceuticals. Figure 2.4 shows the year-over-year performance of oil

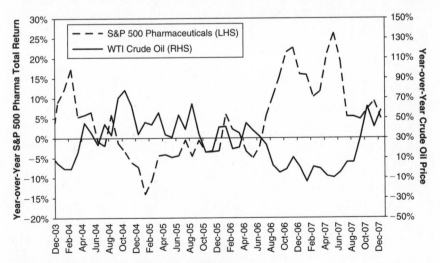

Figure 2.4   Oil vs. Pharmaceuticals
Source: Thomson Datastream.

prices compared to the year-over-year performance of the S&P 500 Pharmaceutical Index. Historically, when oil prices rise, the performance of pharmaceutical stocks tends to fall, and vice versa.

Forecasting Oil Demand

Forecasting oil demand requires determining each major country's position in the business cycle. Is the country in the growth, mature, or recession stage? Does the business cycle greatly differ when comparing the largest oil-consuming countries to smaller oil-consuming countries? Certainly, the world's giant economies like the US and China will have a much greater impact on oil markets than a smaller one like, say, Zimbabwe will. Forecasting oil demand relies mainly on accurately predicting economic growth in the largest oil-consuming nations. Figure 2.5 shows a common depiction of the business cycle. When a country is contracting (in recession), oil demand is likely to fall. Meanwhile, the expansion stage is likely to see an increase in oil demand.

Forecasting oil demand for specific countries is difficult as it requires a specialized knowledge of how oil use differs. Fortunately, oil demand forecasts from government agencies are widely available through the Energy Information Administration (EIA) and International Energy Agency (IEA). As with any forecast, however, always view them with skepticism and closely scrutinize assumptions and data sources.

It's useful to use oil forecasts and then draw conclusions depending on the differences between your view and the forecasters' outlooks. Ask "Do I agree with their economic growth assumptions?" and "What potential surprises could there be they aren't factoring in?"

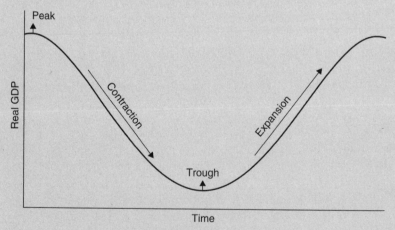

Figure 2.5   Business Cycle

Therefore, while oil demand appears price inelastic, it does not act like a traditionally defensive sector. Oil-related stocks tend to do well when the economy is growing. In fact, as evidenced by the data, combining energy firms sensitive to oil prices and pharmaceutical firms could be a good hedging strategy.

Contributions to Demand

We know energy demand is very important, but who are the biggest demanders? Tables 2.1 and 2.2 show the countries with the largest percentage of oil consumption and imports.

The US dominates world oil consumption, representing nearly 25 percent of oil demand. The next is China with 8.6 percent, followed by Japan with 6.2 percent. Developed nations historically are the world's largest oil consumers. However, the mix between developed and developing markets' oil use is changing rapidly.

Table 2.1   Top 10 Oil Consumers

Rank	Country	Consumption (mil bbls/day)	% of Total Consumption
1	US	20.7	24.3%
2	China	7.3	8.6%
3	Japan	5.2	6.2%
4	Russia	3.1	3.7%
5	Germany	2.6	3.1%
6	India	2.5	3.0%
7	Canada	2.2	2.6%
8	Brazil	2.2	2.6%
9	Korea, South	2.2	2.5%
10	Saudi Arabia	2.1	2.4%
	Rest of the world	34.6	40.9%
	World total	**84.6**	**100.0%**

Source: Energy Information Administration, as of 12/31/06.

Table 2.2   Top Oil Importers

Rank	Country	Net Imports (mil bbls/day)	% of Total Imports
1	US	12.2	26.8%
2	Japan	5.1	11.2%
3	China	3.4	7.5%
4	Germany	2.5	5.4%
5	Korea, South	2.2	4.7%
6	France	1.9	4.1%
7	India	1.7	3.7%
8	Italy	1.6	3.4%
9	Spain	1.6	3.4%
10	Taiwan	0.9	2.1%
	Rest of the world	12.6	27.6%
	World total	**45.6**	**100.0%**

Source: Energy Information Administration, as of 12/31/06.

As economies transition from developing to developed markets, they generally change from manufacturing-based to service-based economies. Developed nations tend to see their economies' reliance on oil diminish over time as a percentage of overall spending. Improvements in energy efficiency also help reduce an economy's oil reliance. The US is an example of how a primarily service-based (non-manufacturing) economy's GDP growth is much less dependent on energy than it was 20 years ago. The same can be said about most developed economies.

Meanwhile, strong economic growth from manufacturing-based emerging economies like China has caused oil demand to soar. After years of booming GDP growth driven by industrial and manufacturing activity, China is now the second-largest oil consumer in the world. Other developing nations like India, Brazil, South Korea, and Saudi Arabia have also emerged as major oil consumers.

The difference between oil demand growth in developed and developing economies in recent years has been substantial. Figure 2.6

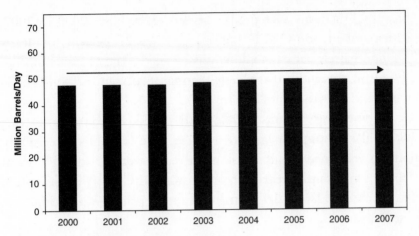

Figure 2.6   OECD Oil Consumption
Source: Energy Information Administration.

shows the annual oil consumption of developed nations, represented by the Organisation for Economic Co-operation and Development (OECD). (Note: OECD is a group of 30 developed economies including the US, Japan, and most of Europe.) Notice how oil demand has been virtually flat the last several years.

Meanwhile, oil demand in developing economies (non-OECD nations) is growing rapidly. Figure 2.7 shows oil demand growth in

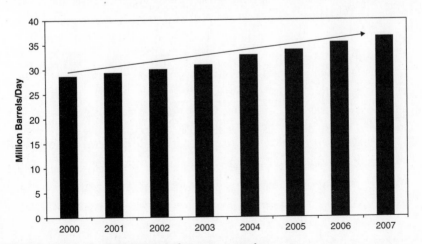

Figure 2.7   Non-OECD Oil Consumption
Source: Energy Information Administration.

non-OECD nations over the last several years. From 2000 to 2007, oil demand in non-OECD nations grew by 27 percent, or nearly 8 million barrels per day.[1] China was by far the largest driver of non-OECD oil demand growth, representing 36 percent of non-OECD oil demand growth from 2000 to 2007.[2]

As emerging nations develop, they'll likely continue driving world oil consumption growth too. Because OECD oil consumption has remained about constant in recent years (and likely won't change significantly year-over-year), non-OECD oil consumption may be an even larger determinant of future prices, warranting close observation.

Oil as a Financial Instrument

While oil is primarily demanded for its physical use, it is also used as a financial instrument. Just like any stock or bond, oil is traded daily by investors hoping to profit from its price fluctuations. Some have invested in oil and other commodities as a way to diversify their portfolios. The result has been rampant speculation and the creation of several financial products.

Oil can act as a hedge against the dollar. (This is true for any dollar-denominated commodity.) As oil prices are primarily denominated in dollars, a foreign investor can trade their currency for dollars, buy a specific number of barrels of oil, and then sell those barrels for dollars at a later date. Should the dollar depreciate against the foreign investor's home currency, they would receive a foreign currency gain in the transaction plus the difference in the price of crude oil. The same would be true if a foreign investor bought a US stock or bond.

Investors may also demand oil as a hedge against inflation. Just like gold, oil is one of the many physical assets and commodities investors tend to flock to when they expect an increase in inflation. When inflation rises, they expect nominal prices of commodities to increase correspondingly, preserving the value of the dollar or any other currency used to purchase oil.

However, demand for oil as a hedge against inflation or the dollar is likely only a short-term phenomenon, and there are many instances where this strategy does not play out as expected. In the long term, oil prices will be determined by supply and demand fundamentals of the commodity itself.

Breakdown of Oil Use

There are five predominant uses for oil in today's world economy. Oil use can vary greatly depending on the country, but a breakdown of oil use in the US is:

1. Transportation (69 percent)
2. Industrial (24 percent)
3. Residential (4 percent)
4. Electricity Generation (2 percent)
5. Commercial (1 percent)[3]

Transportation The vast majority of oil use is for transportation. The US uses 69 percent of its oil for transportation via gasoline and diesel.[4] US gasoline and diesel unit demand generally grows at a pace proportional to, but slightly slower than, GDP growth.

What could possibly upset the historical relationship between long-term GDP growth and gasoline demand? For one, demand could increase if long-term per capita wealth in developing nations causes a surge in auto use. With 1.2 billion people, China represents one of the fastest-growing markets for new automobiles, which will become increasingly affordable as the country's citizens become wealthier. However, demand could sink if new advanced technologies in automobiles or alternative transportation fuels suddenly emerge (though this is unlikely in the short run). Similarly, economies experiencing a shift toward less transportation-intensive activities like financial services or healthcare might also impact this relationship.

Seasonality also plays a role in the demand for transportation fuels. In the US, demand traditionally increases in the summer as vacationers drive farther distances than during other times.

Industrial Besides transportation, oil products are used to power industry—factories, power plants, you name it. Industrial use also varies greatly by country. As mentioned previously, industrial activity makes up a much larger percentage of GDP in certain developing economies than in many developed economies. Thus, surging economic growth in China will have a much larger effect on oil demand growth than surging economic growth in Europe or the US.

Residential   Residential oil comes mainly in the form of heating oil. In many parts of the world, heating oil is still a popular method to warm homes in frigid winter months. Heating oil demand is typically seasonal and varies based on differences in climate.

Electricity Generation   Although oil represents a small proportion of total electricity generated in the US, many countries still use it to make electricity. Oil use by utilities firms can vary significantly due to the wide availability of substitutes like coal, nuclear energy, and natural gas—which are viable and close competitors in this industry.

Commercial   The smallest proportionate oil user is the commercial sector. These are service businesses like local governments or private and public organizations not included in the manufacturing industry. Service industries are generally not energy intensive, so oil demand in this area is fairly constant.

OIL SUPPLY DRIVERS

One could spend a career (and many have) analyzing oil supply. We don't have time for that. Instead, our goal is to provide an overview of oil supply basics and show how you can use publicly available data to help make better investment decisions.

In the short term, oil supply is relatively fixed—at least for increasing supply. Once found, it takes years for new oil supplies to actually become available to the public. (Recall from Chapter 1 that a company must explore, drill, produce, ship, refine, then market oil products.) Meaningful, unexpected supply additions do not typically occur in a 12 to 18 month period. However, production capacity can decrease almost instantly due to forces like embargoes, hurricanes, strikes, wars, accidents, and so on. In an era of little to no spare production capacity, an *asymmetric risk* has developed—in the short run, there is little chance of an unexpected increase in supply, but there is significant risk of unexpected decreases.

Important oil supply drivers covered in this section are:

- World oil production
- Crude oil reserves
- Spare capacity
- Oil inventories
- Geopolitics

World Oil Production

Generally, world oil production has kept up just enough to meet demand, rising 1 to 2 percent annually on average, as seen in Figure 2.8. World oil demand has grown at a 1.5 percent average annualized rate

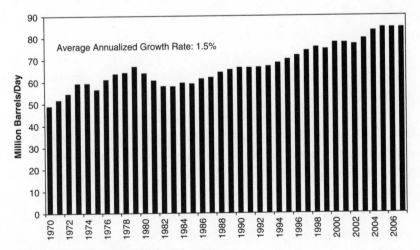

Figure 2.8   World Oil Production
Source: Energy Information Administration.

since 1970. However, though world oil consumption has grown in the last few years, world oil production has been virtually flat.

Total world oil production only tells part of the story. Behind production are two distinct groups with two vastly different incentives—OPEC and non-OPEC. Any analysis of oil production should begin by separating these two and analyzing them discreetly.

OPEC   The Organization of Petroleum Exporting Countries (OPEC) was formed in 1960 to provide a unified voice on oil industry issues. The group consists of 13 developing nations whose economies rely on oil export revenues including Saudi Arabia, Iran, Iraq, Kuwait, Qatar, Libya, Nigeria, Algeria, Ecuador, Indonesia, the United Arab Emirates, Venezuela, and Angola.

OPEC's stated purpose is to coordinate oil production policies to stabilize the oil market and help oil producers achieve a reasonable rate of return on their investments. The organization meets twice a year at its Vienna headquarters (but can meet more frequently) to review international oil market supply and demand. Among other things, the group sets production quotas for member nations in an effort to affect world oil prices.

OPEC evolved into a cartel in 1973, about the same time oil production in the US began its decline. Since then, the cartel has maintained a considerable influence on world oil prices. In October 1973, in response to Western nations' support of Israel during the Yom Kippur War, OPEC initiated an oil embargo, sending world oil prices soaring.

OPEC remains a powerful influence on world oil markets today. Table 2.3 lists OPEC's member nations and their production and contribution to world production. The group acts as the *swing* producer, altering production to balance supply and demand. While OPEC mentions price stability as one of its desired goals, it's naturally motivated to keep prices high—the higher the price, the more money member nations make. (This is particularly true since oil demand generally isn't severely affected by price increases.)

Table 2.3 OPEC Members and Production

Country	Location	Production (Mill bbls/day)	% of Total Production
Saudi Arabia*	Middle East	10.7	12.6%
Iran*	Middle East	4.1	4.9%
United Arab Emirates	Middle East	2.9	3.5%
Venezuela*	South America	2.8	3.3%
Kuwait*	Middle East	2.7	3.2%
Nigeria	Africa	2.4	2.9%
Algeria	Africa	2.1	2.5%
Iraq*	Middle East	2.0	2.4%
Libya	Africa	1.8	2.1%
Angola	Africa	1.4	1.7%
Qatar	Middle East	1.1	1.3%
Indonesia	Asia	1.1	1.3%
Ecuador	South America	0.5	0.6%
Total OPEC supply		35.8	42.4%
Total non-OPEC supply		48.8	57.6%
Total world production		**84.6**	**100.0%**

Source: Energy Information Administration, as of 12/31/06.
*Founding Members

Non-OPEC Supply Non-OPEC supply refers to production from publicly traded oil firms, national oil companies (NOCs) from non-OPEC nations, and privately held exploration and production firms. While OPEC nations tend to artificially restrain output (because that's what cartels do to keep prices high), non-OPEC nations try vigorously to expand output. It hasn't always been a successful endeavor.

Figure 2.9 shows annual oil production of non-OPEC nations (bar chart) and the percentage of world output non-OPEC nations represent (line). Non-OPEC production has grown at an average annualized rate of 2.1 percent since 1970. As the figure shows, non-OPEC sources

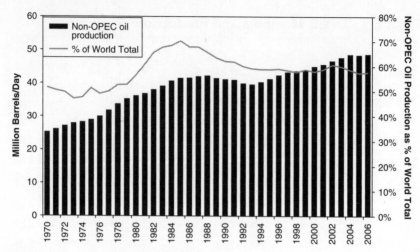

Figure 2.9   Non-OPEC Production
Source: Energy Information Administration.

represent just under 60 percent of world oil production, despite having far fewer reserves than OPEC nations.

The outcome of non-OPEC supply growth is critical to world oil prices. When non-OPEC supply growth is unable to meet world oil demand growth, the world is forced to rely increasingly on OPEC to cover the shortfall. This reliance on OPEC member nations—who have every incentive to keep supplies tight—is one reason world oil prices have escalated in recent years.

Overall Supply Contributors   Setting aside OPEC versus non-OPEC, who are the world's biggest oil suppliers? These are the countries that have the biggest impact on world oil supplies and, thus, should be followed closely. For example, a significant drop in production from one of these countries would require a corresponding increase in production from others to maintain world output. Table 2.4 shows top oil producers. World oil production is dominated by a few major countries, most notably Saudi Arabia and Russia. But note: The US, Canada, and Mexico are also major oil producers—a fact many investors forget.

Table 2.4   Top 10 Oil Producers

Rank	Country	Production (mill bbls/day)	% of Total Production
1	Saudi Arabia	10.7	12.6%
2	Russia	9.7	11.4%
3	US	8.3	9.8%
4	Iran	4.1	4.9%
5	China	3.8	4.5%
6	Mexico	3.7	4.4%
7	Canada	3.3	3.9%
8	United Arab Emirates	2.9	3.5%
9	Venezuela	2.8	3.3%
10	Norway	2.8	3.3%
	Rest of the world	32.4	38.3%
	World total	**84.6**	**100.0%**

Source: Energy Information Administration, as of 12/31/06.

Beyond looking at who's producing, it's vital also to note who's exporting (Table 2.5). When countries don't produce enough oil to meet domestic demand (like the US, Japan, and China), they must rely on exporters, giving the exporters bigger clout in oil markets. Seven of the 10 largest oil exporters in the world are OPEC members. Russia, Norway, and Mexico are the largest exporters outside the cartel.

Crude Oil Reserves

The vast majority of oil reserves are held by just a handful of countries. Any geopolitical events, wars, or other supply disruptions in the world's largest holders of reserves have the power to move markets substantially. Table 2.6 lists the top oil reserve holders by country. OPEC nations hold the vast majority of the world's oil supply by a long shot, with 70 percent of total reserves.[5] Yet OPEC nations only account for 42 percent of world production.[6]

Table 2.5   Top 10 Oil Exporters

Rank	Country	Net Exports (mill bbls/day)
1	Saudi Arabia	8.5
2	Russia	6.9
3	United Arab Emirates	2.6
4	Norway	2.6
5	Iran	2.5
6	Kuwait	2.3
7	Venezuela	2.2
8	Nigeria	2.1
9	Algeria	1.8
10	Mexico	1.7

Source: Energy Information Administration, as of 12/31/06.

Table 2.6   Top 10 World Oil Reserves by Country

Rank	Country	Reserves (Billion Barrels)	% of Total Reserves
1	Saudi Arabia	262.3	19.9%
2	Canada	179.2	13.6%
3	Iran	136.3	10.3%
4	Iraq	115.0	8.7%
5	Kuwait	101.5	7.7%
6	United Arab Emirates	97.8	7.4%
7	Venezuela	80.0	6.1%
8	Russia	60.0	4.6%
9	Libya	41.5	3.1%
10	Nigeria	36.2	2.7%
	Rest of the world	207.7	15.8%
	World total	**1317.4**	**100.0%**

Source: Energy Information Administration, as of 12/31/07.

Unconventional Reserves

The world is known to have trillions of barrels of additional oil in unconventional reserves like oil sands and oil shale, but it is very difficult to extract and produce large quantities economically. These reserves, currently being developed, will take decades before they contribute meaningfully to supply. As a result, unconventional reserves are not a significant driver of oil supply at present, though they will no doubt play an ever-increasing role in the future. (For more information on unconventional resources, see Chapter 4.)

Note: While Canada is listed as the second-largest holder of world oil reserves with 179 billion barrels, 173 billion of those come from its oil sands.[7] If looking only at conventional oil reserves, then Canada should be removed from the top reserve holders.

Spare Capacity

Spare oil production capacity is the amount of oil currently not being produced, but could be if needed. It represents the world's supply "cushion." Generally, the greater the world's spare capacity, the lower the potential for prices, and vice versa.

There is virtually no spare capacity in non-OPEC nations because they already attempt to increase production to the greatest extent possible. As a result, the only current spare production capacity today is within OPEC nations, and for the most part, it truly only resides in Saudi Arabia.

Figure 2.10 shows how world spare oil capacity has changed over the last several years. Upon reaching a peak in 2002 following a global recession, spare capacity plunged as economic growth—and oil demand with it—rebounded sharply.

Spare oil capacity was abundant in decades past and a key reason why oil prices remained in such a narrow band for so long. If there was a surge in demand, oil-producing nations could simply ramp up production to meet it. Nowadays, spare capacity has fallen dramatically to around 1 to 3 million barrels/day.

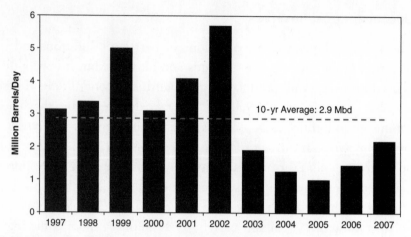

Figure 2.10   OPEC Surplus Oil Production Capacity
Source: Energy Information Administration.

When OPEC nations decide to reduce target output, it immediately creates spare capacity. OPEC generally reduces output to keep world oil supply and demand in "balance," but it's usually skewed to sustain high prices.

The greater the spare capacity, the greater the world's ability to weather potential supply shocks. The current lack of spare capacity makes oil markets more sensitive and vulnerable to oil supply shocks than in years prior. Any supply disruptions (hurricanes, war, etc.) make it nearly impossible to compensate for any lost supply in the short run.

Oil Inventories

Changing oil inventories around the world are an indicator of how oil supply balances with oil demand. Inventories held by the largest consuming nations are watched on a weekly basis to predict short-term price moves. The logic goes like this: Growing inventories might signal excess supply to meet demand, suggesting prices should fall. Conversely, shrinking inventories generally predict higher prices. (But, as always, seasonal factors must also be accounted for.)

Data for oil inventories is most widely available for developed nations, specifically the OECD. Figure 2.11 shows the history of OECD

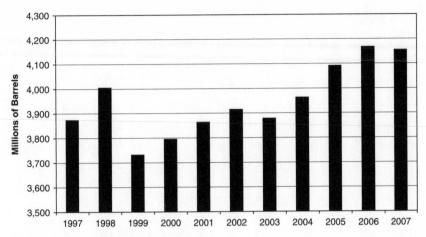

Figure 2.11   OECD Inventories
Source: Energy Information Administration.

commercial inventories over the last several years. Because OECD oil demand has been virtually flat recently, oil inventories have actually been increasing. While historically rising inventories would normally lead to falling prices, oil prices have continued to rise mostly because of strong demand in non-OECD nations.

Geopolitical Examples

What are some examples of geopolitical issues that have affected oil supply?

- Oil embargo (Middle East, 1973)
- War and the potential of war (Iraq invasion of Kuwait, 1990)
- Nationalization of oil reserves (Venezuela, 2007)
- Militant attacks against pipelines and oil workers (Nigeria, 2007)
- Contract renegotiations between governments and international oil firms (Russia, 2008)

One of the most significant geopolitical events in the past 30 years was the Iran-Iraq war beginning in September 1980. Iraq's invasion caused oil production in Iran to nearly halt, while Iraq's oil production was also severely cut. With two of the largest oil-producing nations' supplies dramatically curtailed, prices around the globe soared. Oil prices behaved similarly following Iraq's invasion of Kuwait in 1990.

Geopolitical events are impossible to forecast, but they're unquestionably a force driving oil prices.

Geopolitics

Geopolitical issues are increasingly important to oil markets. Oil supply disruptions are routine around the world, whether they be from labor strikes, weather, civil unrest, terrorism, or wars. With limited spare oil capacity in the world, global events are instantaneously reflected in prices as investors worry about supply disruptions. As with other supply analyses, it's important to scrutinize the events surrounding the largest reserve holders, producers, exporters, and consumers.

NATURAL GAS DEMAND DRIVERS

The differences between crude oil and natural gas markets are numerous. Natural gas and oil are not perfect substitutes, as natural gas is used for different purposes than oil. Natural gas is also difficult to transport from the largest reserve regions to global end users. As a result, natural gas prices are largely determined in regional markets, not on a global scale.

These factors and more make the supply and demand situation for natural gas very different from oil and often more difficult to predict. We will cover major factors affecting natural gas prices, taking a close look at the world's largest natural gas market—North America.

In short, natural gas demand is driven by a combination of economic activity and weather. Natural gas is used not only to power industrial plants, but also to fuel electric power plants and heating needs.

World natural gas consumption has grown at an annual rate of 2.7 percent on average since 1980, as shown in Figure 2.12.[8] Even though natural gas use in a country can fall or rise substantially due to abnormal weather, the global trend has been a steady increase. While the natural gas market is not as large as the oil market, it still makes up a substantial part of most upstream oil and gas companies.

Contributions to Demand

Though there are many differences between oil and natural gas, the world's major consumers remain similar. Like oil, the US is by far the world's largest natural gas user, representing 20 percent of world

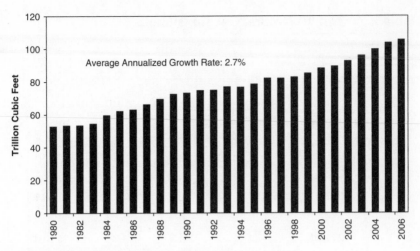

Figure 2.12   World Natural Gas Consumption
Source: Energy Information Administration.

Forecasting Demand

Forecasting regional natural gas demand in the short term is especially challenging given its dependence on weather. Assuming weather remains within a normal historic range, natural gas—like oil—will depend heavily on the strength of regional economic growth driven by industry.

In addition to oil forecasts, the IEA and EIA also produce government forecasts of natural gas demand across the world. These forecasts can serve as a starting point when determining the relative attractiveness of natural gas, but just like oil forecasts, they should be viewed with skepticism, and assumptions should be closely scrutinized.

consumption.[9] Tables 2.7 and 2.8 show the world's largest natural gas consumers and importers. Because Russia's and Iran's natural gas markets are government controlled, it's not surprising the vast majority of publicly traded natural gas E&Ps reside in the US. As shown in Table 2.8, the US, Japan, and countries in Europe are the largest natural gas importers. This makes them most vulnerable to supply conditions in the largest natural gas export markets.

Table 2.7   Top 10 Natural Gas Consumers

Rank	Country	Natural Gas Consumption (trillon cf)	% of Global Natural Gas Demand
1	US	21.8	20.7%
2	Russia	16.6	15.7%
3	Iran	3.7	3.5%
4	Germany	3.6	3.4%
5	Canada	3.3	3.1%
6	United Kingdom	3.2	3.1%
7	Japan	3.1	3.0%
8	Ukraine	3.1	3.0%
9	Italy	3.0	2.8%
10	Saudi Arabia	2.6	2.5%
	Rest of the world	41.4	39.2%
	World total	**105.5**	**100.0%**

Source: Energy Information Administration, as of 12/31/06.

Table 2.8   Top 10 Natural Gas Importers

Rank	Country	Imports (Million Cubic Meters)	% of Total Natural Gas Imports
1	US	118.6	13.6%
2	Germany	93.7	10.7%
3	Japan	88.6	10.1%
4	Italy	77.4	8.9%
5	Ukraine	50.2	5.8%
6	France	45.3	5.2%
7	Spain	34.4	3.9%
8	Korea, South	33.0	3.8%
9	Turkey	30.2	3.5%
10	Netherlands	25.2	2.9%
	Rest of the world	276.4	31.7%
	World total	**873.0**	**100.0%**

Source: International Energy Agency, as of 12/31/06.

But just because the US and Russia are the biggest consumers doesn't necessarily mean they'll pay the same price for natural gas. Since natural gas prices are generally determined in regional markets, natural gas consumption in the US and Russia will have little effect on the prices the other nation pays.

Breakdown of US Natural Gas Use

Natural gas is generally used for five purposes:

1. Industrial (35 percent)
2. Electricity generation (29 percent)
3. Residential (20 percent)
4. Commercial (13 percent)
5. Transportation (3 percent)[10]

Industrial   The largest industrial use for natural gas is running factories, where it's used for heat, power, or chemical feedstock. Industrial activities include manufacturing, mining (including oil and gas extraction), and construction. Natural gas is also used in agriculture as a major feedstock for fertilizer.

Unlike oil, natural gas can be substituted to some degree by alternatives like fuel oil. Some large-volume customers (primarily industrial consumers and electricity generators) can switch between natural gas and oil, depending on the prices of each. Because of this interrelation between fuel markets, demand shifts toward natural gas when oil prices rise.

Electricity Generation   Natural gas can be used as a major input for power generation. In fact, about 20 percent of all electricity generation in the world comes from natural gas.[11]

Gas-fired plants have gained popularity over coal-fired and nuclear plants in recent decades. Why? First, natural gas prices were consistently low and gas-fired plants were relatively inexpensive to build years ago. Second, burning natural gas results in much lower CO^2 emissions than coal, making it more environmentally (and therefore, politically) attractive. Finally, nuclear power fell greatly out of favor following the nuclear power plant accidents at Three Mile Island and Chernobyl. As a result, nearly 90 percent of all new power plants built since 1995 in the US are natural gas-fired plants.[12]

For years, natural gas prices remained around $2 per million cubic feet (MMcf) due to abundant US supplies, imports, and relatively stable consumption. But natural gas prices began an upward trajectory as massive amounts of generating capacity came online in 2000. Today, natural gas is still a preferred power generation source and is expected to gain an even greater share of the pie in the future.

Residential   Natural gas is also used for residential home heating. In the US, over half of all homes use natural gas as their main heating fuel.[13] Natural gas is also a main fuel source for other home needs, like stoves, furnaces, water heaters, clothes dryers, and so on.

Since it's used for heating purposes, natural gas demand is also driven by weather and seasonality. Winter months usually see rising prices and falling inventories, while summer months generally see the exact opposite. An abnormally hot or cold climate can dramatically affect demand, making price forecasting much more difficult. Weather unpredictability is one of the reasons natural gas prices are so volatile, and also why many natural gas producers use hedging strategies to mitigate risk.

Seasonality and Scams

The seasonal pattern of spot natural gas prices tempts financial hucksters to promote "surefire investing strategies" to uninformed investors. They claim buying natural gas futures contracts before winter will yield huge gains as the seasonal price increases occur. Unfortunately, the futures market efficiently anticipates this pattern, thereby eliminating the prospect of a risk-free investment opportunity. Don't fall for this trap.

Commercial   The commercial sector uses natural gas for nonman-
ufacturing purposes, primarily for the sale of goods or services. This
includes service industries like hotels, restaurants, and wholesale and
retail stores. Additionally, federal, state, and local governments and
other private and public organizations like religious, social, or frater-
nal groups use natural gas—but this number is comparatively small.
Common uses of natural gas in this sector include space heating, water
heating, cooking, and running a wide variety of other equipment.

Transportation   Transportation amounts to the smallest percentage
of natural gas use and will likely remain so in the future. There are
some buses, trucks, and cars with the capability to run on natural gas
in place of gasoline, but they are few.

    While it may be considered cleaner than gasoline, widespread
natural gas use in the transportation industry is unlikely. Other than
the fact natural gas is a finite, depleting hydrocarbon, just like oil, it
would take far too much new infrastructure and too many automo-
bile modifications to make it economical on a mass scale.

NATURAL GAS SUPPLY DRIVERS

Natural gas supply drivers are similar to oil's but must be analyzed
differently. While politics, wars, and production mishaps globally
have the ability to affect oil prices, this is rarely the case with natural
gas. Instead, because it is a more segmented market, regional prices of
natural gas will be determined by the fundamental supply environment tied to local inventories, production, and imports. But this will
not always be the case. As natural gas becomes easier to transport via
liquefied natural gas (covered more in a bit), prices will increasingly be
determined by global forces.

Natural Gas Production

Natural gas production varies depending on the country, but all are
affected by demand, geology, and expected price, among other factors. Historically, world natural gas production has been sufficient in

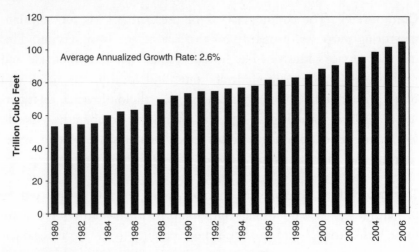

Figure 2.13   World Natural Gas Production
Source: Energy Information Administration.

meeting world demand, rising at an annualized rate of about 2.6 percent[14] as shown in Figure 2.13.

Natural Gas Reserves

Like crude oil, world natural gas reserves are concentrated in a handful of countries. But unlike oil, natural gas is generally not considered to be short in supply globally. Table 2.9 shows the countries with the largest reserves of natural gas in the world.

As discussed earlier, natural gas prices are affected by regional supply and demand conditions, so the largest reserve holders have much less influence on world gas prices than OPEC does over oil prices. Even so, certain reserve holders can still have tremendous influence over regional prices. As a dominant player, Russia can have a heavy sway over natural gas prices in Europe since they are the number one supplier for that region.

Supply Contributors

Natural gas supply is influenced by a country's ability to produce enough domestic gas and also secure sufficient gas imports to meet

Table 2.9   Top 10 Natural Gas Reserves by Country

Rank	Country	Reserves (Trillion Cubic Feet)	% of Total Reserves
1	Russia	1,680	27.2%
2	Iran	974	15.8%
3	Qatar	911	14.7%
4	Saudi Arabia	240	3.9%
5	United Arab Emirates	214	3.5%
6	US	204	3.3%
7	Nigeria	182	2.9%
8	Algeria	162	2.6%
9	Venezuela	152	2.5%
10	Iraq	112	1.8%
	Rest of the world	1,352	21.9%
	World total	**6,183**	**100.0%**

Source: International Energy Agency, as of 12/31/06.

demand. As natural gas is, for the most part, limited by existing pipelines and not easily transportable on ships, countries generally rely on domestic or regional production. Table 2.10 lists the world's largest natural gas producers, showing an even more concentrated market than oil. Russia and the US, responsible for nearly 40 percent of world natural gas production combined, dominate the natural gas market. Notice the world's natural gas is concentrated in different spots than oil. The Middle East, for example, does not have as large a presence in the natural gas market as do parts of Asia, Europe, and North America.

Like the crude oil market, the natural gas export market is also concentrated among a handful of countries. Table 2.11 shows the largest natural gas exporters, led by Russia, Canada, and Norway. While Russia and Norway are responsible for supplying natural gas to Europe—a major gas consumer—Canada meets the needs of the US.

Table 2.10   Top 10 Natural Gas Producers

Rank	Country	Production (Million Cubic Meters)	% of Total Natural Gas Production
1	Russia	656.3	22.0%
2	US	524.4	17.6%
3	Canada	189.2	6.4%
4	Iran	98.1	3.3%
5	Norway	91.8	3.1%
6	Algeria	88.8	3.0%
7	United Kingdom	83.8	2.8%
8	Netherlands	77.3	2.6%
9	Indonesia	72.1	2.4%
10	Turkmenistan	67.1	2.3%
	Rest of the world	1,027.7	34.5%
	World total	**2,976.6**	**100.0%**

Source: International Energy Agency as of 12/31/06.

Table 2.11   Top 10 Natural Gas Exporters

Rank	Country	Exports (Million Cubic Meters)	% of Total Natural Gas Exports
1	Russia	202.8	22.9%
2	Canada	102.1	11.5%
3	Norway	86.2	9.7%
4	Algeria	64.4	7.3%
5	Netherlands	54.7	6.2%
6	Turkmenistan	50.0	5.7%
7	Indonesia	34.9	3.9%
8	Malaysia	31.2	3.5%
9	Qatar	31.2	3.5%
10	US	20.5	2.3%
	Rest of the world	206.5	23.3%
	World total	**884.5**	**100.0%**

Source: International Energy Agency as of 12/31/06.

Natural Gas Supply Disruptions

Hurricanes and tropical storms have the potential to dramatically affect natural gas production and prices in certain parts of the world. This is especially true in the Gulf of Mexico—a region with vast oil and natural gas reserves.

In the summer of 2005, Hurricanes Rita and Katrina along the US Gulf Coast were responsible for halting more than 800 billion cubic feet of natural gas production between August 2005 and June 2006.* At the time, this was equivalent to about 5 percent of US production and about 22 percent of annual production in the Gulf of Mexico. As a result, natural gas prices surged to over $15 per MMcf in the period, as shown in Figure 2.14.

Fortunately, this price spike proved to be short-lived. Once much of the lost production was restored in the following months, prices generally declined throughout 2006. There has not been a comparable storm since, but hurricane threats are now watched more closely by the industry since they can temporarily move natural gas prices in a big way.

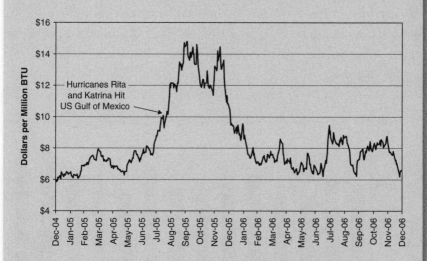

Figure 2.14   US Natural Gas Prices, 2005–2006

Source: Energy Information Administration.

*US Department of Energy, Energy Information Administration, "An Analysis of Price Volatility in Natural Gas Markets," p. 2, August 2007.

Natural Gas Inventories

Like oil, changes in natural gas inventories are an indicator of the balance between supply and demand. But because regional natural gas prices are less affected by global issues, inventory changes tend to have a greater effect on natural gas prices than on oil.

A country's natural gas inventories relative to historical averages tend to affect natural gas prices. In the US, natural gas is injected and withdrawn from underground storage fields while inventories are logged on a weekly basis. Natural gas is injected into these fields primarily from April through October and withdrawn from November through March.

Analysts and traders use weather and economic forecasts to predict gas storage withdrawals or injections. For example, if the US has an abnormally hot winter, more gas will likely be injected into storage, putting downward pressure on prices.

Figure 2.15 shows the trend of average annual US natural gas storage inventories over the last several years. As the graph shows, inventories tend to be volatile year to year, but inventories have grown over the last several years due in part to tepid weather reducing natural gas demand.

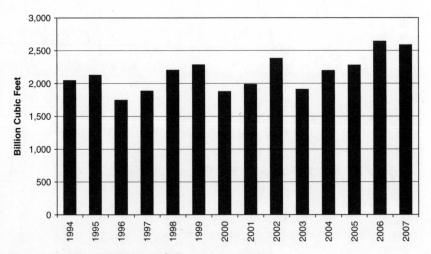

Figure 2.15   US Natural Gas Inventories
Source: Energy Information Administration.

Imports and Liquefied Natural Gas

When a country is unable to meet natural gas demand with domestic production, it will need imports to make up the shortfall. Most countries historically have little difficulty importing sufficient natural gas through pipelines, but this has proved more difficult in the last several years. Problems include pricing disputes between import and export nations, rising natural gas demand in export nations, and general concerns about supply security (several nations are heavily reliant on just one natural gas exporter). As a result, the global liquefied natural gas market is growing in a big way.

To export natural gas outside of pipelines, it must first be transformed into a liquid. Liquefied natural gas (LNG) is stored and transported at atmospheric pressure at a temperature of −260° F. LNG can be placed on special ships and exported to any region of the world. Once the ship reaches its destination, the LNG is sent to re-gasifiers, which convert it back into gas for local distribution via pipeline systems.

LNG as a percentage of natural gas imports in the US is increasing steadily, but still remains a small percentage of total US gas consumption—only 3.3 percent[15] of America's 23,058 billion cubic feet (bcf) in 2007.[16] Although LNG is growing, it will still take years for it to have a substantial effect on the gas market.

Figure 2.16 shows the growing importance of US LNG imports over the last several years. The bar chart shows the absolute LNG import growth, while the line represents LNG imports as a percentage of total US natural gas imports.

LNG's popularity is rising in other nations as well. Japan is currently the world's largest LNG importer with 42 percent of all LNG exports.[17] Europe represents 24 percent of world demand; South Korea, 16 percent; and the US, 9 percent. Since LNG can be transported to any nation in the world, countries compete for LNG supplies based on price.

Geopolitics

Given continued geopolitical conflicts with some of the world's largest natural gas reserve holder nations like Russia, Iran, and Iraq,

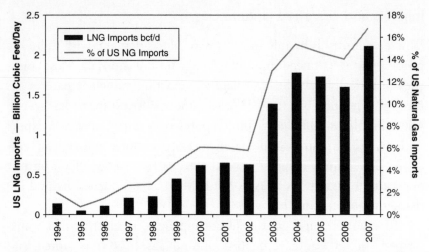

Figure 2.16   LNG as a Percent of US Consumption and Imports
Source: Energy Information Administration.

geopolitics is likely to be an important issue affecting natural gas markets in perpetuity. A country's ability to secure a stable supply of imports to make up shortfalls in domestic natural gas production has a major influence on prices.

This is particularly true for Europe, where geopolitics has recently played a major role in natural gas prices. Russia is in a position of tremendous strength, supplying 25 percent of Europe's natural gas needs via pipelines. Thus, Russia's policies and reliability as a supplier have a great effect on prices. In 2006, Russia temporarily shut off natural gas supplies to certain countries (e.g., Ukraine) over a pricing dispute. Such tactics spur concern about the long-term supply reliability and can push prices higher based on fear.

In the US, geopolitics is a lesser factor since it supplies the vast majority of its demand internally and relies on generally politically stable countries (mostly Canada) for its natural gas imports.

ADDITIONAL DRIVERS

Up until now, we've only discussed commodity prices, but there are additional important drivers impacting Energy earnings and stock prices. While there are many more detailed drivers that affect individual company performance, our goal at this point is to identify high-level sector drivers that affect the majority of Energy firms. Here are additional drivers analysts follow closely.

Oil and Gas Production Growth

After pricing, oil and gas production growth is the most important factor in producer revenues. A company's success at replacing the reserves it produces will determine the long-term sustainability of the company and often influences stock valuations.

Oil firms can increase oil and gas production and reserves in two ways: organically and through acquisitions. *Organic growth* means a firm increases its oil and gas production from its own operations, whether through new discoveries or increased efficiencies at existing wells. *Acquisition growth* entails buying existing oil and gas assets from another company or acquiring a private or public oil company outright.

A widely followed performance measure is the *reserve replacement ratio*. This measures the ratio of a company's increase in reserves to its oil and gas production annually. So a reserve ratio greater than 100 percent shows a growth in reserves. Reserves usually grow or fall due to revisions, changing recovery rates at existing fields, extensions, new discoveries, and production for the year. Purchases and sales of reserves also apply to reserve replacement, but are not part of organic growth. (Reserve replacement ratios of upstream producers are found in the financial statements.)

As explained in further detail in Chapter 4, there are growing challenges to the industry's ability to increase oil and gas production and reserves. The sector's aggregate revenues and earnings should benefit to the extent companies are able to expand oil and gas production consistently without a significant drop in commodity prices.

Finding and Development Costs

Finding and development costs describe the cost of newly booked reserves, typically expressed in dollars per barrel. While commodity prices and oil and gas production growth may drive the top line, costs ultimately drive the bottom line.

Finding and development costs generally rise and fall in concert with hydrocarbon prices. As oil and gas prices rise, demand for labor, equipment, and services rise, pushing up prices of the entire supply chain. This is why Energy sector profit margins have stayed rather stable over the past several years despite the huge run-up in energy prices—while absolute earnings figures may appear tremendous, it costs firms much more to earn them!

In general, the largest integrated oil firms have the size, scale, and influence to somewhat mitigate cost inflation. Smaller firms, however, may find it more difficult to control costs and could be challenged to maintain profit margins.

Firms within the Energy Equipment & Services (EES) industry may benefit directly from rising finding and development costs (which are covered in more detail in Chapter 3). While finding and development costs represent cash outflows for exploration and production firms, they also represent cash inflows to many equipment and services firms. As demand for energy services increases, these firms are able to pass on higher prices for their products and services.

Finding and Development Costs

Finding and development (F&D) costs are usually expressed as dollars per barrel of oil equivalent (BOE). The technical definition is total costs incurred (purchases of properties, exploration costs, and development costs), divided by the summation of annual proved reserves on a BOE basis—attributable to revisions of previous estimates, purchases of minerals in place, and discoveries and extensions. (Note: Some tweak F&D cost calculations to exclude acquisitions of producing reserves. Doing so shows the company's pure operating performance.)

Exploration and Production Capital Expenditures

Exploration and production capital expenditures from the Oil & Gas industry will also be a driver of performance for the Energy

Equipment & Services industry. Periods of rising capital expenditures generally benefit energy services firms providing the rigs, equipment, and services necessary to search for and expand oil and gas production. Firms base their planned capital expenditures on factors like expectations for commodity prices, availability of high-return projects, reserve replacement needs, cost inflation, and balance sheet strength.

However, the more important issue is determining where and how these expenditures will be spent. Is more money now being spent on exploration versus last year? Are firms spending relatively more drilling for natural gas or oil, or both? What regions of the world stand to benefit the most from an increase in spending? Consequently, if capital expenditures fall substantially, which parts of the industry would be hurt most? These kinds of questions should be asked when determining how exploration and production capital expenditures will affect the industry.

As seen in Figure 2.17, world Energy sector capital expenditures have increased significantly along with oil prices over the last several years. The rise in spending has been a boon to the vast majority of firms in the Energy Equipment & Services industry, driving profits higher.

Capital expenditures may also affect Oil & Gas industry performance. If rising capital expenditures eventually lead to higher oil and

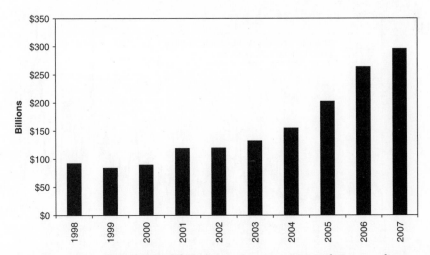

Figure 2.17   MSCI World Energy Sector Capital Expenditures
Source: Thomson Datastream, MSCI, Inc.[18]

gas production, it could be a positive for the industry. Consequently, falling capital expenditures could eventually inhibit long-term production growth.

Refining Margins

Refining margins are the difference between petroleum product prices and the cost of crude oil, usually quoted in dollars per barrel. They are the main earnings drivers for the downstream segment of the Oil & Gas industry.

Refining margins differ greatly depending on the country or region because petroleum product prices differ by country due to regional supply and demand conditions, tax policies, and government intervention (like gasoline price caps in several emerging market nations).

For the world's largest petroleum product market—the US—refining margins can be highly volatile. While crude oil prices fluctuate every day, petroleum product prices can be sticky (i.e., it can take longer for gasoline prices to change versus oil prices).

Figure 2.18 shows a proxy for US refining margins since 1997. Due to a combination of volatile oil and petroleum product prices,

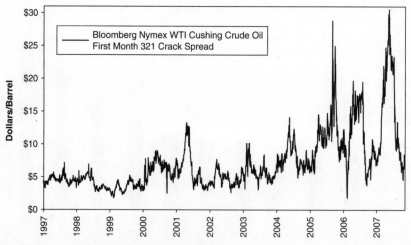

Figure 2.18 US Refining Margins
Source: Bloomberg Finance L.P.

refining margins have swung wildly over the last few years. (We'll discuss refining margins and their drivers in greater detail in Chapter 5.)

Share Buybacks and M&A Activity

Like any sector, industry consolidation and share buybacks can influence stock market performance. With the supply of securities reduced—and assuming demand is constant—prices rise. Oil and gas firms are some of the most profitable firms in the world, with some of the largest cash hoards today, making consolidation and buybacks a major part of sector performance.

Because many oil and gas firms generate tremendous cash flow, they often return cash to shareholders through dividends and share buybacks. All else being equal, many energy firms today can immediately increase earnings per share (EPS) by repurchasing outstanding shares. For instance, Exxon Mobil alone accumulated over $30 billion in cash as of December 31, 2007, and used that giant stash to buy back shares and pay out dividends.[19]

Energy sector consolidation will likely continue to be meaningful as reserve access becomes increasingly difficult. Instead of disputes over contracts or trying to make new, large discoveries, oil firms may find it easier and cheaper to simply buy a competitor. However, a multitude of factors determine the likelihood of increased consolidation, including valuations, financing costs and capital availability, and management attitudes toward consolidation.

Figure 2.19 shows the total number and dollar amount of deals within the world Energy Sector over the last several years. The bar chart shows the deal values while the line chart shows the number of deals. As the chart shows, the rise in oil prices since 2003 has caused a surge in deal activity.

Sentiment

Investor sentiment also has a major effect on sector performance, and Energy is no exception. How firms perform relative to expectations is vital for understanding stock movements. A widely held expectation

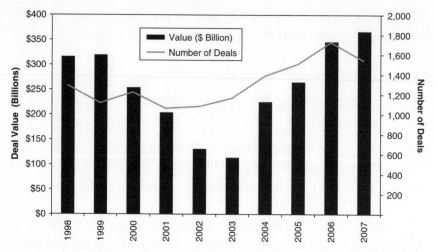

Figure 2.19 World Energy Sector Mergers & Acquisitions
Source: Thomson Reuters.

is likely already discounted into current prices. However, there are still ways to take advantage of sentiment. To gain an advantage, one must glean some information the market doesn't yet know.

In recent years, most industry experts have consistently underestimated future oil prices. When an equity research analyst creates a valuation model for a stock, the analyst forecasts future earnings based on commodity price assumptions. So when oil prices rise higher than consensus estimates, analysts must update their valuation models, revaluing the company at higher prices. Should oil prices trade in a range much lower than expected, valuations will be revised downward. (Note: Futures prices provide easily accessible, but imperfect, proxies for commodity price expectations. The futures markets do not always mimic equity research analysts' consensus views. Use them carefully.)

Thus, there are important questions to ask when evaluating Energy sector sentiment. Do analysts generally expect oil and natural gas prices to rise or fall next year? If the consensus expects prices to rise, what is the expected magnitude of the increase? What are the general assumptions behind the oil and natural gas price forecasts? Do you agree with them? For example, if consensus expects oil prices to reach an average $60/bbl next year but you expect greater than that (and end up being correct), it is likely Energy will perform well as analysts revise their earnings models to reflect higher commodity prices.

Taxes, Politics, and Regulation

Oil and gas firms are consistently the topic of political and regulatory debates around the world. As oil prices and company earnings rise, politicians are quick to propose new taxes, regulations, royalties, and other issues to meddle in free markets.

Taxation, politics, and regulations vary widely depending on the country, but all are important considerations when forecasting future Energy performance. For instance, governments will generally play a greater role in setting prices and policy in emerging market countries than in developed ones. European nations may be more likely to increase taxes on oil firms than the US. Generally, most changes in regulation tend to hurt energy firms during periods of rising commodity prices as governments attempt to grab a greater share of the profits.

There are many ways government involvement can affect future oil and gas company performance. For instance, an implementation of an oil *windfall tax*—where the government gains a greater share of profits should prices hit a predetermined level—has been proposed in the US and other governments on several occasions. The UK has been one of the most aggressive on taxation in recent years, increasing taxes on oil and gas companies from 30 percent in 2002 to 50 percent by 2005.[20] In 2007, Canada's Alberta government announced it would increase royalties on production from oil sands and conventional oil and gas wells. Governments can also increase or decrease subsidies and tax incentives for oil firms. In general, higher taxes and royalties lead to decreased drilling and capital expenditures by the oil and gas industry.

More extreme actions taken by foreign governments include the outright expropriation of assets and forced renegotiation of contracts with private oil firms. For example, Venezuela repeatedly changed the terms of its contracts with foreign oil firms in recent years and, in 2006, mandated private firms to cede majority control of operations to its state oil company PDVSA. When France's Total SA and Italy's

Eni Spa failed to comply with the country's demands, the government sent the military to seize two oil fields from the firms.

Another example includes actions taken by the Russian gas monopoly Gazprom to gain majority control of the Sakhalin 2 oil and gas project in late 2006. Originally, this massive oil and gas project was entirely under control of three non-Russian firms, including the UK's Royal Dutch Shell and Japan's Mitsubishi and Mitsui. But after the firms announced they expected project costs would double to $22 billion—which under the original contract would significantly increase the amount of time before the Russian government would receive royalties—the government's environmental regulatory agency accused the firms of "environmental violations" and threatened to revoke permits. After months of pressure, the three firms agreed to let Gazprom buy control of the project.

Chapter Recap

Identifying and analyzing the Energy sector's key drivers is central in determining whether the sector is currently attractive or unattractive. The sector's largest drivers, by far, are oil and natural gas prices. These are both fundamentally determined by the laws of supply and demand. Other drivers can have an equally large influence on the sector as well (like M&A activity) and must be followed closely.

- High-level drivers will greatly affect the performance of the Energy sector.
- While numerous drivers affect the Energy sector, oil and natural gas prices are by far the most important.
- Oil prices are driven primarily by world supply and demand conditions, but other factors like geopolitics, speculation, and government action can also affect prices.
- Natural gas prices are mostly determined by regional supply and demand issues. Drivers of supply and demand for natural gas differ greatly depending on the region.
- Drivers other than commodity prices—like capital spending, refining margins, and M&A activity—can be equally important to Energy sector returns, especially as they pertain to sub-industries within Energy.

II

NEXT STEPS:
ENERGY DETAILS

3

ENERGY SECTOR BREAKDOWN

Now you've got the general basics and Energy's high-level drivers. But keep in mind a *sector* is really a broad category made of many distinct parts. Any good anthropologist knows "America" is too broad and diverse to understand as a single entity. Instead, one would study regions and states and see how they fit together to understand the whole country. The same is true for the Energy—and any other— sector.

Chapter 1 covered the major industries: Oil & Gas (O&G) and Energy Equipment & Services (EES). But even within those major components, differing sub-industries exist, each with unique characteristics and economic drivers, often interrelated in some way. Before you can make any portfolio decisions, you must understand what a sector looks like and what makes each distinct component tick. This chapter explores the sub-industries and how an investor can form an opinion on each. We'll answer questions like: What economic drivers are important for each industry? How do they fit with the rest of the sector? How do separate industries work in tandem or against each other?

GLOBAL INDUSTRY CLASSIFICATION STANDARD (GICS)

Before we begin, some definitions. The Global Industry Classification Standard (GICS) is a widely accepted industry framework for classifying firms based on similarities. GICS was developed by MSCI, an independent provider of global indexes and benchmark-related products and services, and Standard & Poor's, an independent international financial data and investment services company and provider of global equity indexes.

The GICS structure consists of **10** sectors, **24** industry groups, **68** industries, and **154** sub-industries.[1] This structure offers four levels of hierarchy, ranging from the most general sector to the most specialized sub-industry:

- Sector
- Industry group
- Industry
- Sub-industry

Let's start by breaking down the Energy sector into its different components. According to GICS, the Energy sector consists of one industry group (Energy), two industries, and seven sub-industries. Energy's industries with the corresponding sub-industries are:

Oil, Gas & Consumable Fuels
- Integrated Oil & Gas
- Oil & Gas Exploration & Production
- Oil & Gas Refining & Marketing
- Oil & Gas Storage & Transportation
- Coal & Consumable Fuels

Energy Equipment & Services
- Oil & Gas Drilling
- Oil & Gas Equipment & Services

GLOBAL ENERGY BENCHMARKS

What's a benchmark? What does it do, and why do you need to select one? A *benchmark* is your guide for building a stock portfolio. You can use any well-constructed index as a benchmark—examples are in Table 3.1. By studying a benchmark's (i.e., the index's) make-up, an investor can assign expected risk and return to make underweight and overweight decisions for each industry. This is just as true for a sector as it is for the broader stock market, and there are many potential Energy sector benchmarks to choose from. (Benchmarks will be further explored in Chapter 7.)

So what does the Energy sector investment universe look like? It depends on the benchmark, so choose carefully! The US Energy sector looks very different from that of Europe, Japan, and the Emerging Markets. Table 3.1 shows major global benchmark indexes and the percentage weight of each sector.

Table 3.1   Energy Benchmark Differences

Sector	MSCI World	MSCI EAFE	S&P 500	Russell 2000	MSCI Emerging Markets
Consumer Discretionary	9.8%	10.8%	8.5%	13.5%	4.9%
Consumer Staples	8.8%	8.5%	10.2%	3.0%	4.2%
Energy	**10.9%**	**7.9%**	**12.9%**	**6.7%**	**18.0%**
Financials	22.6%	26.9%	17.6%	18.9%	21.7%
Health Care	8.7%	6.3%	12.0%	14.5%	1.6%
Industrials	11.4%	12.1%	11.5%	15.1%	9.7%
Information Technology	11.0%	5.5%	16.7%	18.3%	10.1%
Materials	7.2%	9.9%	3.3%	5.6%	14.7%
Telecommunication Services	4.9%	6.2%	3.6%	1.5%	11.5%
Utilities	4.7%	5.9%	3.6%	3.0%	3.5%
Total	100.0%	100.0%	100.0%	100.0%	100.0%

Source: Thomson Datastream, MSCI, Inc.[2] as of 12/31/07.

Common Benchmarks

Commonly used benchmarks include the *MSCI World, MSCI EAFE, S&P 500, Russell 2000,* and *MSCI Emerging Markets.* The MSCI World is a market-capitalization weighted index designed to measure the equity market performance of developed markets (encompassing 23 developed markets, including the US). The MSCI EAFE is a market-capitalization weighted index that measures the equity market performance of developed markets excluding the US and Canada. The S&P 500 is a market capitalization weighted index that measures the equity market performance of a basket of 500 stocks that encompass the majority of the US equity universe. The Russell 2000 is a market-capitalization weighted index that measures the equity market performance of the small-cap segment of the US equity universe. Lastly, the MSCI Emerging Markets is a market-capitalization weighted index that measures the equity market performance of emerging markets (encompassing 25 emerging market countries).

The sector weights show the relative importance of each sector in driving overall index performance. While Energy is the second-largest weight in the MSCI Emerging Markets index, it's only the fourth largest in the MSCI World index (made up of developed nations only). But the sector weights aren't fixed and can change over time—due to performance differences, additions and deletions of firms to the indexes, and a variety of other factors. For example, Financials wasn't always the biggest, and for many decades Industrials dominated.

In some countries, Energy is by far the largest sector; while in others, it barely makes up a few percent. Table 3.2 shows the Energy sector percentage weight by country, based on the MSCI World and MSCI Emerging Market indexes. Note the stark differences between developed and emerging market countries. On one extreme, Russia's stock market is dominated by Energy—mainly state-controlled Gazprom. On the other, Germany has no Energy weight at all.

The sector weight can vary, but so can sub-industry weights— sometimes greatly depending on the chosen benchmark. Table 3.3 shows the weight of each Energy sub-industry within each benchmark. (Columns add up to 100 percent.)

Table 3.2 Energy Weight by Country

Country	Energy Weight
Russia	59.9%
Norway	44.3%
Canada	28.3%
Brazil	27.1%
India	20.2%
Italy	19.0%
China	18.4%
United Kingdom	18.2%
Austria	16.7%
South Africa	13.9%
US	13.0%
France	12.5%
Australia	5.3%
Spain	4.6%
Netherlands	2.3%
Greece	2.1%
Korea	2.0%
Finland	1.7%
Japan	1.3%
Sweden	0.8%
Denmark	0.4%
Singapore	0.3%
Belgium	0.2%
Germany	0.0%
Hong Kong	0.0%
Ireland	0.0%
New Zealand	0.0%
Portugal	0.0%
Switzerland	0.0%

Source: Thomson Datastream, MSCI, Inc.[3] as of 12/31/07.

Table 3.3   Energy Sub-Industry Weights

Sub-Industry	MSCI World	MSCI EAFE	S&P 500	Russell 2000	MSCI Emerging Markets
Coal & Consumable Fuels	1.8%	0.3%	1.8%	5.4%	6.8%
Integrated Oil & Gas	63.5%	86.0%	60.5%	0.0%	66.3%
Oil & Gas Drilling	3.5%	0.6%	4.9%	9.1%	0.3%
Oil & Gas Equipment & Services	10.7%	5.0%	15.0%	29.9%	2.0%
Oil & Gas Exploration & Production	14.8%	4.7%	11.6%	43.7%	10.8%
Oil & Gas Refining & Marketing	2.8%	3.2%	3.2%	4.8%	13.3%
Oil & Gas Storage & Transportation	2.8%	0.2%	3.0%	7.1%	0.5%
Total	100.0%	100.0%	100.0%	100.0%	100.0%

Source: Thomson Datastream, MSCI, Inc.[4] as of 12/31/07.

Table 3.4 shows how the global Energy sub-industries are concentrated by region. Using the MSCI All Country World Index (encompassing developed and developing market Energy firms), the table shows how each sub-industry is distributed among regions. It's important to consider the regions as well, because in a top-down context, local economic and political conditions will have a large impact on sector, industry, and sub-industry performance. For example, if you expect the US will perform well overall in the near term, that bodes well for Oil & Gas Drilling and Oil & Gas Equipment & Services, where most of those companies are located. And how you expect Emerging Markets to perform overall should figure into your expectations for Coal & Consumable Fuels.

The main global Energy benchmarks have some notable differences. But in most, the Integrated Oil & Gas sub-industry is by far the largest sub-industry by market cap (see Table 3.3)—most notably in the MSCI EAFE, where it comprises 86.0 percent of the total Energy sector.

Table 3.4 Energy Sub-Industries by Region

Sub-Industry	Canada	EAFE	Emerging Markets	US	Total
Coal & Consumable Fuels	16.0%	3.2%	44.2%	36.6%	100.0%
Integrated Oil & Gas	4.5%	39.4%	17.6%	38.5%	100.0%
Oil & Gas Drilling	2.7%	6.2%	1.6%	89.6%	100.0%
Oil & Gas Equipment & Services	0.7%	16.0%	3.4%	79.9%	100.0%
Oil & Gas Exploration & Production	31.8%	9.8%	13.3%	45.1%	100.0%
Oil & Gas Refining & Marketing	0.0%	27.3%	42.0%	30.7%	100.0%
Oil & Gas Storage & Transportation	39.7%	2.4%	3.4%	54.5%	100.0%

Source: Thomson Datastream, MSCI, Inc.[5] as of 12/31/07.

This is because *supermajor* integrated oil companies (IOCs) all have market caps dwarfing the majority of firms in each index. Previous periods of industry consolidation created the supermajors—familiar firms, like Exxon Mobil, Chevron, Royal Dutch Shell, and BP, characterized by large market caps, geographic diversity, huge reserves, and massive scale. So why are they such a small percentage of the Russell 2000? Because IOCs are generally too large to appear in the small cap Russell 2000 index.

It's also important to note many of the world's most significant Integrated Oil & Gas companies are owned by foreign governments and therefore are neither publicly traded nor reflected in stock market indexes. For example, Saudi Aramco, Saudi Arabia's National Oil Company, is the largest oil company in the world based on production and reserves, but it's not represented in stock market indexes because it's entirely state-owned.

Other items to note from the benchmarks: The majority of publicly traded Oil & Gas Exploration & Production firms are in the US. In general, most of these firms explore for and produce oil and gas (mostly natural gas) within North America. While the sub-industry is the second- or third-largest within most major global benchmarks, it's the largest weight within the small cap Russell 2000 index.

Another US-heavy industry is Energy Equipment & Services, with major energy service firms like Schlumberger and Transocean contributing heavily to the industry's weight. The industry is growing outside the US but still remains a relatively small weight in most foreign benchmarks. Within Emerging Markets, there are virtually no Energy service firms.

The Oil & Gas Refining & Marketing sub-industry is a relatively small weight in all benchmarks except Emerging Markets, where it's the second-largest weight. Geographically, most of these firms reside in emerging markets or the US.

Last, the smallest Energy sub-industries are Oil & Gas Storage & Transportation and Coal & Consumable Fuels. Because these firms are relatively smaller in market cap, they only make up a significant weight in the Russell 2000 and Emerging Markets indexes. In the broader indexes, they're tiny, with little discernable impact. Geographically, Storage & Transportation is almost entirely concentrated in the US and Canada, while Coal & Consumable Fuels is concentrated in emerging markets and the US.

OIL, GAS & CONSUMABLE FUELS INDUSTRY

Once you understand what the benchmarks look like and how they're comprised, you can analyze the main players and key performance drivers in each sub-industry. And we begin with Oil, Gas, & Consumable Fuels (O&G).

In general, O&G firms explore for, produce, transport, store, and refine oil and natural gas. As mentioned in Chapter 1, these firms make up the *integrated* process—the upstream, midstream, and downstream activities. By far, these firms as an industry make up the majority of the Energy sector's market capitalization, including familiar supermajor integrated oil firms like Exxon Mobil, Chevron, Royal Dutch Shell, and BP. This industry is the most directly affected by energy commodity prices. Its sub-industries are:

- Integrated Oil & Gas (upstream and downstream)
- Oil & Gas Exploration & Production (upstream)
- Oil & Gas Refining & Marketing (downstream)
- Oil & Gas Storage & Transportation (midstream)
- Coal & Consumable Fuels (coal and uranium mining)

Integrated Oil & Gas Sub-Industry

The Integrated Oil & Gas sub-industry is where you find the super-majors and other IOCs, engaged in both upstream and downstream activities. In other words, these firms explore for and produce oil and natural gas, refine them into various petroleum products, and sell them through retail gas stations—all parts of the integrated process.

IOCs are some of the largest firms in the world, including the world's largest publicly traded firm, Exxon Mobil (as of December 31, 2007). In periods of high energy prices, IOCs are historically some of the most financially healthy in the world, typified by tremendous cash flows, low debt, and high credit ratings.

State-owned IOCs are known as *national oil companies* (NOCs). NOCs are most often found in places like Saudi Arabia, Iran, Iraq, and Venezuela. Although the majority of the NOCs are not publicly traded, they have tremendous influence on the industry. Ranked on the basis of oil and gas reserve holdings, 14 of the world's top 20 upstream oil and gas firms are NOCs or newly privatized NOCs.[6] State-owned firms are major clients of many of the world's Energy Equipment & Services firms and often partner with IOCs for exploration and production projects. NOCs are often responsible for generating the vast majority of government revenues, especially in the Middle East.

Most IOCs have two business segments: upstream and downstream. As mentioned in Chapter 1, *upstream* involves exploration and production of oil and natural gas resources, which are then sold to the downstream sector. *Downstream* involves converting these resources into petroleum products through refineries and then selling them to consumers. In periods of high energy prices, the upstream division provides the vast majority of earnings to IOCs. The downstream division usually provides the majority of a firm's sales, but profit margins are often much smaller.

IOCs have diverse business operations and geographies, producing oil and natural gas from locations all over the globe, including land, offshore, and unconventional sources. In the downstream segment, in addition to owning refineries globally producing gasoline, diesel, heating oil, and chemicals, IOCs often own hundreds (if not thousands) of retail gas stations. Most IOCs also own midstream assets to transport and store crude oil, natural gas, and petroleum products, but consider the midstream segment to be more of a cost rather than a revenue source. Diversity in product offerings helps stabilize revenues through seasons and broader economic cycles.

IOCs' upstream and downstream activities also serve as natural hedges to overall earnings. When crude oil prices rise, the upstream division makes tremendous profits while the downstream division faces higher costs. In periods of falling crude prices, the opposite is true. Geographic diversity also helps offset shifting currencies, tax rates, interest rates, and geopolitical risks.

Integrated Oil & Gas is relatively concentrated, with the largest publicly traded firms located in the US and Europe. In fact, until recently the largest publicly traded IOCs were almost exclusively American or European. Now that certain countries have opened their stock markets to greater foreign investment, helping drive share prices higher, state-owned firms like Russia's Gazprom have joined the ranks of the majors.

While IOCs' business operations in emerging markets and developed markets are very similar, there are important nonoperating differences. Emerging market IOCs (like Gazprom and PetroChina) are subject to sudden and draconian government involvement not generally seen in the US or Europe. This may include tax rate changes, price controls, or government involvement in the strategic direction of the company. All of this can (and generally will) happen without warning—adding a layer of uncertainty and, thus, increased volatility to these share prices.

Table 3.5 shows the 15 largest publicly traded IOCs in the MSCI All Country World Index (ACWI) as of December 31, 2007.

Table 3.5   15 Largest Integrated Oil Companies

Name	Market Cap (Billions)	Country	% of Sub-Industry
Exxon Mobil	$511.9	US	16.1%
Gazprom	$333.6	Russia	10.5%
Royal Dutch Shell	$269.5	United Kingdom	8.5%
BP	$231.7	United Kingdom	7.3%
Total	$198.8	France	6.3%
Chevron	$197.1	US	6.2%
Petrobras	$149.6	Brazil	4.7%
Eni Spa	$146.7	Italy	4.6%
ConocoPhillips	$141.2	US	4.4%
Rosneft	$101.4	Russia	3.2%
StatoilHydro	$99.2	Norway	3.1%
BG Group	$76.9	United Kingdom	2.4%
Lukoil	$71.9	Russia	2.3%
Occidental Petroleum	$63.8	US	2.0%
Suncor Energy	$50.6	Canada	1.6%

Source: Thomson Datastream, MSCI, Inc.[7] as of 12/31/07.

Oil & Gas Exploration & Production Sub-Industry

Oil & Gas Exploration & Production (E&P) operates exclusively in Energy's *upstream*. These firms engage in the exploration and production of oil and natural gas without any refining or marketing assets.

There are more E&P firms in the world than any other type of Energy firm. While the largest come from foreign nations like China, India, Russia, and Canada, the majority of publicly traded E&P firms are domiciled in the US.

Typical E&P firms are focused on finding, extracting, and producing oil and natural gas, then selling it to the downstream sector. Historically, E&Ps have been subject to wide swings in earnings because revenue is dependent on volatile commodity prices. Thus, many use a variety of hedging techniques to mitigate commodity price exposure. Locking in future production at specific prices allows E&Ps to guarantee sufficient cash flows to fund current and future drilling projects.

E&Ps' long-term success ultimately depends on the ability to secure a consistent and growing level of oil and gas production. There are two main strategies—*organic growth* and *acquisition*. Each strategy has pros and cons.

An organic growth strategy relies on the success in securing attractive drilling sites, making discoveries, and maintaining steady growth in commodity production. This can be a risky venture since drilling speculative wells is costly and may result in failure. For those already holding vast proven resources, there still could be *execution risk*—the ability to extract oil and gas in a cost- and time-efficient manner.

An acquisition strategy removes the uncertainty of making discoveries and execution risks, but requires firms to identify and acquire attractive assets at a fair price. Moreover, an acquisition strategy can be affected by firm credit rating, cash flow sustainability, and cost of capital. In periods of rapidly rising commodity prices, energy firm valuations may rise in concert, making financially attractive acquisitions more difficult to find.

Because oil and gas reserves are usually found together, many E&P firms produce at least some amount of both oil and natural gas, but they tend to focus on one depending on geography and reserve access. Because the US has much greater natural gas reserves than oil reserves, the majority of US E&P firms focus primarily on natural gas. Canada has vast oil sands reserves, but those are not easily extracted. Hence, the largest Canadian E&Ps also focus on natural gas. In general, most of the largest E&P firms produce more natural gas than oil based on barrels of oil equivalent (BOE). (Note: BOE is used by oil and gas companies to combine oil and gas reserves and production into a single measure.)

The E&P sub-industry is also highly fragmented. Firms in the sub-industry range from large, state-owned firms with access to vast reserves to small, wildcat producers whose success is determined by

Table 3.6   15 Largest Oil & Gas Exploration & Production Companies

Name	Market Cap (Billions)	Country	% of Sub-Industry
CNOOC	$75.5	China	9.9%
Oil and Natural Gas Corp	$67.1	India	8.8%
EnCana	$51.4	Canada	6.7%
Surgutneftegas	$44.3	Russia	5.8%
Canadian Natural Resources	$39.7	Canada	5.2%
Devon Energy	$39.6	US	5.2%
Apache	$35.8	US	4.7%
Anadarko Petroleum	$30.6	US	4.0%
Woodside Petroleum	$30.5	Australia	4.0%
INPEX Holdings	$25.6	Japan	3.4%
XTO Energy	$24.8	US	3.3%
EOG Resources	$22.0	US	2.9%
Talisman Energy	$19.0	Canada	2.5%
Canadian Oil Sands Trust	$18.8	Canada	2.5%
Chesapeake Energy	$18.6	US	2.4%

Source: Thomson Datastream, MSCI, Inc.[8] as of 12/31/07.

new discoveries. Table 3.6 shows the 15 largest publicly traded Oil & Gas Exploration & Production firms in the MSCI ACWI as of December 31, 2007.

Oil & Gas Refining & Marketing Sub-Industry

Oil & Gas Refining & Marketing (R&M) firms engage exclusively in *downstream* activities. These firms focus on processing and refining crude oil into petroleum products for sale to wholesale or retail customers.

R&M has the second-fewest publicly traded firms in the industry, after the Integrated Oil & Gas sub-industry. This is mostly because refining and marketing in the US is dominated by the downstream divisions of the big IOCs. As a result, most R&Ms are non-US firms.

R&M consists of two basic businesses: refining and retail sales. The retail division delivers petroleum products to independently or company-owned retail outlets (like gasoline stations), where the products are sold to the end user.

But R&M firms' main assets are the refineries, where crude oil is obtained from local or imported sources, processed, and sold on the wholesale market to a wide variety of customers over an extensive network in the form of multiple petroleum products. These products include gasoline and diesel, jet fuel, heating oil, propane, chemicals, and more. As mentioned in Chapter 1, refineries choose what mix of petroleum products they will produce based on local supply and demand. Refineries also change their product mix based on seasons—producing more gasoline during the summer driving season and more heating oil during the winter.

Refineries also vary in their complexity, or ability, to process different grades of crude oil (see Chapter 1). Heavier, sour crudes are typically cheaper than light, sweet crudes as the former are more difficult and costly to refine. Refineries are often built to process the most readily available type of crude, but larger refineries can often process multiple grades of crude.

R&M firms in general make the vast majority of their earnings through their refining divisions. The main earnings driver, the refining margin, is determined by the spread between crude oil costs and petroleum product prices. Because both crude oil and petroleum products can be highly volatile, these firms often see the Energy sector's most wild earnings swings. To temper this, many firms also use a variety of techniques to hedge their exposure to crude oil, natural gas (used to power the refineries), and petroleum product prices.

In order to grow, R&M firms must acquire other refineries, build new ones, or expand refining capacity at existing sites. It can be politically difficult, if not downright impossible, to build a grassroots refinery in some countries (the US hasn't built a new refinery since 1976).[9] Many choose to expand capacity at existing sites or upgrade plant complexity to refine more types of crude oil. This growth strategy—at least in the US—will likely continue for the foreseeable future. Despite recent complaints about high gasoline prices, it's unlikely we'll see a new refinery built in the US anytime soon due to political barriers, environmental group opposition, government red tape, uncertain economics, and the so-called "not-in-my-backyard" mentality from consumers.

The R&M sub-industry varies greatly depending on geography. In the US, there are relatively few independent refiners because IOCs handle most of the nation's refining. The few large publicly traded US refining firms are focused exclusively on the domestic market, producing mainly gasoline and diesel. In other countries—especially emerging markets—some refineries produce mainly chemicals and sell their products to multiple countries.

Table 3.7 shows the 15 largest publicly traded R&M firms in the MSCI ACWI as of December 31, 2007.

Table 3.7   15 Largest Oil & Gas Refining & Marketing Companies

Name	Market Cap (Billions)	Country	% of Sub-Industry
Reliance Industries	$106.3	India	33.1%
Valero Energy	$38.5	US	12.0%
Formosa Petrochemical	$27.7	Taiwan	8.6%
SK Energy	$17.7	Korea	5.5%
Nippon Oil	$11.9	Japan	3.7%
S-Oil	$9.5	Korea	3.0%
Neste Oil	$9.0	Finland	2.8%
Polski Koncern Naftowy ORLEN	$9.0	Poland	2.8%
Sunoco	$8.5	US	2.7%
Tupras Turkiye Petrol Rafine	$7.3	Turkey	2.3%
Tesoro	$6.5	US	2.0%
Nippon Mining	$6.0	Japan	1.9%
GS Holdings	$5.8	Korea	1.8%
TonenGeneral Sekiyu K.K.	$5.6	Japan	1.7%
Thai Oil	$5.2	Thailand	1.6%

Source: Thomson Datastream, MSCI, Inc.[10] as of 12/31/07.

Oil & Gas Storage & Transportation Sub-Industry

Oil & Gas Storage & Transportation (S&T) is the *midstream* segment of Energy. These firms store and transport crude oil, natural gas, petroleum products, and more by way of pipelines, storage terminals, and crude tankers.

These firms are relatively few, with the majority domiciled in the US and Canada. The largest are mainly North American pipeline firms (most non-North American pipelines are state-owned). While some IOCs and E&Ps own their own midstream assets, there are several large publicly traded midstream firms.

Generally, segments within S&T are not directly affected by commodity prices. Instead, S&T services are generally fee-based and driven by volume. For example, pipeline firms charge fees for using their pipelines, earning greater revenues as the pipeline use increases. Thus, rising and falling commodity prices only affect revenues to the extent prices change the volume demanded.

The storage business involves owning and operating fields and storage facilities for a variety of products including crude oil, natural gas, and petroleum products. For example, underground natural gas storage provides pipelines, local distribution firms, producers, and pipeline shippers with inventory management, seasonal supply backup, and access to natural gas needed to avoid imbalances between pipeline network receipts and deliveries.

Pipeline operators tend to be heavily regulated by government agencies. In the US, firms are regulated by the Federal Energy Regulatory Commission (FERC) for their interstate pipelines and by various state bodies for intrastate pipelines. With regulated tariffs, many firms are akin to public utilities. As such, they tend to have high dividends and consistent cash flows, making them attractive to income-oriented investors.

Many US pipeline operators are structured as Master Limited Partnerships (MLPs). This structure exempts them from US federal income taxes but requires payout on the majority of operating income to shareholders. Shareholders are then responsible for paying income taxes

Table 3.8   15 Largest Oil & Gas Storage & Transportation Companies

Name	Market Cap (Billions)	Country	% of Sub-Industry
TransCanada	$22.2	Canada	22.7%
Williams Cos.	$21.2	US	21.7%
Spectra Energy	$16.3	US	16.7%
Enbridge	$14.9	Canada	15.3%
El Paso	$12.1	US	12.3%
Frontline Ltd	$3.6	Norway	3.7%
Transneft Pref.	$3.1	Russia	3.2%
Dampskibsselskabet TORM	$2.6	Denmark	2.6%
Euronav	$1.9	Belgium	1.9%

Source: Thomson Datastream, MSCI, Inc.[11] as of 12/31/07.

on the distributions. When researching S&T firms, it's important to note which are structured as MLPs, as these securities will have different tax implications.

Pipeline MLPs generally grow by building new pipeline networks or acquiring other pipeline networks—both subject to regulatory limits. MLPs generally carry large debt burdens, funded by steady cash flows.

Another type of S&T firm operates crude oil and petroleum product transportation fleets. This includes firms with large tankers—the largest of which can carry up to two million barrels of crude oil.

Table 3.8 shows all the publicly traded Oil & Gas Storage & Transportation firms in the MSCI ACWI as of December 31, 2007.

Coal & Consumable Fuels Sub-Industry

Coal & Consumable Fuels (CCF) firms primarily mine and sell coal and uranium. While they are in some respects similar to the Materials sector, coal and uranium firms remain classified in Energy and are a relatively small weight in most major Energy indexes. For simplicity's sake, because uranium (used for nuclear power) is the smaller fuel in the sub-industry, we will focus primarily on coal.

The CCF investment universe is very small in developed nations but is more significant in emerging markets. China has several of the world's largest coal firms, including China Shenhua Energy (the world's largest as of December 31, 2007, after its 2007 IPO).

Coal firms own and operate coal mines, selling their output mainly to utilities firms. Coal mining is a cyclical commodity industry characterized by high capital intensity and volatile costs and prices. Success is often based on many factors outside company control, including coal prices, transportation costs, environmental policies, and labor costs.

Coal is used primarily for power generation. Worldwide, 65 percent of coal is for power generation, 31 percent is for industry, and most of the remaining 4 percent is used by residential and commercial consumers.[12] In the US—the world's largest reserve holder and second-largest coal consumer after China—about 92 percent of its coal[13] is responsible for 50 percent of all power generation in the country.[14] The largest consumer and producer of coal, China, consumes 56 percent of its coal for electricity generation through coal-fired plants.[15] Coal is also used in the steelmaking process and for making plastics, tar, fertilizers, and medicine.

When coal is burned, it emits carbon dioxide—the main greenhouse gas many link to global warming. Burning coal also produces emissions such as sulfur, nitrogen oxide, and mercury—substances that pollute water. As a result, firms burning coal are generally subject to strict environmental regulations and high scrutiny.

Unlike oil, coal is not considered to be in short supply. The world is currently estimated to have 998 billion tons of recoverable coal, with 67 percent of that amount located in four countries: the US (27 percent), Russia (17 percent), China (13 percent), and India (10 percent).[16]

Coal mining takes two forms: surface mining and underground mining. In *surface mining*, coal is extracted from surface mines generally less than 200 feet underground. *Underground mining* is anything

200 feet or more below the surface. Surface mining is less expensive than underground mining and comprises the majority of US coal production.

After coal is extracted and processed, it's ready for transport. Most coal in the US is moved by train, but it can also be shipped via barges, ships, and trucks. In fact, coal can be so cheap, it's not uncommon for the cost of shipping to be more than the cost of mining.

Most publicly traded coal firms serve local markets, but the coal export market is growing rapidly. Some emerging market nations like Indonesia have government-regulated domestic coal prices. Thus, the coal export market can be much more profitable than the domestic market.

Table 3.9 shows all the publicly traded Coal & Consumable Fuels firms in the MSCI ACWI as of December 31, 2007.

Table 3.9   15 Largest Coal & Consumable Fuels Companies

Name	Market Cap (Billions)	Country	% of Sub-Industry
China Shenhua Energy	$20.3	China	17.5%
Peabody Energy	$16.4	US	14.1%
Cameco	$13.8	Canada	11.9%
CONSOL Energy	$13.0	US	11.2%
China Coal Energy	$12.9	China	11.1%
Bumi Resources	$12.4	Indonesia	10.7%
Arch Coal	$6.4	US	5.5%
Uranium One	$4.2	Canada	3.6%
Yanzhou Coal Mining	$3.9	China	3.3%
Paladin Energy	$3.7	Australia	3.1%
Banpu	$3.2	Thailand	2.8%
Inner Mongolia Yitai Coal	$3.2	China	2.8%
Massey Energy	$2.8	US	2.4%

Source: Thomson Datastream, MSCI, Inc.[17] as of 12/31/07.

ENERGY EQUIPMENT & SERVICES INDUSTRY

That takes care of the O&G industry and its sub-industries. As discussed in Chapter 1, the Energy Equipment & Services (EES) industry assists O&G in the exploration, production, and refining of oil and natural gas. The main difference between the two industries is EES firms' main businesses are support products and services—not the selling of hydrocarbons or petroleum products.

While EES is much smaller than O&G in terms of both market capitalization and revenue, it still consists of sector stalwarts like Schlumberger, Halliburton, and Baker Hughes. Unlike O&G, EES firms are only indirectly affected by commodity prices—instead, capital expenditures from the O&G industry drive results.

EES sub-industries include:

- Oil & Gas Drilling (contract drilling)
- Oil & Gas Equipment & Services (oil field products and services)

EES is considered the Energy sector's *high beta* play. When energy prices surge, EES generally sees the greatest year-over-year change in earnings. When energy prices fall, the opposite is true, and many firms even go bankrupt.

Oil & Gas Drilling

Oil & Gas Drilling (OGD) firms own and operate the rigs responsible for exploration and production activities. Their main customers include public and private oil and gas exploration and production firms, IOCs, and NOCs.

The OGD investment universe consists of the fewest firms in the Energy sector and is virtually dominated by US firms. Transocean is the largest player, and after its acquisition of GlobalSantaFe in late 2007, it now has over twice the market capitalization of its next-largest competitor.

OGD firms' main business is contract drilling. The most common type of contract is a *daywork* contract, where drillers lease their rigs to oil and gas firms for a length of time at a specified rate, known as a *dayrate*. Oil firms can secure rigs via a short- or long-term contract, usually with an option to extend. Other types of contracts include *turnkey* contracts, where a driller receives a lump sum after a well is completed, and *footage* contracts, where operators pay a rate per foot drilled.

OGD firms tend to have diverse rig fleets. Rigs vary by type but are mainly classified as either *land* or *offshore*. These also vary by drilling depth capacity and how far offshore they can drill. The following is a basic description of the main types of rigs:

1. **Land rig.** Designed to drill on dry land, categorized by size and drilling depth capability. Heavy-duty land rigs can drill over 30,000 feet.
2. **Submersible.** Offshore rig floating on water when moved, but is submerged so the lower part of the rig hits the seafloor. This rig typically operates in wetlands and swamps and is capable of operating in water depths up to 85 feet, drilling over 30,000 feet.
3. **Jack-up.** Offshore rig with legs extending to the sea floor, used to "jack up" the hull to sit above the height of the highest anticipated waves. This rig generally operates in shallow waters less than 400 feet deep but can drill over 30,000 feet.
4. **Semi-submersible.** Offshore rig submerged a few feet below the water's surface, using air-filled steel floats on which the rig sits, held in place by anchors. This rig operates in intermediate to deepwater and can drill more than 30,000 feet, in water up to 10,000 feet deep.
5. **Drill ship.** Ship drilling while floating on the water's surface. Drill ships can drill more than 30,000 feet, in water up to 10,000 feet deep.

Drill ship.
Source: © Getty Images, Inc.

Offshore oil platform.
Source: © Getty Images, Inc.

Semi-submersible rig.
Source: © Getty Images, Inc.

Another type of rig, a *workover*, is designed specifically to provide periodic maintenance as well as major repairs and modifications of oil and gas wells. Workovers use a variety of tactics to keep oil and natural gas flowing efficiently after a well is drilled, including modifying well depths, repairing leaks, and sealing off depleted zones.

Rigs are also classified by the type of hydrocarbon extracted—mainly oil or natural gas. In the US, around 80 percent of all active rigs drill for natural gas, with the remainder drilling for oil.[18] In the international market, it's the reverse—around 75 percent of international rigs drill for oil.[19] Combined, the world's roughly 3,100 rigs (as of 12/31/07) are about evenly split between oil and natural gas rigs.[20]

OGD firms have two growth strategies: building new rigs organically or growth through acquisition. Both strategies have several challenges. In an organic strategy, building new rigs can mean rising costs and delays. While land rigs can be built relatively quickly, deepwater rigs take years and can cost upwards of $600 million. In periods of strong rig demand, shipyard delays are common and costs rise due to tight rig building capacity. Growth through acquisition faces the challenges of obtaining financing and purchasing firms or rigs at acceptable valuations.

Historically, drilling is a boom-bust industry. In boom periods—usually following a surge in oil and/or natural gas prices—demand and prices for rigs soar, causing drilling firms to increase their rig fleet. In bust periods—usually following a steep decline in oil and/or natural gas prices—demand and prices for rigs plummet, forcing firms to take rigs out of service. Because drilling contracts are traditionally awarded on a competitive bid basis, intense price competition occurs among industry participants. As a result, OGDs are characterized by highly volatile earnings.

Table 3.10 shows all the publicly traded OGD firms in the MSCI ACWI as of December 31, 2007.

Table 3.10   15 Largest Oil & Gas Drilling Companies

Name	Market Cap (Billions)	Country	% of Sub-Industry
Transocean	$45.4	US	35.3%
Diamond Offshore Drilling	$19.7	US	15.3%
Noble Corp	$15.2	US	11.8%
Seadrill	$9.7	Norway	7.6%
Ensco International	$8.6	US	6.7%
Nabors Industries	$7.8	US	6.0%
Pride International	$5.7	US	4.4%
Rowan Cos.	$4.4	US	3.4%
China Oilfield Services	$3.5	China	2.7%
Patterson-UTI Energy	$3.0	US	2.4%
Ensign Energy Services	$2.4	Canada	1.8%
Precision Drilling Trust	$1.9	Canada	1.5%
Ocean Rig	$1.2	Norway	1.0%

Source: Thomson Datastream, MSCI, Inc.[21] as of 12/31/07.

Oil & Gas Equipment & Services Sub-Industry

Oil & Gas Equipment & Services (E&S) firms provide basically all products and services to the O&G industry, with the exception of rigs. (Note: There are some E&S firms that offer rigs, but that's not generally their main business.) Similar to drillers, E&S firms' main customers also include public and private oil and gas exploration and production firms, IOCs, and NOCs, as well as drillers.

The E&S investment universe is extremely diverse, with the majority of firms residing in North America. The largest E&S firm, Schlumberger, dominates the investment universe with over three times the market capitalization of its next-largest competitor.

E&S firms assist the O&G industry in every aspect of the exploration and production process. The types of products and services offered by E&S are many, but the main functions are to assist in drilling, evaluation, and completion of oil and gas wells. Because this type of expertise is unique and requires specialized equipment, oil and gas producers find it most cost effective to contract this work out to E&S firms rather than develop them internally.

Some of the many E&S products include drill bits, drilling fluids, drill pipes, casing, and tubing. All these and more are vital to drilling and maintaining oil and gas wells. Service offerings are also varied. Examples include pressure pumping services, wireline services, directional drilling, seismic imaging, and marine support vessels such as boats, helicopters, and submarines. Some E&S firms—mostly foreign—are responsible for building oil and gas facilities like liquefied natural gas (LNG) plants, offshore platforms, and refineries. These firms perform engineering and construction services in a wide variety of locations—onshore, offshore, and subsea. (Descriptions and detailed explanations of these services and more are provided in most E&S firms' annual reports and financial statements like the 10-K.)

Although E&S firms provide many different types of products and services, many of these firms have highly diversified business segments, offering a one-stop shop product and service solution to the global O&G industry. Others focus specifically on specialized market segments or geographies.

Table 3.11   15 Largest Oil & Gas Equipment & Services Companies

Name	Market Cap (Billions)	Country	% of Sub-Industry
Schlumberger	$117.6	US	30.4%
Halliburton	$33.4	US	8.6%
Tenaris	$26.3	Argentina	6.8%
National Oilwell Varco	$26.2	US	6.8%
Baker Hughes	$25.8	US	6.7%
Weatherford Intl.	$23.1	US	6.0%
Saipem	$17.7	Italy	4.6%
Smith Intl.	$14.8	US	3.8%
Cameron Intl.	$10.5	US	2.7%
WorleyParsons	$10.5	Australia	2.7%
Technip	$8.5	France	2.2%
CGG Veritas	$7.8	France	2.0%
FMC Technologies	$7.4	US	1.9%
Aker Solutions	$7.3	Norway	1.9%
BJ Services	$7.1	US	1.8%

Source: Thomson Datastream, MSCI, Inc.[22] as of 12/31/07.

E&S is highly fragmented. A common feature of the largest E&S firms is globally diverse business operations, employing thousands of people in offices around the world, with very diverse clients. Table 3.11 shows the 15 largest publicly traded E&S firms in the MSCI ACWI as of December 31, 2007.

SUB-INDUSTRY DRIVERS

Now comes a key part of the top-down investment process: identifying and analyzing portfolio drivers. In general, the basic business operations within each Energy sub-industry don't vary much; as a result, high-level sub-industry drivers tend to affect peer groups similarly and very often determine performance dispersion among the sub-industries.

However, drivers will differ in relative importance depending on the sub-industry. For example, while commodity prices affect all Energy firms to some degree, upstream firms are more directly affected than others. In the remainder of this chapter, we'll list and discuss main drivers and explore how each sub-industry might affect others.

Integrated Oil & Gas, Exploration & Production, and Refining & Marketing Sub-Industry Drivers

Because the Integrated Oil & Gas sub-industry is a combination of the Exploration & Production (E&P) and Refining & Marketing (R&M) sub-industries, similar drivers apply to all three sub-industries. The most important drivers for firms engaged in upstream and downstream segments of the industry are:

- Oil and natural gas prices
- Oil and gas production growth
- Finding and development costs
- Exploration and production capital expenditures
- Share buybacks and mergers and acquisitions (M&A) activity
- Regulatory environment
- Refining margins
- Light/heavy spreads

Oil and Natural Gas Prices   As the majority of Integrated Oil & Gas firms' earnings usually come from the upstream division, oil and natural gas prices greatly affect results. Many years ago, most major Integrated Oil & Gas firms sold much of their natural gas assets to focus on international oil exploration. So in terms of relative importance, oil prices tend to be more significant than natural gas prices to the giant integrated firms.

Because E&P firms don't have downstream assets, commodity prices affect them more than any other sub-industry. (But as discussed earlier, hedging activities can help mitigate risk and guarantee cash flows for future projects.) In general, E&P firms are influenced more by natural gas than oil prices, mostly because the majority of E&Ps produce more natural gas than oil, especially in North America.[23] For these firms, higher commodity prices lead to higher profits.

On the flip side, downstream R&M firms tend to be negatively affected by rising oil and natural gas prices. Because refiners' main input is oil, rising oil prices can negatively affect margins to the extent those costs cannot be passed on via higher petroleum product prices. This happens because product prices can be sticky—some estimate it takes three to six months for higher oil prices to work their way through to product prices. Moreover, many refineries use natural gas as their main power source. The higher the natural gas price, the higher the operating cost.

Thus, rising commodity prices mostly benefit upstream firms while hurting downstream firms. However, Integrated Oil & Gas firms have less earnings variability, as one division's results can offset the other.

Oil & Gas Production Growth   Increasing production growth is vital for Integrated Oil & Gas firms. However, absent a large acquisition, the sheer production volume from most Integrateds makes it unusual to report large year-over-year production growth. So most integrated firms target a modest 1 to 4 percent annual production growth, and many find even that to be challenging.

Production growth, reserve replacement, and new discoveries are significantly more important to pure E&P firms than the big Integrateds due to their relative size. Without the same vast, globally diverse reserves of the Integrateds—as well as downstream assets—upstream results make or break E&P company earnings. It's not uncommon to see E&P firms report strong double-digit, year-over-year production growth or, conversely, big declines.

The importance of production growth comes down to size and reserves. For smaller E&P firms—including private ones—there's a much higher degree of business risk because success depends upon discoveries or acquisitions. Larger E&Ps tend to have big resources and geographic diversity, thus creating less variability in production growth.

Finding and Development Costs Finding and development metrics describe the cost of newly booked reserves. Finding and development costs typically rise and fall with commodity prices because of changing demand for labor, equipment, rigs, and energy services necessary to increase production and reserves. While changing costs usually affect the entire industry, some are better equipped to handle them than others, usually because of scale and efficiency.

Costs can also vary dramatically based on drilling location and reserve type. For instance, some firms focus on high-cost locations like North America's oil sands or oil shale. Others may drill for conventional oil and gas resources in lower-cost offshore regions like the Gulf of Mexico. So while cost inflation (or deflation) tends to affect the industry as a whole, it can also vary greatly depending on the type of reserves and location.

Integrated firms have the scale, global diversity, market share, and financial clout to mitigate cost inflation. For example, if one region of the world proves too costly, a globally diverse integrated oil firm can easily switch to other projects or another part of the world.

Finding and development costs affect E&P firms much more than the Integrateds. Without the same advantages of scale and asset diversity, it's tougher for E&Ps to mitigate cost increases. Thus, some may choose to sacrifice production growth to maintain profit margins.

Falling oil and natural gas prices affect the highest cost producers the most since they have the slimmest profit margins. Operators in high-cost regions like the oil sands, oil shale, and deepwater regions can find their operations to be uneconomic should oil prices experience a prolonged downturn.

Operating Costs and Exploration Expense

While finding and development costs are a key operating measure widely followed in the industry, individual company costs are usually broken down between *operating costs* and *exploration expenses*.

(Continued)

Operating costs include labor and energy costs, repair, maintenance, taxes, insurance, and depreciation. Also called *lifting* or *production* costs, operating costs aggregate the field-by-field costs for extracting oil and gas from the ground.

Exploration expenses are costs incurred when exploring a region for oil and gas resources, including drilling costs and non-drilling costs (such as seismic surveys). Exploration expenses can vary significantly due to the great differences in oil field characteristics (such as deepwater versus land).

Exploration and Production Capital Expenditures Exploration and production capital expenditures will have a major affect on cash flows and future production growth. Firms vary greatly in how cash flows are used year to year. If the Oil & Gas industry decides to significantly increase capital expenditures in a given year, it will reduce cash reserves but potentially increase future production growth. Firms could also reduce capital spending but increase share buybacks and dividends, pay down debt, or make acquisitions. Reduced exploration and production spending in general without increased share buybacks and dividends would likely mean firms are forecasting tough times ahead.

Due to their size, the vast majority of exploration and production capital expenditures come from the Integrated Oil & Gas sub-industry. These firms have a greater emphasis on oil production and tend to spend more money in remote foreign locations than their independent E&P counterparts (who generally concentrate spending in the North America gas market). Both sub-industries generally increase or decrease capital expenditures in concert, but occasionally diverge due to different drilling plans for natural gas versus oil.

Share Buybacks and M&A Activity In general, share buybacks and M&As benefit stock prices—all stock prices, not just Energy—by reducing equity supply. Basic economics tell us reducing supply of something while holding demand constant will cause prices to rise. This holds true for stock prices, as well as for a barrel of oil or any other good traded on an open market.

Share buybacks directly affect earnings per share. Among other things, oil and gas firms divide cash flows between exploration and production projects, share buybacks, dividends, acquisitions, and debt reduction. Should firms decide to buy back a meaningful chunk of shares, they can immediately increase earnings-per-share (EPS) by reducing outstanding shares. Integrated Oil & Gas firms often use this tactic to increase EPS. Because E&P firms tend to be so focused on increasing production growth and reserve replacement, significant share buybacks are somewhat rare. Therefore, significant share buyback announcements can be a significant sign of optimism for an E&P firm.

Acquisitions drive higher stock prices (for the acquiree) when a firm bids for a competitor at a premium. Acquisitions also have the effect of increasing speculation of what the next takeover will be, helping to increase prices across the industry or sector. But these effects are generally temporal. Between the three sub-industries, M&A activity may be more important to the E&P sub-industry due to the sheer number of potential targets and sub-industry fragmentation. It's becoming increasingly difficult for firms to access significant reserves from foreign governments, so the easiest way to grow oil and gas production may be to acquire an independent E&P company. Antitrust concerns, lack of viable acquirers, and difficulty in completing mergers of size could limit major acquisition activity within the Integrated Oil & Gas sub-industry in the future. Antitrust concerns could limit further consolidation in US Refining & Marketing as well.

Regulatory Environment   The major IOCs are often the subject of new legislation and media scrutiny in periods of high energy prices. (Think of how many headlines skewer Big Oil for price gouging and the like as gasoline has gotten pricier.) Governments may increase or decrease taxes, subsidies, royalties or drilling rights depending on the public's sentiment. This is often more applicable in emerging market countries, where high taxes and government involvement are prevalent. As IOCs operate within multiple countries, they can be susceptible to multiple punitive legislative risks around the globe.

Similar to the IOCs, the E&P sub-industry also faces new and changing taxes, royalties, subsidies, and access to reserves set by governments. As mentioned previously, these higher or lower costs tend to affect smaller firms more than the larger ones, thus E&P firms may be more affected than IOCs.

Government involvement in the R&M sub-industry can have dramatic effects on earnings as well. In some emerging markets like China, the government caps the price of petroleum products. So as crude oil prices climb, refineries are unable to pass on the extra costs, forcing firms to operate at a loss (though many receive government subsidies to help offset this loss).

Other forms of government regulation focus on environmental issues. Environmental regulations in the US in recent years have caused refineries to change fuel specifications in an attempt to reduce emissions and pollution. Changes include reducing sulfur content in diesel and mandating a larger ethanol component in gasoline. Additional environmental legislation may force refineries to invest millions in compliance with new fuel standards, reduce current supplies, and cause upward pressure on prices.

Refining Margins With both major upstream and downstream divisions, refining margins are important to IOCs, but not the most important earnings driver. In general, refining margins are driven by world crude oil prices and the supply and demand balance of petroleum products in regional markets. Since IOCs own refineries and gas stations throughout the world, refining margins vary widely. While crude oil costs remain fairly universal, each refinery will be subject to a different demand and mix of petroleum products and supplies.

However, the refining margin is the most important earnings driver of the independent R&M sub-industry. Unlike integrated firms, most independent R&M firms do not have upstream assets to offset volatile refining margins. So they tend to go through boom and bust periods, with little ability to mitigate earnings volatility. Hedging is possible using futures or forwards contract, but these tactics only offset risk for modest periods into the future.

Light/Heavy Spreads   Refineries vary in complexity—the ability to process different types of crude—thus the cost spread between light and heavy oil greatly affects earnings. The greater a refinery's ability to process cheaper, heavier crude, the greater the advantage it has during periods of large spreads in light and heavy crude oil.

The spread between light and heavy crude oil prices changes in response to changes in heavy oil production, primarily by OPEC. When OPEC decides to reduce production, it first reduces production of cheaper, heavier crude oil, reducing supply and increasing prices, thus closing the gap between heavy and light crude. When OPEC increases production, it raises supply of heavy crude, reducing prices and increasing the gap between light and heavy oil. So light oil tends to sell at a premium to heavy oil in periods of strong global oil demand.

Due to its greater reliance on refining margins for its earnings, the independent R&M sub-industry is relatively more affected by light/heavy spreads than IOCs.

Oil & Gas Storage & Transportation Sub-Industry Drivers

Unlike upstream and downstream players, which are directly impacted by oil and gas price shifts, midstream firms are only indirectly affected by oil and gas prices. This sub-industry's firms have more unique business lines (such as pipelines and tankers, two very different businesses) than other parts of the Energy sector. As a result, high-level drivers affecting the sub-industry as a whole are a bit more difficult to identify. A few of the important drivers for the Oil & Gas Storage & Transportation sub-industry are:

- Hydrocarbon volumes
- Interest rates
- Demand for defensive/high income-yielding securities

Hydrocarbon Volumes   Midstream earnings depend primarily on the volume of hydrocarbons transported—and volume is propelled by demand. Particularly strong economic growth—as seen recently in

China—could cause surging crude oil import demand. In recessionary periods, petroleum demand and crude oil import growth may wane, reducing volumes for midstream firms.

Supply conditions also play a role. For example, hydrocarbon volumes will increase following the completion of new oil and gas pipelines, whereas a damaged pipeline or other disruption could cause volumes to fall. When Hurricanes Katrina and Rita in 2005 temporarily halted production of crude oil, natural gas, and petroleum products in the US, demand for imported energy supplies surged. Tanker firms saw demand for their services increase sharply, allowing them to temporarily charge higher prices.

Interest Rates   Interest rates will affect certain Storage & Transportation (S&T) firms in two ways. As mentioned earlier, many pipeline operators carry large debt loads to fund acquisitions and build new pipelines. Changing interest rates affect interest expense and future growth plans.

Because firms like MLPs are high-dividend-yielding securities, they also tend to act as bond proxies. Income-oriented investors usually invest in MLPs and utilities because they offer high dividends, lower risk, and potential equity appreciation. When interest rates rise, these become relatively less attractive compared with long-term bonds. When interest rates fall, the opposite is true.

Demand for Defensive/High Income Yielding Securities   Because many S&T firms have relatively low risk, long-term earnings stability, and high dividend yields, they are also attractive to income-oriented investors. They are also sometimes considered defensive investments in unstable or recessionary environments due to consistent earnings and cash flows, as these firms are relatively unaffected by hydrocarbon prices.

Coal & Consumable Fuels Sub-Industry Drivers

The Coal & Consumable Fuels sub-industry is the Energy sector's most unique and, without a direct relationship to oil or natural gas prices, has its own unique drivers. But like natural gas, the coal industry is more affected by regional conditions versus global ones. The most important drivers of the Coal & Consumable Fuels sub-industry are:

- Coal prices
- Transportation costs and bottlenecks
- Exports/imports
- Legislation/environmental regulation
- Relative costs of alternative fuels

Coal Prices   Similar to natural gas, coal prices are set regionally and depend on country-specific supply and demand conditions. Supply conditions depend on the region, but in general, coal supply is plentiful and inhibited mainly by transportation and bottleneck issues.

Due to its use primarily for electricity generation and industry, coal demand is driven by economic growth, especially from manufacturing-based economies. Coal demand will likely continue to increase steadily as increasing interest in energy security and independence drives more economies to expand use of their substantial coal supplies.

Transportation Costs and Bottlenecks   Because transportation costs of coal can be more than extraction costs, shipping can be a major factor. In a booming economy, coal firms must compete for space on trains with other commodities and goods. The sheer tonnage of coal demanded by the power industry can cause bottlenecks in regions with limited rail capacity.

Exports/Imports   Much like oil, imports are an important factor for setting coal prices in countries where domestic production falls short of demand. Coal exports may slow as some of the largest coal exporters—Indonesia, Russia, and South Africa—keep more coal at home for domestic use.

Legislation/Environmental Regulation   Because coal emits carbon dioxide (CO^2)—a greenhouse gas—it's subject to legislation and intense environmental regulations. With new government regulations designed to reduce emissions, firms around the world spend billions for environmental upgrades. Additionally, in some regions like the European Union, utility firms are required to buy CO^2 emission credits for each ton of CO^2 produced.

Coal will continue to be subject to new environmental laws designed to reduce usage or emissions. New legislation harmful to coal users could have a material impact on demand and prices.

Relative Costs of Alternative Fuels For power generation and industrial use, coal can be substituted to a degree with other fuel sources such as natural gas and oil. As a result, alternative fuel prices will have an effect on coal demand and price. A dramatic rise in natural gas prices, for example, would likely increase demand for coal.

As mentioned previously, some countries have imposed a cost of pollution for the use of coal. Therefore, firms must compare the combined cost of coal with its pollution costs relative to alternative fuels. Should the cost of pollution increase, it would decrease the demand for coal.

Energy Equipment & Services Drivers

Both sub-industries of the Energy Equipment & Services (EES) industry—Oil & Gas Drilling and Oil & Gas Equipment & Services—are affected by the same high-level drivers. The actions of their customers—the Oil & Gas industry—will be the main determinant of the industry's performance. The following drivers are what we believe to be the most important specifically to the Energy Equipment & Services Industry:

- Upstream capital expenditures
- Oil and natural gas prices
- Worldwide rig count
- Dayrates

Upstream Capital Expenditures   By far, the largest EES industry driver is spending by the Oil & Gas industry. Total annual revenue for the EES industry should closely equate with aggregate upstream capital expenditures of the Oil & Gas industry. When oil firms are willing to spend a greater part of their budget on exploration and production, they'll naturally require more rigs, drilling products, and services. In periods when firms decide to spend less on exploration and production, or decide to spend more on share buybacks and dividends, EES demand falls.

Firms allocate their upstream capital expenditures between three main segments: exploration and development of new properties, acquisitions, and production from existing assets. In periods of rising oil and natural gas prices, firms tend to first increase drilling activity at existing sites to maximize production and profits. In periods of declining oil and natural gas prices, firms tend to reduce drilling activity and focus more on acquisitions and developing new reserves. In the last several years, continued high oil prices have allowed firms to allocate more capital to all three segments, though the vast majority of capital expenditures in general continue to go to increasing current production.

Oil and Natural Gas Prices   Oil and natural gas prices affect the EES industry indirectly, mainly by impacting demand. Due to the tighter supply conditions of oil, swings in oil prices tend to not affect drilling demand in the short term. Because natural gas is relatively more plentiful, natural gas drilling activity is more sensitive to price swings.

Because oil and natural gas are abundant in some places and scarce in others, each will affect regional drilling demand differently. For example, due to North America's abundant onshore natural gas reserves, higher natural gas prices tend to benefit US and Canadian land rig operators. In contrast, higher oil prices tend to benefit rig operators with presence in international regions with more oil supplies, such as rigs in the Middle East, Russia, or offshore West Africa.

Consequently, when oil and natural gas prices diverge, rig operators tend to see part of their fleet in high demand while others are forced out of operation. This is common among firms with diverse global rig fleets. For example, due to generally falling natural gas prices in North America in 2006 and 2007—caused in part by high natural gas supplies and tepid demand—natural gas drilling activity in the region slowed or declined. In the meantime, oil's rapid rise toward $100 a barrel in the same time period spurred (or rapidly advanced) oil drilling activity in international markets.

Worldwide Rig Count   Rig demand is driven primarily by oil and natural gas prices. At first, high commodity prices will increase drilling demand at sites already in production as oil firms hope to extract as much oil and gas as possible. Should prices stay high, firms may wish to also increase exploration for new supplies. Also, many fields in the world require more drilling to offset the effects of aging fields experiencing depletion. This phenomenon is likely to accelerate as peak production at the field, and more consequentially, on a global level, approaches. Sustained periods of low commodity prices have the opposite effect—reduced drilling demand.

When rig demand increases or decreases, the industry's supply response is to build new rigs or take rigs out of service. Rig supply will vary greatly depending on the type of rig. (In general, the most common types of rigs are land rigs, followed by jack-ups, semi-submersibles, and drill ships.) It may take months to build a new land rig, but years to build a new drill ship.

Rig supply also varies by region. For example, if a large, resource-rich nation such as Saudi Arabia decides to increase drilling for oil, Middle Eastern rig supply will naturally increase. But if, at the same time, natural gas prices fall dramatically in North America—thereby reducing natural gas drilling demand—rig supply in the region would fall. Moreover, rigs may move from one region to another where dayrates are higher.

Rig supply depends on rig utilization, which measures to what extent a company's rig fleet is being used to capacity. When rig utilization is high, it means the supply of rigs is tight, creating opportunities for building new rigs. Should drilling demand fall or many new rigs come online, rig utilization will fall, causing less demand for new rigs.

Utilization may also be affected by firms taking rigs out of operation for maintenance or modification.

Dayrates   Rig dayrates—determined by the supply and demand for rigs in a region—are the most important driver of drilling company earnings because they make up the majority of revenues.

Since it may take months or years to increase the supply of rigs, rising drilling demand—usually due to rising commodity prices—tends to increase dayrates. Dayrates generally decline when drilling demand falls or if the supply of available rigs increases.

Dayrates vary widely depending on the type of rig and location. The most expensive rigs tend to be the ultra-deepwater drill ships and semi-submersibles, capable of drilling in 10,000 feet of water to more than 30,000 feet below the surface. There are relatively few deepwater rigs in the world, and they take years to build. For the most coveted deepwater drill ships, it is not uncommon to see dayrates exceed $600,000 a day. The least expensive rigs are the land and shallow water rigs, with less drilling depth capability. These rigs are more plentiful and more easily and less expensively built.

Chapter Recap

While the Energy sector investment universe is a diverse group of thousands of firms, it breaks up into the Oil & Gas firms and Energy Equipment & Services firms. But depending on the Energy sector benchmark used, each industry and sub-industry will have varying degrees of impact on the benchmark's performance. In general, the Integrated Oil & Gas sub-industry has the largest impact on the Energy sector's overall performance because it makes up the majority of the sector's market capitalization. However, the other six sub-industries—each with unique characteristics—should not be overlooked.

The performance of each Energy sub-industry is affected by high-level drivers, many of which are listed for you. Analyzing drivers and how they affect each sub-industry will be key to identifying the most and least attractive segments of the Energy sector.

- The Energy sector is comprised of one industry group, two industries, and seven sub-industries.

(*Continued*)

- Use benchmarks as a guide to help with portfolio construction, analysis, and performance monitoring.
- Depending on the benchmark, the Energy sector can look very different. Each benchmark will have different relative weights between the sub-industries.
- The Oil & Gas industry includes all the firms in the upstream, midstream, and downstream segments of the sector. This industry is most directly affected by commodity prices.
- The Energy Equipment & Services industry provides all the engineering, construction, tools, and services necessary to assist the Oil & Gas industry in the integrated process. These firms are less directly affected by commodity prices, but rather capital spending.
- The performance of each sub-industry is affected by high-level drivers, the greatest of which are commodity prices and capital spending.

WHY WE'LL NEVER RUN DRY

Will the world run out of oil? If yes, when? Are we close to a peak in world oil production? Will stratospheric oil prices cause a global economic depression and subsequent collapse of society as we know it?

These are just a few questions raised while oil prices surged in recent years. With prices surpassing $145 per barrel (as of July 2008), questions about our oil supply sustainability will likely only intensify in coming years. Whether you believe the hype or not, the world's ability to supply enough oil to meet forecasted demand has vast implications for investors, the oil industry, and global economic development.

Numerous theories abound. Investors could occupy themselves with countless books and industry reports on "peak oil" alone. Few have time or patience for that, but successful Energy investors still need at least a general understanding of peak oil theories and potential implications. Suggestions for further reading are provided at the end of this chapter.

THE WORLD WILL NEVER RUN OUT OF OIL

Will the world ever run out of oil? No. Never! While the physical amount of oil in the ground is indeed finite, the laws of supply and demand ensure the last barrel will never be consumed. The future of oil supply is simply a matter of economics and politics.

Trust Supply and Demand

Good-old Economics 101: the law of supply and demand. Once we get down to the last drops of oil, few will be able to afford them. With supply so scarce, prices will skyrocket so only the most critical oil uses will be employed. End users will curb usage and/or find alternatives.

Oil makes up such a large percentage of the world's energy consumption today because it's historically one of the most cost-efficient energy resources. When using oil becomes inefficient (i.e., too costly because of supply scarcity), the world will have to adapt. If oil hits $10,000 a barrel by 2110, it's virtually certain people won't be driving gasoline-powered cars—the only use would be running antique 2010 Ferraris in museums. (Picture an eccentric museum curator shuffling around the display floor and telling first-graders: "Centuries ago, humans used to mine icky black oil from the ground and burn it to make autos run. Strange but true!") In the end, the world will likely adapt to meet future energy needs in ways not even our best scientists have yet envisioned.

This process of adaptation also goes by the economic term *substitution effect*. That is, the higher the oil price, the greater the incentive to reduce oil demand by using other energy sources. Viable substitutes aren't found overnight, so suddenly higher oil prices in the short term could cause a period of serious pain to many parts of the economy. Whole industries could be crushed while consumers would be forced to alter their consumption habits. Ironically, the faster the pain happens, the faster the pain is over (like ripping off a Band-Aid). The rate of substitution will be a function of how fast prices rise and how damaging they are to the economy.

Think of all you could do if gasoline prices quadrupled overnight. It might make financial sense to trade in your SUV for a smaller car or hybrid, carpool to work, work from home, move closer to work, do more online shopping, walk or bike more, and so on. Those changes could be done quickly. However, if it takes 30 years for gasoline prices to quadruple, society might only make a few changes over the years since it wouldn't make financial sense (not to mention the inconvenience) to employ those drastic changes all at once.

It might sound crazy, but in a market-based capitalist system, a spike in oil prices can be a huge *opportunity*. Entrepreneurs the world over would suddenly have an unprecedented incentive to profit from developing lower-cost alternative energy. (They're already well on their way in this process.) Autos have already begun a period of significant change, which is likely to intensify in coming years. For example, auto firms globally are working to perfect cars running on gasoline-electric hybrid technology, ethanol, hydrogen, and electricity. The only reason these cars are not already mass produced is because there was never a real need or demand for them without high oil prices.

Other alternative energy technologies like wind, solar, and hydro-electric can also make great strides to shift the world's mix of traditional energy sources. And while these technologies may be years from significantly changing the game, continued high oil prices create incentives to eventually make them viable. The world has a remarkable history of speeding innovation when challenged by necessity or when great profits can be made. Ah, the power of capitalism!

High oil prices will also increase efforts to stretch existing supplies and explore for new reserves. Despite myriad "authoritative" studies proclaiming as much, we have no way of knowing for certain what the world's total oil supply is—and never have. For example, in 1980, the world was estimated to hold 645 billion barrels of conventional oil reserves. Today, that number is over 1.3 trillion barrels, despite the world consuming over 700 billion barrels in the same period.[1] That "new" oil didn't fall from the sky—it was just hidden. This expansion happened because oil firms found it economical to invest in exploration and new technology to find more oil.

Below some price level, spending more on exploration is not cost effective. In such times, many supermajor oil firms will instead opt to use their cash to buy back shares or hoard cash. (Exxon currently has over $30 billion in cash on its balance sheet.)[2] But once the price gets high enough and reserves low enough, firms will again become motivated to find new reserves. Thus, exploration and drilling activity is highly cyclical—rising and falling along with oil and natural gas prices.

High oil prices also spur efforts to develop previously uneconomical petroleum sources like oil sands and oil shale (see box below). These resources combined are estimated to contain trillions of barrels of oil and natural gas, but with current technology, they are very difficult and costly to extract. As conventional prices rise, these resources will continue to be developed, and methods to extract them in significant quantities will undoubtedly be improved.

More Oil than Saudi Arabia!

Do you know who has more oil than Saudi Arabia? We do! Way more—roughly 10 times more—all sitting in oil shale. Our Canadian friends also have known reserves that rival Saudi Arabia—all in oil sands. Unfortunately, the problem with both oil shale and oil sands is extracting it in useful forms and in significant quantities.

Oil Sands

Oil sands are deposits of *bitumen*—a heavy, thick, sticky form of crude oil that must be rigorously treated to convert into a usable form for refineries. While conventional crude oil is pumped from the ground using drilling rigs, oil sands must be mined or recovered in situ. (Note: Meaning "in place," in situ recovery involves steam-heating deposits buried deep down to bring the bitumen to the surface.)

Hydraulic and electrically powered shovels scoop up the oil sand, load it into enormous trucks, and haul it to special treatment facilities for processing. This is an extremely capital-intensive and costly system. About two tons of oil sands must be dug up, moved, and processed to produce just one barrel of oil.[*]

However, global oil reserves held within oil sands are tremendous, estimated to be about 3.7 trillion barrels,[†] though not all of it is recoverable. Oil sands are found in many countries, but the largest deposits are found primarily in Canada's Alberta region and Venezuela. The world currently produces 1.6 million barrels per day (Mbd) from oil sands, with 1.1 Mbd coming from Canada.[‡] If you count Canada's 173 billion barrels of proven crude oil sand reserves, it's the second-largest holder of oil reserves in the world after Saudi Arabia.[**] Today, firms around the globe are spending billions to develop the oil sands in Canada. By 2020, production from the country's oil sands is expected to reach almost 4 Mbd.[††]

Oil Shale

Oil shale is a sedimentary rock containing solid bituminous materials called *kerogen*, from which liquid hydrocarbons can be extracted when the rock is heated. Oil shale is mined and then heated to high temperatures to separate the hydrocarbons. However, due to the complexity and high costs of mining and extracting energy from the oil shale, the resource is not being exploited to a significant degree today.

Global oil shale deposits are equally sizable to the oil sands, conservatively estimated at *2.8 trillion barrels* of recoverable oil.[‡‡] The vast majority of the world's known oil shale is located in the US, under portions of Colorado, Utah, and Wyoming. Count that, and the US is the world's largest holder of oil reserves.

While producing large amounts of oil from shale remains uneconomic even at today's oil prices, the resources are known and have barely been touched. Extracting them is simply a matter of economics, technological advancement, and political impediments.

---

[*]Alberta Department of Energy, Government of Alberta, "What Is Oil Sands."
[†]U.S. Department of Energy, Energy Information Administration, "When Will World Oil Production Peak?" slides 15–17.
[‡]World Energy Council, "Natural Bitumen and Extra-Heavy Oil," Survey of Energy Resources 2007 (September 2007), p. 131.
[**]Alberta Department of Energy, Government of Alberta, "Oil Sands Statistics 2006."
[††]Canadian Association of Petroleum Producers, "Oil Sands Resources, Production and Projects."
[‡‡]See note 5, p. 105.

Political Posturing

As with most things these days, politics play a large role in the amount of oil we consume and the prices we pay. Governments throughout the world wreak havoc with the price of oil by changing taxes, subsidies, mandates, environmental restrictions, city planning, and energy policies.

Today's world oil consumption is the result (at least in part) of a series of political decisions made decades ago. For example, over 30 years ago, the French decided the way to energy independence was to build a large network of nuclear power plants (currently generating over 75 percent of the country's electricity).[3] Combined with its already extensive public transportation network, the country has seen its oil consumption continually fall—it consumes less oil today than 30 years ago.[4] The US, with its extensive network of interstate highways and lack of efficient public transportation, obviously took a much different route.

Governments also affect oil consumption through petroleum product taxes. For example, one reason the US consumes 25 percent of the world's oil is because US gasoline taxes are so low. By comparison, Europe's gas taxes make a gallon of gasoline two to three times more expensive than the US.[5] So Europeans drive much less, rely more on public transportation, and drive smaller, more fuel-efficient automobiles. If the US government truly wanted to reduce oil consumption, it could raise gasoline taxes to be on par with Europe. However, this tax policy comes at a cost: Higher taxes artificially force consumers to use less energy—which might seem good, but can actually decrease productivity (e.g., increasing commute times through substituting cars for public transportation). Moreover, higher taxes burden them with additional costs.

Another government policy affecting petroleum product use is fuel economy standards. From 1975 to 2000, Americans cut their fuel use by the equivalent of 2.8 Mbd partly due to the Corporate Average Fuel Economy (CAFE) laws.[6] In December 2007, Congress passed the Energy Independence and Security Act of 2007, raising CAFE standards to 35 miles per gallon (mpg) by 2020.[7] This type of legislation—intended to increase production of smaller, more fuel-efficient automobiles—could affect future gasoline consumption. (Note: It's still unclear whether higher CAFE standards will cause the intended changes in fuel economy from auto producers and, hence, fuel consumption because the target may be unrealistic. The auto industry today is nowhere near capable of producing an auto fleet with such fuel economy absent a change in technology or drastically changing fleet production to smaller, lighter vehicles.)

In developing countries like China and parts of the Middle East, fuel demand is artificially high because their governments cap prices on petroleum products. Thus, consumers drive far more than they would in a free market system. As more people in developing countries are able to afford cars, the potential for those countries to significantly affect world oil demand growth is high. Additionally, besides causing greater government revenues to be spent subsidizing fuels, price caps cause countries to periodically suffer fuel shortages. Allowing prices to be governed by market forces would do much to help reduce growing oil demand in those countries and prevent shortages or other disruptions.

Governments can also reduce oil consumption by offering subsidies, tax breaks, or other benefits to encourage alternative energy use or conservation. These incentives have been used in varying degrees to promote billions of investment dollars to mixed results. Because most alternative energy is currently uneconomic without subsidies and thus not subject to completely free market forces, government capital doesn't always flow to the most efficient resources and often causes more economic inefficiency than gain.

However, sleep tight knowing the oil spigot will never run dry. The powers of supply and demand mean we will one day find and use an appropriate replacement. How fast we shift away from oil will depend on how quickly oil prices rise. The faster and greater the pain, the faster and greater the efforts to reduce that pain. While there may be a physical limit to oil, there essentially is no limit to energy.

THE TIPPING POINT?

Instead of questioning *if* we will run out of oil, a better question to ask is *when* will oil production *peak*?

Peak Oil refers to the theoretical point in time when global oil production reaches its peak, after which the rate of production cannot increase and enters an irreversible decline. It's got to happen sometime—but exactly when is extremely difficult to guess.

Assuming global oil consumption continues to increase each year, crude oil prices should rise dramatically if supply eventually fails to meet demand. Many peak oil theorists postulate this period of markedly higher oil prices will cause a global economic collapse as the world becomes unable to afford the "lifeblood" of its economies. Peak oil, some surmise, will usher in a period of unprecedented economic, social, and political unrest, and potentially war.

Peak oil theory originated from M. King Hubbert in 1956, who correctly predicted oil production *in the US* would peak between 1965 to 1970. It peaked in 1970.[8]

Figure 4.1 shows US crude oil production from 1940 through 2007. Production has been on a steady decline ever since output peaked in 1970. The result has been an increasing reliance on foreign oil imports.

Dubbed *Hubbert's Peak*, the theory assumes the production rate of a limited resource follows a bell-shaped curve that declines once reserves are half-depleted. The theory stems from historical observations of oil fields, where production ramps up to a maximum over a period of years,

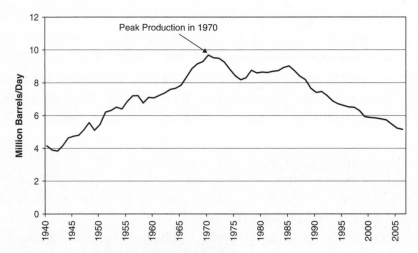

Figure 4.1   US Crude Oil Production
Source: Energy Information Administration.

then gradually declines at a similar rate. Since world oil production is the sum of individual oil fields everywhere, the theory is extrapolated to predict the world's peak. The evidence of peak oil can be seen in individual fields and countries around the world: 33 out of 48 major oil-producing nations have already seen oil production peak.[9] Scary, right?

But hang on—that doesn't settle the issue by a long shot. Industry experts differ widely on when exactly peak oil will occur. Remember, exploration and technological advances over the decades keep yielding discoveries of still more recoverable oil—or more ways to recover known reserves. From a mere geological perspective, the peak could be anywhere from a few years to several decades from now, but a host of other factors also come into play. Some believe the peak will happen much sooner because of limited access to reserves due to geopolitical issues, technological challenges, higher costs, and strains on industry resources. Some even say global oil production has already peaked! While no one knows with certainty when it will happen, geologists generally agree it will no doubt happen eventually.

An immediate concern is when non-OPEC production peaks. Once non-OPEC production hits its top, the world will increasingly rely on OPEC to make up the shortfall. Given the cartel's inherent desire to keep oil prices high by limiting output, a world where oil prices remain in a permanently higher range is possible.

Arguments for Peak Oil

Since the first commercial well was drilled in the US in 1859, the world has consumed about 1 trillion barrels of oil.[10] About half of that was consumed in just the last 20 years.[11] Now the question is how much longer can world production keep up with ever-increasing demand? Indeed, the oil industry is facing some of the toughest challenges in its history to increase supply while demand continues rising. Many believe it can't be done. Here are some of the main arguments supporting the peak oil theory.

Few Discoveries   Many analysts think almost all the easy-to-reach oil and gas supplies are already found and tapped, forcing the industry to search for supplies in increasingly harsh and remote locations. By 1970, the oil industry discovered 10 giant fields that could each produce more than 600,000 barrels a day.[12] In the subsequent 20 years, the industry found only two. Since 1990, only one field was discovered (the Kashagan field in Kazakhstan) with the potential to top the 500,000 barrels a day mark, despite billions spent on exploration. Should the industry maintain this dismal discovery rate, future supply may be unable to meet future demand.

Aging Fields   The majority of world oil production comes from fields discovered decades ago, and production is declining. Over the course of an oil field's life, production rises to a maximum point, plateaus, then gradually declines as ground pressures fall. As a result, today's oil fields are conservatively estimated to be declining at an average of 4.5 percent a year.[13] This means the world needs to add nearly 4 Mbd of new production every year—equal to the current output of Iran—just to maintain current levels.

We Just Can't Get It   Although the world has trillions of barrels of unconventional oil waiting to be tapped (like oil sands and shale), the industry could prove impotent in its ability to extract them in significant quantities. Canada's oil sands are estimated to contain 173 billion barrels of oil reserves, but technological, economic, environmental, and other constraints limit current production to only 1.1 Mbd.[14] Sure, production in the oil sands is estimated to reach 4 Mbd by 2020,[15] but that's still a relatively small amount since current global demands are 85 Mbd and growing. Oil shale is also estimated to contain vast oil and gas reserves—some estimate in the trillions—but is still far too costly and technologically difficult to extract in substantial quantity. Although we may not lack reserves, we do lack the technology to pull them out of the ground fast enough to meet future demand. Who knows? Maybe technological advances will not gain much from here and we're stuck. (But history shows that's quite unlikely.)

No Trespassing   Most of the major oil supplies in the world are off-limits to the world's major integrated oil companies (IOCs). Blame it (as you can with many things) on the government. In fact, over 75 percent of the world's oil reserves are held by government-controlled national oil companies (NOCs).[16] Many of the world's most promising oil reserves reside in politically unstable countries like Nigeria, Iran, Iraq, Libya, Venezuela, and Sudan. Wars and government restrictions make most of these oil-rich nations underexplored, and they produce far below their potential.

Given soaring oil prices over the last several years, you would think these foreign governments would lighten their grip and allow greater production. Nope! Instead, they've tightened their grasp, further restricting supplies, re-negotiating contracts with IOCs, and even nationalizing reserves. This is particularly detrimental to world oil supply growth because firms with the greatest technical know-how, capital, and experience (and thus best capable of achieving production growth) take back seats to inefficient, government-controlled operations. What a shame.

There are also regions in the world known to contain vast quantities of oil and gas, but they are government-restricted. For example, the US bans drilling in the Arctic National Wildlife Refuge (ANWR) in Alaska—estimated to contain over 10 billion barrels of oil.[17] The US also restricts exploration of the Outer Continental Shelf, an area potentially containing billions of undiscovered oil and gas resources.

Profit Fears   Up to the point where supply meets demand, the oil industry generally lacks incentives to increase output, fearing it may put downward pressure on prices and jeopardize profits. If the industry continuously produced more oil than needed, global oil inventories would build and the price of oil would fall. Thus, increasing oil volume for its own sake is simply not the best use of capital for most firms.

OPEC's Incentive to Restrain Output

Today, the incentive to restrain output really only applies to OPEC nations. Why? Non-OPEC nations, including the major IOCs, are doing everything they can to increase output, but are still struggling to replace reserves. Because OPEC has spare oil capacity, it has the option of decreasing oil output to its benefit. As OPEC nations derive a great majority of government revenues from oil exports, it's in their best interest to keep prices high (though maybe not so high as to cause a global recession). This reduces their desire to increase oil production (absent a glaring supply shortage) as it would put downward pressure on prices.

Arguments Against Peak Oil

There's no doubt increasing world oil production will be challenging in the face of growing geological and political barriers. But today isn't unique. The world has frequently fretted about oil supplies over the last century. Recall the Arab oil embargo of the 1970s, when similarly dire predictions about peak oil abounded. The world responded by making new oil discoveries, increasing oil reserves, lifting oil production, developing alternatives, and increasing energy efficiency. Then, peak oil theorists were proven wrong.

Fallout from that botched prediction has kept peak oil theory from gaining widespread acceptance among industry veterans. Most feel peak oil is too far off to be of dire concern today. After all, if the theorists have been proven wrong so many times before, what would make them right now?

It's difficult to say who's right, but in either case, the spirit of skepticism is always encouraged for good investing. It's dangerous to categorically dismiss anything unless you're absolutely sure about it (which is an important reason for diversifying any portfolio). Here are some primary arguments against peak oil theory.

There's More Out There   Peak oil theory is generally based on assumptions about conventional oil reserves *without* taking unconventional reserves into account. That's likely a mistake. Estimates of conventional and unconventional resources vary widely throughout the industry; and while there's really no telling precisely how much unconventional oil we'll be able to ultimately use, it's highly likely it will make a major difference.

The official estimate of conventional oil reserves is 1.3 trillion barrels as of December 31, 2007,[18] but some industry experts foresee total oil reserves (conventional and unconventional) in the 12 trillion to 16 trillion barrel range.[19] As technology is continually developed to exploit the world's unconventional reserves, the peak in conventional oil production may become less important than originally feared.

As mentioned earlier, even with big strides in technology and newer, more precise seismic and other measuring instruments, no one has ever accurately calculated oil reserves. Oil firms have always found ways to increase reserves when prices become high enough. The question is whether that will continue. In either case, history shows we have always underestimated reserves, and it's plausible we'll continue to do so.

For example, it may not be entirely correct to assume the days of giant oil field discoveries are long past us. Recently, there have been three major discoveries that could eventually be classified as giant fields, once more testing is completed. The Jack Field, discovered in the Gulf of Mexico in 2006, is estimated to contain up to 15 billion barrels of oil. The Jidong Nanbao field, discovered off the coast of China in 2007, is estimated to contain seven billion barrels of oil. The Tupi Field, discovered off the coast of Brazil in 2007, is estimated to hold between five to eight billion barrels of oil.

We're Getting Better   Predictions of the peak rest on big assumptions. That's one reason they can vary tremendously, because analysts base their models on widely differing assumptions of oil decline rates and oil recovery rates. After all, not all oil is recoverable and production in any one field will eventually decline.

While the industry struggled over the past century to recover a majority of reserves in most oil fields, modern science and new technologies will likely increase recovery efficiency in the future.

For example, while a typical oil company is able to extract only one out of every three barrels in the ground historically, enhanced contemporary oil recovery techniques pull two out of three barrels.[20] Some estimate even a 10 percent gain in extraction efficiency on a global scale could unlock 1.2 to 1.6 trillion barrels of extra resources.[21]

Cambridge Energy Research Associates (CERA)—a prominent independent energy research consultancy—has long dismissed an imminent peak in world oil production. Based on a field-by-field analysis, the company predicts global production capacity could rise from 91 Mbd in 2007 to as much as 112 Mbd by 2017, when demand will be 101 Mbd.[22] CERA also notes there is no evidence oil field decline rates will increase suddenly, as suggested by some peak oil theorists.

Demand Matters, Too!   Peak oil theory focuses solely on the supply side of the equation, with no regard to how demand might change. The theory assumes demand would continue on an upward trajectory in line with its historical average, eventually reaching a point where supply is unable to meet demand. This shortfall between supply and demand is what will cause prices to spike upward.

As mentioned in the beginning of the chapter, higher prices will eventually elicit a demand response. Higher prices will encourage the use of alternatives, promote conservation, and alter consumer behavior until the pain of higher prices is reduced. If high prices cause enough demand destruction, the world may eventually see peak demand, rendering peak oil insignificant.

PEAK OIL AND YOU

What should investors make of peak oil theories and predictions? How should investment strategies be altered?

If you believe peak oil is decades away or may never occur, then it should not be a factor in your investment decisions today. The market doesn't discount information decades into the future. At most, markets discount information three to seven years ahead, and perhaps even less. It's much more helpful to analyze the supply and demand balance of oil for the period immediately ahead, which is approximately the next 12 to 18 months. This perspective will tie back more easily to company earnings and stock prices than theories, which may or may not pan out in the distant future.

If you believe peak oil will be a reality within the next several years—or that it has already occurred—there are a number of possible actions you can take. The beginning of peak oil suggests a period of rapidly rising oil prices. At first, this would be a good reason to overweight the Energy sector as firms reap huge profits on an ever-increasing price for their good, while giving up little or no sales volume. But at some price point—after an indeterminate period of months or years—oil will negatively affect several sectors and, eventually, the overall global economy. The global economy could go through a period of pain, including a recession, as it adjusts to markedly higher oil prices and would likely coincide with a downturn in global stock markets. Should this happen, it would be more prudent to sell most, if not all, of your stocks and prepare for a prolonged bear market. But as the world undergoes substitution effects to compensate for oil's rapid rise, there are likely to be as many winners as losers.

Another strategy is to take advantage of public sentiment. The popularity of peak oil theory has risen and fallen over time depending on oil prices and worries about oil market tightness. In this strategy, whether peak oil eventually does occur is not as important as investors' perceptions of whether it will. Depending on the shift in investor sentiment, investors may cause short-term swings in a variety of industries. For example, if the majority of investors come to believe peak oil is imminent, they might bid up the prices of crude oil, oil and gas producer stocks (especially those with long-life reserves), and alternative energy stocks, or dump shares of economically sensitive firms in anticipation of a global recession. However, trying to determine the level of public sentiment and whether it is justified is very difficult and always fickle. Expect wild swings within short periods.

PEAK OIL READING

For more information on possible peak oil outcomes and investment opportunities, some publications are listed below. However, be forewarned: These are scary reads! Remember that most involve worst-case scenarios, not inevitable outcomes.

1. *Profit from the Peak: The End of Oil and the Greatest Investment Event of the Century* by Brian Hicks and Chris Nelder.
2. *The Coming Economic Collapse: How You Can Thrive When Oil Costs $200 a Barrel* by Stephen Leeb and Glen Strathy.
3. *Peak Oil Survival: Preparation for Life After Gridcrash* by Aric McBay.
4. *Hubbert's Peak: The Impending World Oil Shortage* by Kenneth S. Deffeyes.
5. *Twilight in the Desert: The Coming Saudi Oil Shock and the World Economy* by Matthew R. Simmons.

Chapter Recap

Taking all the arguments together, how can we know when peak oil will occur? The answer is: *We can't!* No one needs to figure out exactly when peak oil will occur because no central planning is necessary or able to solve the challenges that would arise (though governments will surely try). Instead, market forces will appropriately respond to the balance of supply and demand, whether the peak happens in days, months, years, or never.

So don't run to the hills fully stocked with guns, food, and fuel just yet. The world still has plenty of oil, and we will never completely run out of it. Whether peak oil happens tomorrow or never, market forces will continue to restore balance to supply and demand.

- The world will never run out of oil. The laws of supply and demand, substitution effects, and politics will ensure we never consume the last barrel.
- Peak oil theory attempts to identify the future date when global oil production peaks, at which point the rate of production cannot increase and begins an irreversible decline.

- Arguments for peak oil include a lack of new discoveries, oil field decline rates, and concentration of world oil reserves by NOCs.
- Arguments against peak oil include its failure to consider unconventional resources, demand-side responses, and more optimistic assumptions about global reserves and oil field decline rates.
- Peak oil alone should not affect your investment strategy unless you believe it will occur in the next several years.
- If peak oil does occur in the next several years, this initially would be positive for the Energy sector. At some point though, high oil prices will take a toll on global economic growth, which could be bad for the stock market.

STAYING CURRENT

Tracking Industry Fundamentals

Energy is a big, diverse sector made up of thousands of firms globally. How can you stay current? What are the most important issues to stay abreast of? What kind of data should you track and analyze when identifying high-level portfolio drivers?

This chapter covers vital industry fundamentals used by pros to interpret, analyze, and forecast the next big Energy moves. We'll also provide a summary of quantitative data followed closely by analysts and investors to forecast commodity prices and Energy sub-industry performance. An extensive list of industry data sources is also provided in the Appendix so you can perform your own research and analysis.

CRUDE OIL MARKET FUNDAMENTALS

As with any commodity, crude oil prices are determined fundamentally by the laws of supply and demand. But while crude oil prices have historically tracked these fundamental indicators, it is not uncommon for prices to respond to non-fundamental factors in the short term (like speculation for supply disruptions due to wars or terrorist attacks). In the long term though, fundamental supply and demand indicators should have the greatest influence on prices. This is why it's important to closely follow any indicator that may affect global oil supply or demand.

The primary quantitative factors influencing oil prices, which we'll cover in more detail in this chapter, are:

- Oil demand
- OPEC oil production
- Non-OPEC oil production
- Spare oil production capacity
- Global refining utilization
- Global oil inventories

But how do these factors impact oil? Table 5.1 provides bullish drivers—those likely to drive oil higher—and bearish drivers—those likely to drive oil lower.

Oil Demand

Oil demand is followed closely by energy investors and analysts. Using regional GDP forecasts, macroeconomic indicators, and studying past oil consumption patterns, analysts forecast how economic growth (or recession) will affect oil consumption. The greater the outlook for global economic growth, the greater the probability oil demand accelerates.

Table 5.1   Bullish and Bearish Drivers of Oil

Bullish Oil Drivers	Bearish Oil Drivers
Rising oil demand	Falling oil demand
Falling OPEC oil production	Rising OPEC oil production
Falling non-OPEC oil production	Rising non-OPEC oil production
Falling spare oil production capacity	Rising spare oil production capacity
Rising global refining utilization	Falling global refining utilization
Falling global oil inventories	Rising global oil inventories

While aggregate global oil data are available, it's usually more useful to break down demand regionally because demand varies significantly by country due to the differing oil dependencies. Particularly, the economic outlook for the largest oil-consuming nations should be scrutinized.

Historically, oil demand growth is driven by developed world economies, notably the US. But this has changed. Global demand growth today is primarily driven by emerging market economies like China, India, and the Middle East. In fact, China represented 21, 55, and 36 percent of world oil demand growth in 2005, 2006, and 2007, respectively.[1] Global demand has been driven by very strong relative economic growth in developing nations versus developed nations over the past several years.

Figure 5.1 shows oil consumption by the US, OECD excluding the US (developed world), and non-OECD (developing world). While oil consumption has been virtually flat in the US and the developed world over the last several years, oil consumption in non-OECD countries has been rising steadily. Thus, a significant contraction in economic growth in non-OECD nations would likely have the largest effect on oil demand growth in future years.

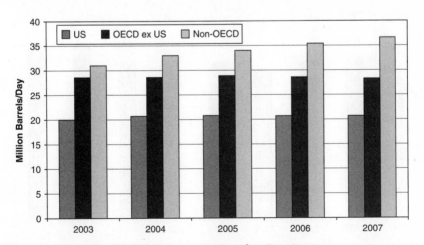

Figure 5.1   World Oil Consumption by Region
Source: Energy Information Administration.

OPEC Production

The Organization of Petroleum Exporting Countries' (OPEC) production target decisions will continue having a major effect on oil prices in the foreseeable future and should be closely watched. Investors and analysts pay close attention to OPEC's public announcements, using any available information to forecast the group's actions.

OPEC's production levels are notoriously difficult to predict. Analysts typically estimate OPEC's production by taking the difference between forecasted world oil demand and non-OPEC production (referred to as the *call on OPEC*). To the extent OPEC is willing and able to meet this shortfall, world inventories will rise or fall.

Figure 5.2 shows OPEC production over the last several years. After ramping up oil production following the surge in global economic growth in 2003, production from the cartel has declined since 2005. Despite the continued rise in oil prices, the cartel has shown little interest in increasing supply.

Non-OPEC Production

Non-OPEC production determines how much the world will rely on OPEC crude oil production. In recent years, non-OPEC nations

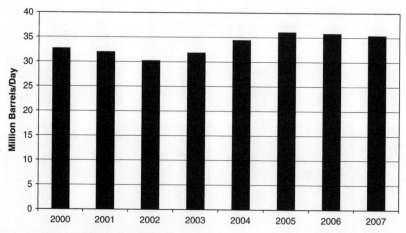

Figure 5.2   OPEC Production
Source: Energy Information Administration.

have had great difficulty increasing production. Supply growth has been challenged by maturing oil fields, rising costs, limited access to reserves, and relatively few major discoveries. Moreover, incremental growth from some countries is usually offset to some degree by declines in countries with maturing fields.

Figure 5.3 shows the production of crude oil from non-OPEC nations over the past several years. Despite their greatest effort, overall non-OPEC oil production has just barely increased since 2003.

The difference between world oil demand growth and non-OPEC supply growth is the amount required from OPEC without drawing down inventories. While world oil demand grew 7.2 percent from 2003 to 2007,[2] non-OPEC supply only grew 3.4 percent.[3] The difference was met by OPEC nations.

Figure 5.4 shows year-over-year non-OPEC oil production growth versus world oil consumption growth over the last several years. From 2000 to 2003, non-OPEC oil production growth more than covered world oil demand growth. However, this trend reversed sharply from 2004 to 2006, forcing greater reliance on OPEC. The greater the reliance on OPEC in future years—which has a huge incentive to keep prices high—the greater the likelihood prices stay high.

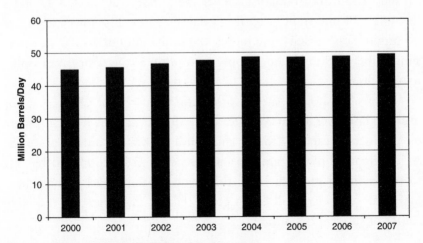

Figure 5.3   Non-OPEC Oil Production
Source: Energy Information Administration.

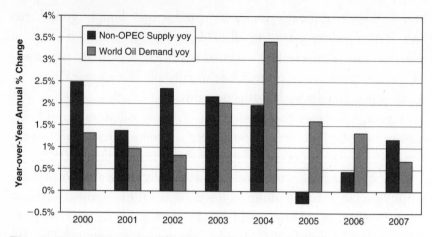

Figure 5.4   Non-OPEC Oil Supply vs. World Oil Demand
Source: Energy Information Administration.

Spare Oil Production Capacity

Spare oil production capacity—the world's ability to respond to increases in demand or shocks to supply—is becoming increasingly important. Strong global oil demand since 2003 caused surplus capacity to shrink dramatically over the last several years, reaching a low point of one million barrels a day in 2005. The lower the spare oil production capacity, the higher the probability of a spike in prices should there be any major supply disruption like war or catastrophic natural disaster.

Figure 5.5 shows spare oil production capacity of OPEC nations over the last several years. (Note: Only OPEC nations have any spare oil production capacity today, and Saudi Arabia has almost all of it.) As the figure shows, spare capacity plummeted in 2003 and has yet to regain much ground. Until this spare capacity reaches more normal levels, oil prices will face a greater likelihood of a spike if a large source of supply goes offline.

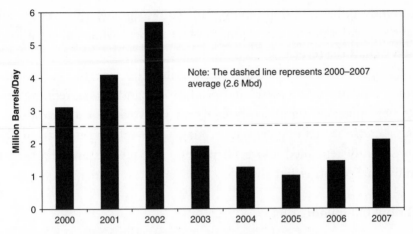

Figure 5.5   OPEC Spare Oil Production Capacity
Source: Energy Information Administration.

Oil Data Reliability

Statistics on global oil supply and consumption are widely available and comprehensive, perhaps more so than for any other commodity. However, industry data are notoriously unreliable and, in many cases, incomplete. For example, while respectable authorities like the Energy Information Administration (EIA) and International Energy Agency (IEA) offer very detailed oil data, reports from the two organizations can show different trends. The data are also frequently revised. Many emerging market nations—those that have been driving demand the last several years—do not report statistics in a timely manner. Saudi Arabia has the world's largest conventional oil reserves, but the country does not publish any data.

Use crude oil fundamental data as a tool for your analysis, but know the data can be suspect—especially in the short term.

Global Refining Utilization

Global refining utilization is an indicator of petroleum product demand, revealing the percentage of the world's refining capacity currently utilized. Rising refining utilization signifies rising crude oil demand and a tighter petroleum product market, while falling utilization signals the reverse.

Figure 5.6 shows global refining utilization over the last several years. Due to surging petroleum product demand, global refining utilization increased significantly in recent years without a corresponding increase in refining capacity. Today, while refining utilization has consistently remained above 80 percent globally, it's even higher in individual countries like the US.

Global Oil Inventories

Global oil inventories indicate the supply–demand balance and are also a determinant of prices. In general, when inventories rise, prices fall; and when inventories fall, prices rise. Good inventory data for every country are very sparse and often opaque, so inventories are generally analyzed based on stocks held in OECD (developed) nations only. Analysts track absolute levels of inventories relative to average ranges (shown in Figure 2.11 in Chapter 2) and commercial oil stock *days of supply*—measuring how many days of inventory are available to meet demand.

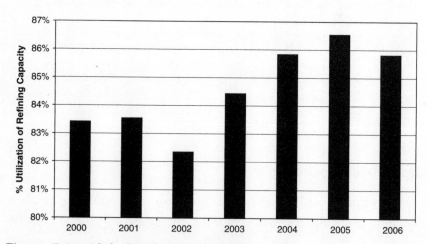

Figure 5.6   Global Refining Utilization
Source: BP.

Figure 5.7 shows commercial oil stock days of supply in OECD nations. The shaded band is the five-year minimum and maximum range for each month, representing the average range. When days of supply are near the lower end of its average range, it signifies a "tighter" market. Based on days of supply data, oil inventories began trending near the lower end of its range from 2003 to 2006, returning to more normal or above-average levels after that.

Historically, oil prices and global oil inventories have a strong negative correlation. Figure 5.9 shows the historical relationship between total crude oil stocks of OECD nations versus oil prices since 1995. Consistent with the historical trend, the late 1990s showed a sharp rise in inventories coinciding with a drop in oil prices. Beginning in 2004, this relationship broke down. Despite a steady rise in oil inventories in OECD nations, oil prices generally remained on an upward trajectory. It has yet to be seen if oil prices and inventories will regain their historical negative correlation.

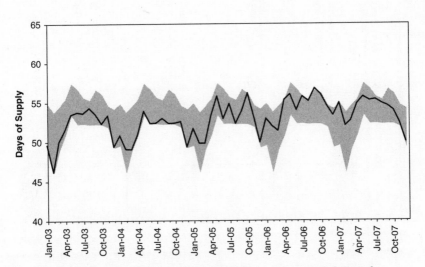

Figure 5.7   OECD Days of Supply Commercial Oil Stocks
Source: Energy Information Administration.

Strategic Petroleum Reserves

Strategic petroleum reserves are nations' emergency oil stockpiles. They serve as a last-resort source of crude oil in the event of natural disasters, wars, or anything potentially disrupting supply. While not usually a supply driver year-to-year (and why it's not in our bullish/bearish table for oil), they do occasionally have the power to move prices.

Fears of supply shortages due to terrorist attacks and geopolitical conflicts in major oil-producing regions have spurred nations to establish new strategic petroleum reserves or increase existing reserves. This is especially true in the US where, after the September 11, 2001 attacks, President Bush pledged to fill the Strategic Petroleum Reserve to its maximum of 700 million barrels. This served as another incremental oil demand growth driver of late.

Should a true oil supply crisis happen, countries with strategic reserves could alleviate the shortfall for a short period. Figure 5.8 shows the growth of US strategic petroleum reserves over the last several years. After rising steadily following September 11th, reserves were tapped briefly in late 2005 following Hurricanes Ivan, Katrina, and Rita, since production in the Gulf of Mexico was temporarily disrupted.

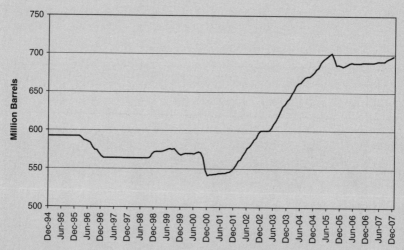

Figure 5.8   US Strategic Petroleum Reserve Inventory
Source: Energy Information Administration.

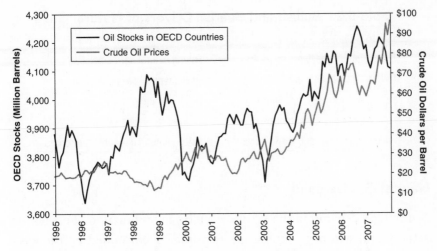

Figure 5.9   OECD Oil Inventories vs. Oil Prices
Source: Energy Information Administration.

NATURAL GAS MARKET FUNDAMENTALS

As mentioned in previous chapters, the natural gas market is not as global as oil due to difficulties in shipping supplies overseas. As a result, analysts and investors analyze the natural gas market by studying supply and demand conditions within specific regions.

For simplicity, we'll discuss fundamentals in the world's largest natural gas market—the US. This is also the region where natural gas data are the most easily accessed, detailed, and timely.

The primary quantitative factors influencing natural gas prices are:

- Natural gas demand
- Natural gas production
- Natural gas/liquefied natural gas (LNG) imports
- Natural gas storage inventories
- Prices of natural gas substitutes

On a high level, how each of these impacts natural gas is shown in Table 5.2.

Table 5.2   Bullish and Bearish Drivers of Natural Gas

Bullish Natural Gas Drivers	Bearish Natural Gas Drivers
Rising natural gas demand	Falling natural gas demand
Falling natural gas production	Rising natural gas production
Falling natural gas/LNG imports	Rising natural gas/LNG imports
Falling natural gas inventories	Rising natural gas inventories
Rising natural gas substitute prices	Falling natural gas substitute prices

Natural Gas Demand

Natural gas demand in the US is driven by a combination of economic activity and weather. Natural gas is primarily consumed by the electric power, industrial, commercial, and residential sectors. While the largest user of natural gas is the industrial sector (driven by economic activity), weather-related demand in the other sectors can make consumption variable and unpredictable. Along with economic growth forecasts, some analysts and investors even try to predict weather patterns to forecast demand.

Figure 5.10 shows how US natural gas demand has differed among the four major end users. While natural gas demand increased

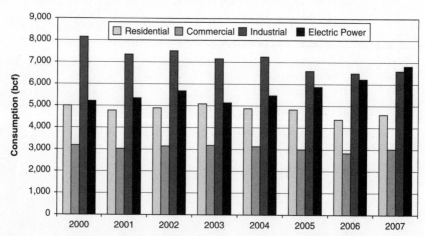

Figure 5.10   US Natural Gas Consumption by End User
Source: Energy Information Administration.

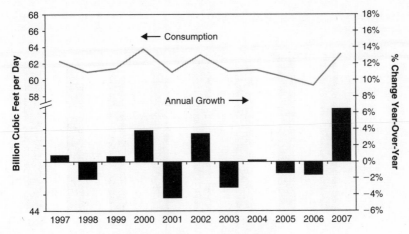

Figure 5.11 US Natural Gas Consumption
Source: Energy Information Administration.

in the electric power sector over the last several years, it's generally remained static or declined in other sectors. Greater proportional use by the electric power sector may make natural gas demand more tied to economic growth and less to weather.

Figure 5.11 shows both total US consumption of natural gas and year-over-year change in consumption. While total US consumption has been about flat the last 10 years, annual demand use has varied significantly year-to-year due in part to weather. These shifts in demand move prices.

Natural Gas Production

The US is currently able to meet about 85 percent of its domestic demand with domestic production. The rest is met by pipeline imports and LNG.

Figure 5.12 shows US natural gas production over the past several years. US natural gas production is similar to demand, remaining about static the last 10 years. However, production most recently peaked in 2001 and has declined since. This has forced the US to rely more on LNG and imports from Canada to make up the shortfall.

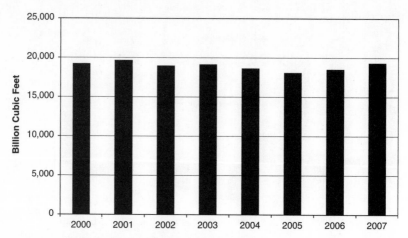

Figure 5.12   US Natural Gas Production
Source: Energy Information Administration.

Natural Gas and Liquefied Natural Gas Imports

Natural gas pipeline imports and LNG imports are gaining importance by helping the US meet demand amid weak domestic supply growth. US natural gas prices are greatly affected by the ability to secure sufficient natural gas imports to meet demand.

The majority of US natural gas imports come from Canada via pipeline. LNG imports come mainly from Trinidad, Egypt, and Nigeria and are gaining as a percentage of total imports. Figure 5.13 shows total US natural gas imports and LNG as a percentage of imports over the last several years. As shown by the line graph, the proportion of LNG imports to the total has increased substantially over the last several years.

Natural Gas Storage Inventories

Natural gas inventories are an indicator of demand, but they can be highly volatile in the short term due to weather variability. In general, natural gas inventories build from March to October, before the onset of winter, and decline from October through March. Abnormally cold or hot weather or changes in supply from domestic or imported sources will cause changes in inventories.

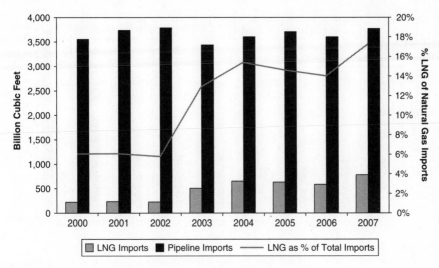

Figure 5.13   US Natural Gas Imports by Type
Source: Energy Information Administration.

Figure 5.14 shows US natural gas inventories on an annual basis over the last several years. Inventories have been generally rising since 2003, trending above average in 2006 and 2007. Analysts typically analyze inventories as they relate to a five-year average range. Inventories significantly above or below average ranges will likely affect prices.

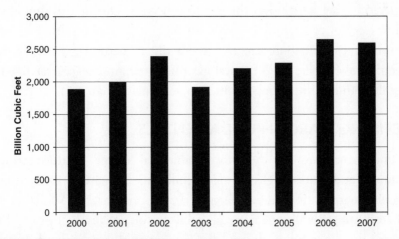

Figure 5.14   US Natural Gas Inventories
Source: Energy Information Administration.

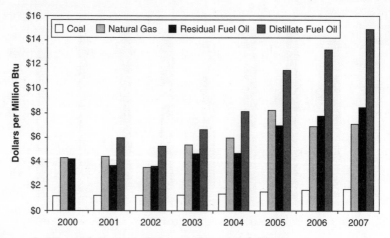

Figure 5.15   US Power Generation Fuel Costs

Source: Energy Information Administration.

Natural Gas Substitute Prices

To some extent, industrial and electric power generators can choose to switch between natural gas and other fuels depending on prices. So when substitute fuel prices fall, natural gas becomes relatively unattractive. This has the power to affect natural gas prices year to year.

Figure 5.15 shows how prices have changed for each power-generation fuel source over the last several years. During this time, fuel oil saw prices rise rapidly along with oil prices. The resulting substitution effect contributed to the recent rise in natural gas use by the electric power sector. US natural gas prices remain cheaper relative to distillate and residual fuel oil but more expensive than coal.

REFINING MARGIN FUNDAMENTALS

Refining margins are the most influential driver of downstream (refining and marketing) earnings. Similar to the natural gas market, refining margins differ depending on the regional market. While crude oil costs are generally the same globally, petroleum product prices differ greatly. Since we've already discussed supply and demand drivers for oil, the industry fundamentals discussed in this section focus on petroleum products. For simplicity, we'll continue using the US—the world's largest petroleum product market—as our primary example.

The primary quantitative factors influencing refining margins are:

- Petroleum product demand
- Crude oil prices
- Refining utilization
- Petroleum product inventories
- Petroleum product imports
- Light/heavy spread

An overview of how these factors impact refining margins is shown in Table 5.3.

Table 5.3   Bullish and Bearish Drivers of Refining Margins

Bullish Refining Margin Drivers	Bearish Refining Margin Drivers
Rising petroleum product demand	Falling petroleum product demand
Falling crude oil prices	Rising crude oil prices
Rising refining utilization	Falling refining utilization
Falling petroleum product inventories	Rising petroleum product inventories
Falling petroleum product imports	Rising petroleum product imports
Rising light/heavy spread	Falling light/heavy spread

The Crack Spread

In order to approximate refinery gross profit margins, a commonly used ratio is the 3-2-1 *crack spread* (the term *crack spread* comes from the stage of the refining process in which molecules are split—cracked apart—to separate what will become different final products). This ratio refers to the proportion of gasoline and heating oil produced for each barrel of oil—for three parts oil, two parts are made into gasoline and one into heating oil.

Petroleum Product Demand

Petroleum product demand is driven by a combination of economic activity and weather. Strong petroleum product demand generally translates into higher prices, while lower demand translates into lower prices. US petroleum products are gasoline, jet fuel, and distillate fuel (diesel and heating oil). Due to changes in weather, economic growth, and travel demand, consumption growth in each can look very different. However, most petroleum products are used in the transportation sector, thus overall demand is fairly inelastic to prices. As a result, while demand does change somewhat year to year, petroleum product demand increased steadily along with GDP growth.

Figure 5.16 shows US petroleum product consumption over the last several years. Total product demand has grown slightly since 2000, but has remained about flat the last few years.

Crude Oil Prices

Crude oil price changes can cause wide swings in refining margins because they're the main feedstock of refineries. Petroleum product prices are sticky—it can take weeks for changes in oil prices to work

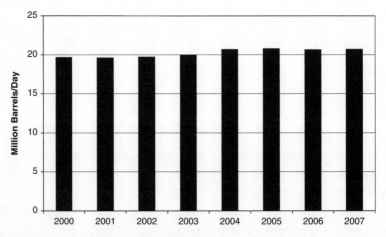

Figure 5.16   US Petroleum Product Consumption
Source: Energy Information Administration.

their way into petroleum product prices. Thus, refining margins generally fall when crude oil prices rise, and vice versa.

It's important to note crude oil costs are just one side of the equation for refining margins (the other being product prices). So over the long term, crude oil prices and refining margins have an inconsistent relationship. In the short term though, this relationship is more relevant.

Figure 5.17 shows the relationship between US refining margins and crude oil prices over the last several years. The inconsistency of the relationship is evident over the last several years, with wide swings in refining margins in a variety of crude oil price environments. This is due to differences between supply, demand, and inventory movements for crude oil versus those for each refined product.

Refining Utilization

While we mentioned earlier in the chapter how global refining utilization affects crude oil prices, refining utilization in individual countries will have a greater effect on petroleum product prices. Refining utilization is an indicator of petroleum product demand. Generally, when

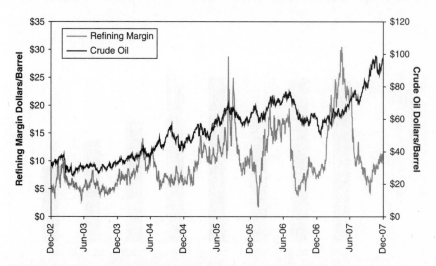

Figure 5.17   US Refining Margins vs. Crude Oil Prices
Source: Bloomberg Finance L.P., Thomson Datastream.

refining utilization is high, it shows refineries increased production to meet demand. This is usually bullish for refining margins.

Refining utilization may also tell us something about the supply situation. Utilization may be low due to unexpected outages and maintenance or repairs, meaning refineries are not producing as much as they would under normal circumstances. Or oil firms may reduce output in response to low refining margins, reducing refining utilization.

In these cases, low refining utilization may also be bullish for refining margins. Understanding what currently drives refining utilization is more important than focusing on absolute numbers.

Figure 5.18 shows US refining utilization over the last several years. On an absolute basis, US refining utilization has been running at high levels (88 to 93 percent), but utilization has been on the decline since peaking in 2004.

Petroleum Product Inventories

Similar to crude oil, petroleum product inventories are also used as a demand indicator. Inventories are usually analyzed based on the days of supply of petroleum product stocks—measuring how many days of inventory are available given current or projected demand—and

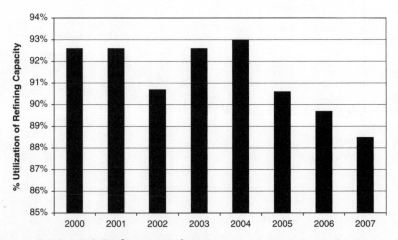

Figure 5.18   US Refining Utilization
Source: Energy Information Administration.

on an absolute basis. Moreover, inventory data are available for each petroleum product separately. In general, low days of supply and inventories signify a tight petroleum product market.

These data are usually analyzed based on year-over-year changes and relative to a five-year average range. Inventories build seasonally over the course of the year, rising during the spring before the peak summer driving season and falling throughout the year into the following January.

Here are two examples of how to track supply data, using US gasoline as an example (though this is also done for other products like distillate and propane). Figure 5.19 shows US gasoline days of supply since 2000. While days of supply data fluctuate significantly over the course of the year, the data show a general downward trend over the last several years. Gasoline days of supply data are typically followed weekly by analysts to gauge whether supplies are increasing or decreasing.

The other way to analyze supplies is to track absolute inventory levels, usually relative to an average range. Figure 5.20 shows the absolute level of US gasoline inventories over the last several years. While the figure fluctuates every week, gasoline inventories have been

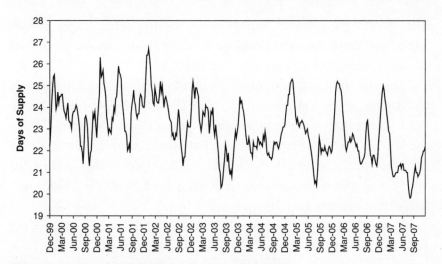

Figure 5.19   US Gasoline Days of Supply
Source: Energy Information Administration.

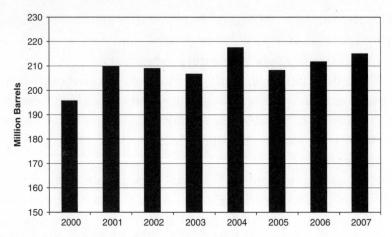

Figure 5.20   US Gasoline Inventories
Source: Energy Information Administration.

steadily rising since 2005. When supplies get to be above their average range, it typically means product prices will remain flat or decline, pressuring refining margins.

Petroleum Product Imports

The petroleum product market is becoming increasingly global. When petroleum product prices are relatively higher in any given part of the world, it typically attracts imports.

Due to the combination of weak US refining capacity growth and strong petroleum product demand growth, US petroleum product imports have been increasingly important over the years. When the US has seen particularly strong petroleum product demand or a major downstream supply shock (like the 2005 hurricanes in the Gulf of Mexico), petroleum product imports helped to alleviate the shortfall between supply and demand.

Figure 5.21 shows the absolute level of US petroleum product imports over the last several years. As the figure shows, imports have been rising steadily since 2002. In the short term, above-average imports have the potential to put downward pressure on product prices.

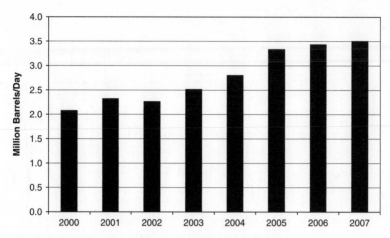

Figure 5.21   US Petroleum Product Imports
Source: Energy Information Administration.

Light/Heavy Spread

The spread between light and heavy crude oil prices affects the profitability of complex refineries capable of processing cheaper heavy crude oil. When the spread increases, complex refineries can take advantage of the cheaper, heavier crude, increasing margins.

The spread between light and heavy crude oil prices generally changes in response to changes in world heavy oil production, primarily by OPEC. When OPEC reduces production, it first reduces production of cheaper, heavier crude oil. This reduces heavy crude supply, increasing prices and closing the gap between heavy and light crude. When OPEC increases production, it raises supply of heavy crude oil, reducing prices and increasing the gap between light and heavy oil.

Figure 5.22 shows the light/heavy spread as calculated by the difference between West Texas Intermediate (light) and Arab Heavy (heavy), though other crude oil benchmarks can be used. The spread began to widen in 2003 after OPEC increased heavy oil production to meet demand, making heavy prices relatively cheaper than light. This benefited Refining & Marketing firms with more complex refineries, increasing refining margins. The spread narrowed as OPEC reduced supplies after 2005.

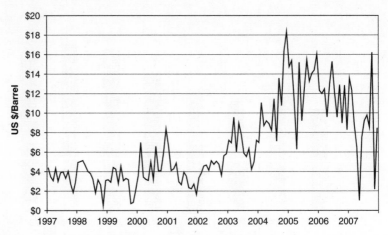

Figure 5.22   Crude Oil Light/Heavy Spread
Source: Thomson Datastream.

ENERGY EQUIPMENT & SERVICES FUNDAMENTALS

As mentioned in earlier chapters, the Energy Equipment & Services (EES) industry is indirectly affected by oil and gas prices because those prices affect industry demand for oil and gas drilling, and equipment and services. EES demand is ultimately quantified by aggregate spending by the Oil & Gas industry.

Other fundamental data followed by analysts and investors are the supply and demand environment for just about every product and service in the industry. This includes the supply of just about every type of rig, supply boat, seismic vessel, and more in nearly every region of the world. Moreover, analysts and investors even forecast future supply of energy equipment and services to help make investment decisions. Because there are too many products and services in the industry to cover (not to mention a lack of easily available aggregate data!), only the broadest fundamental indicators affecting the industry are included.

The primary quantitative factors that influence EES are:

- Energy sector capital expenditures
- World rig count

Table 5.4   Bullish and Bearish Drivers of Energy Equipment and Services

Bullish Industry Drivers	Bearish Industry Drivers
Rising energy capital expenditures	Falling energy capital expenditures
Rising world rig count	Falling world rig count
Rising rig utilization	Falling rig utilization
Rising dayrates	Falling dayrates

- Rig utilization
- Dayrates

Table 5.4 shows how these impact EES on a high level.

Energy Sector Capital Expenditures

As mentioned in Chapter 2, the main driver of EES is capital expenditures from the Energy sector. The amount spent on exploration and production by the oil and gas firms should roughly equate to the revenues received by the EES sub-industry.

Energy firms tend to increase and decrease capital expenditures in response to prolonged periods of high or low energy prices or expectations of future price moves. However, it's important to note all regions of the world do not benefit equally from the spending surge. This could be due to the relative attractiveness of crude oil versus natural gas, new discoveries in a region, geopolitical uncertainty, or differing cost profiles among regions. For example, capital expenditures could increase by double digits in oil-rich regions of the Middle East in a period of high oil prices. However, it could fall in North America should US natural gas prices fall substantially or costs rise significantly. The spending differences will affect EES firms differently based on their relative exposure to different regions.

Figure 5.23 shows aggregate capital expenditures of MSCI World Energy constituents over recent years. In response to rapidly rising oil prices, aggregate annual capital expenditures by global Energy firms have more than doubled since 2003. Because this type of data is not

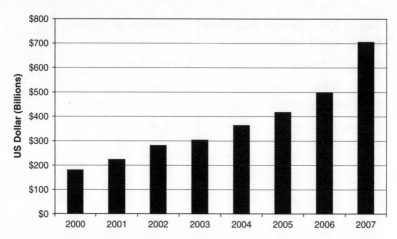

Figure 5.23   Aggregate Capital Expenditures of MSCI World Energy Companies
Source: Thomson Datastream, MSCI, Inc.[4]

available on a real-time basis (firms usually announce capital expenditure plans once a year), analysts typically look to Energy firms' spending surveys from independent research firms to forecast how the next year will look for EES firms.

World Rig Count

World rig count is an indicator of drilling demand. This data can be dissected by region, individual country—even rig type (land or offshore). Like Energy capital expenditures, rig count tends to rise and fall along with oil and natural gas prices. However, each commodity will affect specific types of rigs differently. For example, most offshore rigs are more influenced by oil prices since they tend to drill for oil. US land rigs, however, tend to drill for natural gas and are more influenced by gas prices.

In general, an increasing number of operating rigs worldwide is a positive indicator for the EES industry. As rig demand increases, oil and gas drilling firms are generally able to charge more for their rigs. Moreover, as more rigs enter service, oil and gas equipment and services firms benefit from the greater demand for equipment, services, and labor to operate those rigs.

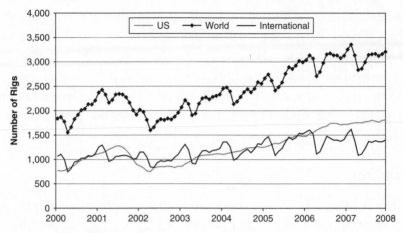

Figure 5.24   World Rig Count
Source: Baker Hughes, Inc.

But a rising worldwide rig count is only positive for the industry as long as rig supply does not outpace demand. Should too many rigs enter the market, dayrates would likely suffer, rigs will eventually be taken out of service, and the industry could suffer some pain as the balance is restored between rig supply and demand. This is why analysts comb through a variety of data sources and follow rig count trends to try and forecast what the future supply and demand balance will be like for each rig type.

Figure 5.24 shows the world rig count over the last several years, breaking out the US and international rigs. Rig count growth in the US has outpaced international growth, with both contributing to a world rig count more than doubling since 2000. The rig count increase has been a boon to the EES industry, especially when the rig count experienced its greatest acceleration.

Rig Utilization

Rig utilization measures the percentage of active rigs out of total rig supply. Rig utilization is often analyzed based on rig type (jack-up versus semi-submersible) or geography (Gulf of Mexico versus North Sea). Rising rig utilization is often characterized by strong rig demand, rising dayrates, and limited rig supply growth. Falling rig utilization is characterized by weak rig demand, falling dayrates, and rigs taken out of service.

Individual drilling firms generally disclose their utilization rates in their financial statements. Rig utilization rates can also be found in some market research firms like ODS-Petrodata (www.ods-petrodata.com) and RigZone (www.rigzone.com).

Dayrates

The vast majority of rigs work on dayrate contracts. Dayrates are driven by supply and demand for rigs and differ greatly depending on the rig type, age, and geography. In general, sustained periods of high oil and gas prices generally lead to higher rig demand and dayrates.

Dayrates can change dramatically over the course of an energy cycle. Over the last several years, dayrates for most types of rigs surged due to high demand, limited supply, and limited ability to build new rigs. However, in 2001, dayrates plummeted as low oil and natural gas prices curbed drilling demand, causing firms to take rigs out of service.

Dayrates also tend to be an indicator of the future rig supply. When dayrates remain high or are rising for a certain rig type, it typically follows that more of those rigs will be built and enter service. Low or falling dayrates typically put on hold plans to build new rigs.

While data for dayrates are compiled in aggregate by subscription services (like ODS-Petrodata), oil and gas drilling firms typically release dayrate information in their financial statements.

Chapter Recap

Industry fundamentals are analyzed thoroughly and monitored closely by Energy analysts and investors. These quantitative data are used to make forecasts for oil and natural gas prices, refining margins, capital spending, and ultimately assist in making investment decisions. But do not limit yourself to the examples shown in this chapter in your quest to analyze the current fundamentals of the Energy sector—these are just the main data series that are widely followed. Using the data sources provided in the Appendix, you should be able to analyze nearly any aspect of the Energy sector.

- Crude oil market fundamentals are followed largely to determine how global supply and demand drivers will move prices.
- Natural gas market fundamentals are also followed to determine supply and demand drivers, but largely on a region-by-region basis.
- Refining margin fundamentals include tracking both the crude oil market and supply and demand drivers for petroleum products in specific regions.
- For the Energy Equipment & Services industry, the most important industry fundamental is capital spending by the Oil & Gas industry.
- Within the EES industry, other fundamentals to follow include supply and demand for the products and services offered, like rigs, equipment, and seismic vessels.

ALTERNATIVE ENERGY

Rapidly rising energy prices. Carbon emissions. Pollution. These are just a few hot-button issues surrounding the drive toward sustainable energy sources. Interest in alternative energies has soared in recent years, and this rapidly growing category received investments of more than $100 billion globally in 2007, as the world invested in renewable energy capacity, manufacturing plants, and research and development.[1]

While this book is centered on investing in the traditional oil and gas sector, we feel compelled to provide a brief overview of the alternative energy landscape, as it will no doubt grow over time. It's important to note *most alternative energy company stocks do not even fall in the Energy sector*. General Electric, for instance, has one of the largest alternative energy divisions in the world, but it doesn't show up in any Energy index. Neither does Toyota's technological advancements of hybrid auto manufacturing.

In this chapter, basic definitions are discussed, along with concepts behind most common types of alternative energy and how they fit into the world's energy consumption mix. Also discussed are limitations and potentials of alternative energy now and in the future.

Like other parts of Energy, there are basic drivers and themes of alternative energy firms from an investment standpoint worth considering. Finally, we'll provide a glimpse into the investment universe of alternative energy firms, including a list of pure-play firms (those 100% focused on alternative energy) and those with indirect alternative energy investments.

WHAT IS ALTERNATIVE ENERGY?

Before we delve into alternative energy investing, it's necessary to highlight some important points and risks.

Investors commonly make the mistake of focusing too much on small, sexy, attention-grabbing, budding industries like those within alternative energy. In reality, many alternative energy firms are unprofitable, inefficient, government-dependent entities whose futures are far from certain. In fact, the current alternative energy investment environment reminds us of the dot-com era of the late 1990s. Then, as now, investors flocked to an investment class with seemingly limitless growth potential, funding firms with questionable economics and sky-high valuations. While there were a few firms that managed to grow dramatically despite the ensuing bust, there were hundreds more that went bankrupt. In any fledgling industry, just picking the survivors is a low probability game. Sure, there will be a few big winners, but there will be far more losers.

Many investors invest in alternative energy firms and other speculative investments thinking, "In the next 30 years, this will be the next big thing for sure!" But markets are too fickle to wait 30 years. Markets discount company-specific information out one to maybe five years—certainly not 30. Unless the firm's technology or products become widely distributed and profitable within a reasonable period, you're basically making a bet on a temporary fad. Doing so is no different than betting on a spinning roulette wheel. And even if you can pick an alternative energy company with a winning technology or strategy, it's likely the firm faces a slew of new competition. Nothing attracts competition faster than huge profits. So correctly forecasting alternative energy winners will not necessarily lead to huge stock returns. You still need to find firms who operate well, execute, and make good on their competitive advantages.

Another investment strategy—one currently employed by many deep-pocketed private equity and venture capital firms—is making large bets on alternative energy firms while hoping government mandates, subsidies, or tax policies will benefit them. Investors may then spend an exorbitant amount of time and effort lobbying Congress to implement legislation that directs public money to their investment. While there's nothing technically illegal about this, it requires investors to take a different approach when analyzing alternative energy firms. Instead of focusing on business fundamentals like strategic attributes, cash flows, and company strategy, one must investigate how politics affects alternative energy. This, too, is very difficult to predict with certainty.

Alternative energy investing therefore requires great scrutiny and caution, and it should not make up a substantial portion of your investment portfolio unless you desire high risk. This is especially true if managing against an energy benchmark, of which alternative energy will be a tiny part, if any.

Regardless, there are indeed potentially profitable long-term alternative energy investments, and it's vital to understand where new competition and technology might eventually spring.

Defining Alternative Energy

Alternative energy (a.k.a. renewable energy) refers to sources of energy other than those generated through fossil fuels like oil and natural gas. Alternative energy replaces conventional fuels in four distinct sectors: power generation, hot water and space heating, transport fuels, and rural (or *off-grid*) energy. The largest of these sectors in terms of overall global consumption is power generation (e.g., wind, solar, biomass, hydroelectric power).

While alternative energy sources have been around for decades, they still make up a relatively modest percentage of the world's total energy consumption and an even smaller percentage of the investment universe. Figure 6.1 shows the world's total energy consumption by energy source. On an energy equivalent basis, petroleum, coal, and natural gas dominate global energy use. Renewables represent about 7 percent of the world's consumption.[2]

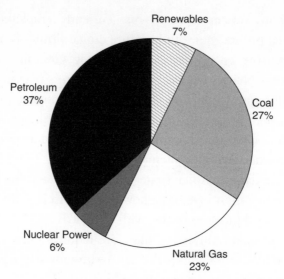

Figure 6.1   World Energy Consumption by Fuel Sources
Source: Energy Information Administration.

Due to the world's current dependency on traditional energy sources, future energy needs, and the difficulty expanding alternative energy sources on a massive scale, the current energy consumption mix is unlikely to change significantly in the foreseeable future. According to the 2007 International Energy Outlook released by the EIA, the renewables share of total world energy consumption is expected to rise from 7 percent in 2005 to only 8 percent in 2030,[3] mostly from mid- to large-scale hydroelectric plants either planned or under construction in several emerging market nations. (Note: This could very well be an undershot due to substitution effects from high oil and natural gas prices, as covered in Chapter 4.) Renewable energy will certainly continue to grow in absolute terms, but so will the use of traditional energy sources (and from a much larger base). Thus, alternative energy sources help at the margin, but none today have the potential to make a significant difference in current global energy consumption in the next several decades.

Don't let alternative energy media hype steer you. For countless investors, politicians, and lobbyists, the message is clear: The world's energy needs will continue to be met by the conventional energy sources—oil, coal, natural gas, and nuclear—for the foreseeable future.

Still, alternative energy has grown rapidly in recent years, gaining increasing notoriety and interest from governments and investors due to rapidly rising energy prices, increasing demand for cleaner energy, and a desire for energy security. As long as these conditions persist—along with advancements in technology—it is likely interest and investment opportunities will continue emerging as well.

Renewable Energy Uses

Renewable energy is used primarily for electricity generation. Believe it or not, the world's power plants generate more electricity through renewables than nuclear power—currently the third-largest fuel source after coal and natural gas. Figure 6.2 shows the world's electricity generation fuel sources as of 2004. While renewables may not make up a substantial percentage of world energy consumption, renewables most definitely play a big role in world electricity generation.

In the US, renewable energy is also used primarily for electricity generation, which accounts for 70 percent of total US renewable energy consumption. 25 percent is used in industrial processes and

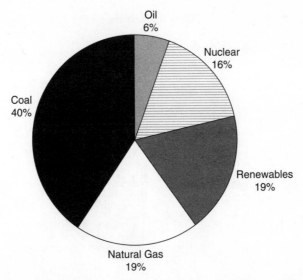

Figure 6.2   World Electricity Generation Fuel Sources
Source: International Energy Agency.

heating and cooling buildings, and the remaining 5 percent is used for transportation fuels.[4]

Compared to the world, the US generates a much smaller percentage of its electricity from renewables, relying more on coal and nuclear power. Figure 6.3 provides the electricity generation fuel sources for the US as of 2006. (Note: We have broken up the renewables section into hydroelectric and other renewables to glean a clearer breakdown.)

In both the US and the world, the vast majority of renewable electricity generation is hydroelectric power. In fact, hydroelectricity makes up over 80 percent of all renewable energy consumed in the world.[5] While it's estimated other electricity generation sources like solar, wind, biopower, and geothermal will increase in the future, they're unlikely to significantly shift the world's reliance on hydroelectric power as its main renewable energy source in the near future.

Transportation fuels like ethanol and biodiesel have an even smaller impact on today's energy consumption mix, as both ethanol and biodiesel combined make up only about 1 percent of the world's transportation fuel supply.[6] According to the Renewable Fuels

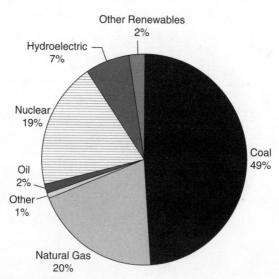

Figure 6.3   US Electricity Generation Fuel Sources
Source: Energy Information Administration.

Association, ethanol currently displaces a little more than 200 million barrels of crude oil annually in the US, or about 10 days of normal oil consumption in the US. Government mandates, subsidies, and tax incentives promote more renewable transportation fuels, but the reality is they won't make a significant impact anytime soon.

Other types of alternative energies within the transportation sector include new energy sources for autos like fuel cells and electric cars. These technologies are mostly experimental and in their infant stages today, but could very well become viable should technological advancements accelerate in the future. But again, such happenstance is many years away at best.

Where Does it Come From?

Renewable energy uses natural resources like the sun, water, and wind that can be replenished in perpetuity. These resources have the ability to provide clean, sustainable energy while reducing the world's fossil fuel reliance.

However, the problem with renewable energy is scale. While each resource contributes to the world's energy needs to some degree, we simply cannot produce enough energy from them fast enough to significantly offset the world's future energy demand needs.

The world is doing what it can to increase its use of renewable energy. Here are the main renewable energy sources and how they contribute to the world's energy needs.

Water   Hydroelectric power is the leading renewable energy source today. Energy is produced by directing, harnessing, or channeling moving water. In most structures, water flows through a pipe, turning blades in a turbine. The turbine then spins a generator and produces electricity. As of 2005, hydroelectric power accounted for 6 percent of world energy consumption and 80 percent of renewable energy consumption.[7]

Hydroelectric generation has the advantage of being a cheap, reliable source of power capable of running 24 hours a day without producing air pollution. While hydroelectric power has been around

Hydroelectric dam.
Source: © Getty Images, Inc.

since the 1800s, it's becoming even more attractive today given the world's increasing demand for cleaner energy.

Yes, hydroelectric power has its advantages, but it also has limitations. For example, power generation can be unpredictable year to year as droughts or limited rainfall might cause utilities to rely on backup power generation sources. (This is because electricity generally can't be stored.)

Moreover, environmental concerns abound regarding hydroelectric's effects on plant, fish, and animal life due to damming rivers and streams. Last, there's a natural limit to the number of hydroelectric plants that can be built in the world because, logistically, there are only certain places viable to harness moving water. There are still plenty of countries in the world with undeveloped hydroelectric resources, but most developed countries have already built out all significant hydroelectric sites.

Other much smaller power generation sources using water are tidal and wave energy (a.k.a. ocean energy). This type of power can be generated through such methods as channeling waves directly into spin turbines. While promising in theory, ocean energy is in its infant stages and will need significant advancements in technology to efficiently produce significant quantities of energy.

Ethanol and Other Biomass/Waste   Biomass energy is produced from non-fossilized materials derived from plants like wood, crops, garbage, landfill gas, and alcohol fuels. Biomass contains stored energy from the sun via photosynthesis. When burned, chemical energy in biomass is released as heat. Biomass fuels provide about 3 percent of the energy used in the US.[8]

There are three main types of biomass: wood, waste, and biofuels. While biofuels like ethanol probably are the most publicized, the biomass generating the largest amount of energy is wood.

- **Wood energy** (mainly burning wood) is used not only to heat residential homes but also to generate energy for electric power producers, industries, and commercial businesses.
- **Waste energy** (mainly burning types of garbage) is generated through means of waste-to-energy plants or capturing gas from landfills to be used as a fuel source.
- **Biofuels** are mostly transportation fuels like ethanol and biodiesel.

Ethanol is an alcohol fuel made from the sugars in a variety of biomass. There are several ways to make ethanol, but it's most often produced from corn or sugar cane. Almost all global ethanol production comes from two countries—about evenly split between the US and Brazil.[9] In the US, corn is the main ethanol ingredient because it's abundant and historically cheap. In Brazil, ethanol is made mainly from its plentiful supply of sugar cane. Another type of ethanol—cellulosic—is made by breaking down cellulose in woody fibers from plant material like grasses, woods, and agricultural wastes. However, production of cellulosic ethanol is still in its beginning stages and will need advancements in technology in order to be economically mass produced.

Ethanol can be used as a total or partial replacement for gasoline. About 99 percent of ethanol produced in the US today is used to make E10, or a mixture of 10 percent ethanol and 90 percent gasoline.[10] There are also more concentrated blends of ethanol and gasoline like

E85, made with 85 percent ethanol and 15 percent gasoline. Any gasoline-powered engine can use E10, but only specially made vehicles can run on E85. While these vehicles are extremely rare in the US, they are highly prevalent in Brazil since the country has embraced E85 and other biofuels for years.

Similar to ethanol, biodiesel is a renewable fuel but is made from grain oils and animal fats. While the majority of biodiesel today is made from soybean oil, it can also be made from used oils or fats like restaurant grease.

Biodiesel can be used as a total or partial replacement for diesel. The fuel is most often blended with petroleum diesel in ratios of 2, 5, or 20 percent, but can also be used as 100 percent pure biodiesel. Unlike ethanol, all biodiesel fuels can be used in regular diesel vehicles without making engine modifications.

While biofuels hold tremendous promise in helping to solve the world's future transportation fuel needs, there are some significant challenges to overcome.

The Ethanol Movement   Recently embraced by the US government as a solution to the reliance on foreign oil, ethanol appears to be a cure worse than the disease. It's a classic case of politics overruling rational science and economics.

Ethanol gained momentum with President Bush's Advanced Energy Initiative in the 2006 State of the Union Address. In it, he stated a goal to reduce America's reliance on foreign oil by increasing alternative fuel use and funding new and existing technologies. Government officials argued that by mandating the use of 35 billion gallons of renewable and alternative fuels in 2017, an estimated 15 percent of projected gasoline consumption could be replaced.[11] Congress then seized the opportunity to extend tax credits for farmers producing biofuels, as well as implementing a 54 cents per gallon tariff on imported ethanol. They also mandated 7.5 billion gallons of the nation's fuel should come from biofuels by 2012.

A later piece of legislation, the Energy Independence and Security Act of 2007, increased this mandate further by requiring fuel producers to supply 36 billion gallons of biofuels by 2022.[12] The act also mandated that at least 21 billion gallons come from feedstock other than corn (a.k.a. cellulosic ethanol, an industry that barely exists today). After an 80 percent rise in US ethanol production in the past two years to seven billion gallons,[13] the industry has already suffered some major growing pains and seen numerous unintended market disruptions. This has raised serious doubts over ethanol's environmental benefits.

While ethanol is the most economically viable of the transportation fuels capable of large-scale production, the fuel has limitations and consequences for several industries. Because most US ethanol is made from corn, increasing ethanol production causes global corn prices to soar. This has a widespread effect on numerous industries reliant on the grain. For example, many food staples have seen their prices increase as well because corn is a common ingredient in a variety of packaged food products. Corn is also the main ingredient in livestock feed, leading to increases in meat and dairy products. This food-for-fuel trade-off raises legitimate questions about whether the benefits of ethanol are worth the costs.

The reason ethanol production hasn't increased substantially until recent mandates is because it's not profitable without subsidies, import tariffs, and tax credits. In other words, it doesn't work in a free market environment. Rising corn prices makes ethanol production even more unprofitable, leading to the shelving of several planned ethanol plant construction projects. The fuel also has lower energy content than gasoline, is difficult to transport (currently, it only ships through truck or rail), and its production requires a significant amount of land and water sources.

Even if all farmers found it profitable to switch to ethanol production, it would still barely make a dent in US energy needs. According to National Geographic, if the entire US corn and soybean crop were turned into biofuels, it would replace just 12 percent of gasoline and 6 percent of diesel (not to mention putting even greater upward pressure on corn prices).[14] The US Agriculture Department projects that by 2010, less than 8 percent of the US gasoline supply will come from corn-based ethanol, but 30 percent of the corn crop will be used to make it.[15] This trade-off is unbalanced and unsustainable.

Numerous academic studies suggest *corn-based ethanol production requires just as much, if not more, carbon-emitting fossil fuel than it creates*. By converting new land to produce alternative fuels from crops and grasses that absorb carbon dioxide from the atmosphere, more CO^2 emissions may be created than the annual savings from replacing fossil fuels. Such deforestation is likely hurting the environment it was intended to preserve!

A better way to handle the current environment would be if the US eliminated the tariff on imported ethanol and allowed markets to trade freely. Brazilian sugarcane ethanol, for example, has far fewer economic and environmental consequences than corn-based ethanol. Based on economic theory, since Brazil has a comparative advantage in ethanol production, it would be mutually beneficial for both parties if the US outsourced domestic ethanol production to Brazil. Of course, this would simply switch our reliance on foreign oil to foreign ethanol, but at least the latter is renewable and from a nation friendly to the US. (But don't hold your breath for such a development.)

Cellulosic ethanol—which doesn't have the food-for-fuel trade-off—also holds tremendous promise. Because it's made using biomass material contained in nearly every natural plant, tree, and bush, the fuel could be produced without agricultural effort or cost needed to make it grow. While it hasn't yet been proven if the fuel can be produced economically in large quantities, further research and technological advancements may eventually bring this cost down.

Ultimately, if ethanol (or some other alternative) solves the renewable energy puzzle, the market will be the first to know. Political meddling in free markets with subsidies and tariffs creates more inefficiencies than benefits and delays potentially meaningful breakthroughs. While increasing our use of cleaner, renewable fuels and reducing our reliance on imported oil is a good goal in theory, it will come at a cost higher than most are willing to pay.

Wind   Wind power systems convert kinetic energy into electricity through wind turbines. Wind turns the wind turbine blades, spinning a shaft, which connects to a generator and makes electricity. Wind energy is often harnessed through the use of large-scale wind farms connected to electrical grids, but individual turbines are also used

Wind turbines.
Source: © Getty Images, Inc.

in isolated locations. Despite its growth in recent years, wind energy produces only 0.4 percent of total US electricity production[16] and 1 percent of worldwide electricity.[17]

Wind energy offers the advantage of producing clean and renewable energy, and wind turbines also have relatively low maintenance costs. New technologies have decreased the cost of producing electricity from wind, while tax breaks and subsidies in the US and Europe help spur new wind power development. According to the World Wind Energy Association, new world wind power capacity has seen a tenfold increase between 1998 and 2007 and is expected to grow more than 21 percent per year through 2010.[18]

There are several limitations to wind energy. Because wind speeds vary depending on the time of day, month, or season, electricity generation can also vary. This requires utilities using wind power to rely on backup generation—usually fossil fuel-based. Moreover, many potential wind farm sites may be far from where the electricity would be used, requiring substantial costs to build new transmission lines.

Wind energy is also opposed by some consumer groups for aesthetic reasons or the belief of negative effects on bird populations.

Solar   Solar energy uses solar radiation to produce either heat (thermal) or electricity (photovoltaic or solar power plants). In the US, over 90 percent of solar energy consumed was used for residential heating, with the rest used for electricity generation.[19] Solar power for electricity generation remains a very small percentage of total electricity generation in the US, representing only 0.02 percent.[20]

Solar thermal devices—typically used for residential heating—can be classified as *passive* or *active*. Passive space heating works by passing air through solar heat surfaces and through the building, using no mechanical equipment. Active heating systems absorb and collect solar radiation through a collector. Fans or pumps then circulate the heated air or heat-absorbing fluid.

Photovoltaic energy converts sunlight into electricity through photovoltaic cells, or solar cells. These cells are usually made from silicon alloys that convert solar energy directly into electrical power. Photovoltaic cells are generally used to power small loads like electronic equipment.

Solar power panels.
Source: © Getty Images, Inc.

Solar power plants produce steam using the sun's heat, which is then converted into mechanical energy in a turbine and into electricity from a conventional generator. The most common type of solar power plant—a parabolic trough—focuses the sun at 30 to 100 times its normal intensity, achieving temperatures over 400° Celsius.[21]

Solar energy has the advantage of capturing energy from the world's largest energy source—the sun—where supplies are unlimited. It also produces no air or water pollution. However, current technology inhibits the world's ability to increase solar power economically and on a massive scale. Additionally, like wind power, the amount of sunlight hitting the earth's surface varies depending on the time of day, month, or season, resulting in variable electricity generation.

Geothermal   Geothermal energy comes from accessing the reservoirs of hot water found far beneath the earth's surface. Geothermal energy utilizes the Earth's heat primarily to produce electricity and heat buildings. Production wells are drilled a mile or more into the earth to bring up hot water as steam at the surface, which is used to drive giant turbines and create electricity. Water is then cooled and sent back underground to recharge the reservoir.

Geothermal plants have the advantage of being able to run 98 percent of the time, providing more affordable, reliable energy than wind and solar power. Moreover, the plants produce little-to-no emissions and require no fuel to operate.

However, there are limitations to the amount of geothermal energy that can be generated as it will depend on available geothermal reservoirs. The US generates the most geothermal electricity of any country, but it accounts for less than 1 percent of the country's electricity needs and is found in only four states.[22]

Nuclear Power

While nuclear power is not a renewable energy source, it's a substitute to traditional hydrocarbons. Nuclear energy is generated from the controlled use of nuclear reactions. Nuclear power is derived by harnessing the energy contained within an atom's nucleus. Energy is released through a process called *fission*, which splits the nucleus of a uranium atom, releasing its neutrons and causing a chain reaction among other uranium atoms. The heat from that chain reaction is used to boil water into steam, which is then used to turn a turbine generator.

The most widely used fuel by nuclear plants for nuclear fission is uranium. While not renewable, uranium is a common metal found in rocks all over the world. Nuclear plants use a specific kind of uranium, U-235, as fuel because its atoms are easily split. Once uranium is mined, U-235 must be extracted and processed before it can be used as fuel.

Nuclear energy is by far the most efficient, abundant, clean, and economical form of energy available in the world today. Unlike solar, wind, or hydroelectric power, nuclear power can produce massive quantities of energy on a large scale economically and run close to peak output continuously. Nuclear power is also considered clean because it does not emit CO^2 emissions or air pollution.

The main drawback of nuclear power is its potentially dangerous by-products: spent fuels and other radioactive materials. These materials are subject to special regulation governing their disposal so they do not harm the environment. In the US, nuclear operators generally store nuclear spent fuel and waste in onsite storage pools or dry storage facilities. The US Department of Energy's long-range plan for the spent fuel is to store it deep in the earth in a geologic repository in Yucca Mountain, Nevada. Unfortunately, the site is still not in operation due to a number of construction delays, underfunding, and opposition from politicians, environmental groups, and Nevada residents.

Currently, there are 439 nuclear power plants around the world generating 16 percent of all electricity.[23] In the country with the greatest absolute nuclear power generation capacity—the US—nuclear power accounts for 19 percent of its power generation.[24]

In the US, nuclear power still faces substantial hurdles preventing the development of new plants. In fact, a new plant hasn't been

France's Nuclear Power

The country currently taking the most advantage of nuclear power is France. France generates over 75 percent of its electricity needs from nuclear power, providing it with low-cost, reliable energy while significantly contributing to the country's energy independence.* France's nuclear power reliance stemmed from the French government deciding in 1974 (right after the first oil shock) to rapidly expand nuclear power capacity. With limited domestic fossil fuel resources but significant engineering expertise, it made sense to turn to nuclear power for its power generation requirements. Now France produces the cheapest, cleanest power in the world.

---

*World Nuclear Association, "French Nuclear Power Program" (April 2007).

constructed for over two decades on US soil. The nuclear industry suffered tremendously following the accident at Three Mile Island in 1979, the worst nuclear accident in US history. And the former Soviet Union's Chernobyl disaster in 1986—the worst nuclear power plant accident in history—sealed the fate of the US nuclear power industry for two decades. While recent efforts to revive the industry in the US are underway, it's likely the industry will face continued environmental opposition, safety concerns, and a NIMBY ("not in my backyard") mentality, making future nuclear power plant construction difficult.

Outside the US, nuclear power is being embraced to meet the world's future energy needs. Currently, over 30 reactors are under construction in 13 countries, mostly in Asia.[25] As of July 2008, there are 93 planned and 219 proposed nuclear reactors around the globe.[26] In the face of rising energy prices and climate change concerns, nuclear power is likely to continue to gain popularity in the years ahead.

ALTERNATIVE ENERGY DRIVERS

Now that you've got a feel for the alternative energy landscape, it's time to turn to main investment drivers. These themes pertain both to financial results and stock price performance. While they are by no means comprehensive, they serve as a good starting point for understanding the category. Analyzing each driver and how each may change in the short to medium term will prove key determinants behind investment decisions. The main drivers are:

- Oil and natural gas prices
- Taxes, politics, and regulations
- Geopolitical environment
- Technological advancements
- Supply chain costs
- Sentiment

Oil and Natural Gas Prices

Because of the substitution effect, the biggest drivers of alternative energy firms are oil and natural gas prices. As the prices of traditional oil and gas increase, demand for alternatives also increases. Conversely, falling prices for oil and natural gas reduce demand for alternatives. So as long as traditional energy prices are considered to be relatively high or a burden to businesses and consumers, there will be a steady demand for alternatives.

Energy Prices and Alternative Energy Stocks

While oil and natural gas prices are the main energy firm drivers, they can be even more important drivers to alternative energy firms. This may seem counterintuitive, but the future profitability of alternative energy firms *depends* on high energy prices because many alternatives (like solar power and fuel cells) have higher costs per unit of energy produced.

Should energy prices fall substantially, demand for alternatives will also fall as investors question the long-term profitability of alternative energy. The stock market discounts future company profits. And if falling oil and natural gas prices threaten the future profitability of alternative energy firms, their stock prices may fall dramatically.

Taxes, Politics, and Regulations

Taxes, subsidies, trade barriers, and other government interventions have a major effect on alternative energy sources. Because many alternative energy sources are not economical without government intervention or subsidies, the industry does not operate in the same competitive fashion as the traditional oil and gas sector. It's therefore vital to understand how politics, regulation, subsidies, and taxes affect an alternative energy investment.

Another way government actions drive alternative energy demand is through implementation of new taxes, costs, or burdens on the traditional energy sector. For example, should the US government impose a punitive carbon tax on coal firms (the main producers of CO^2 emissions), demand for cleaner power generation would increase.

Geopolitical Environment

Geopolitics have become increasingly important to the future of alternative energy. Due to concerns about dependence on foreign oil from unstable governments, countries like the US desire to make a shift toward energy independence. While this may be unfeasible for most countries—especially the US—worsening relationships between oil-consuming nations and the main oil suppliers typically increases the demand for more alternative energy. (Note: As mentioned earlier in the chapter, the Arab oil embargo of 1973 was the catalyst behind France's push for more nuclear power.)

Technological Advancements

Breakthroughs in technology can have major effects on certain types of alternative energy. This not only includes the creation of new alternative energies, but the improvement of current technologies as well. Technological advancements have made several types of alternative energy sources more economical, efficient, and productive over the years, notably in solar power. They can also make other alternative energies obsolete or uncompetitive. Other types of technological advancements help to increase energy efficiency or conservation.

Supply Chain Costs

Broadly speaking, changing costs within alternative energy sources' supply chains can have major effects on the industry. For any alternative energy company, it's important to understand the main inputs and the cost environment for each. For example, soaring energy demand in recent years caused short supplies of just about every kind of fuel, driving up prices of the raw materials involved in making many alternative energies. For biofuels relying on agricultural commodities already facing higher demand as foodstuffs, prices are driven up even higher.

Sentiment

Sentiment for alternative energy waxes and wanes over time, due to changing oil and gas prices, geopolitics, technology, and investment opportunities. Recently, soaring oil and gas prices and climate change concerns caused increased interest in alternative energy projects from venture capital, private equity, hedge funds, and other investors. This was also the case in 1999, when demand for technology IPOs—several touting advancements in alternative energy technologies like fuel cells and solar panels—soared. In a period of low oil and gas prices (like most of the 1990s), alternative energy was rarely on investors' minds as most alternatives were uneconomical without the incentives of high energy prices or significant technological advancements.

ALTERNATIVE ENERGY INVESTMENT UNIVERSE

The alternative energy firm investment universe has expanded significantly in recent years. Investors can now invest in numerous alternative energy mutual funds (a.k.a. *clean energy* or *renewable energy* funds), individual pure-play renewable firms, or firms with alternative energy divisions.

However, the investment universe of alternative energy firms is not well defined, as it's not classified as a singular industry. Instead, most alternative energy revenues come from divisions of much larger firms operating in several sectors. For example, Archer Daniels Midland—in the Consumer Staples sector—is currently America's largest producer of ethanol, but it makes the vast majority of its sales through oilseed processing and other traditional agricultural business segments. Firms operating nuclear power plants and renewable power plants are classified in the Utilities sector. Firms making technology and solar industry products typically fall in the Technology and Industrials sectors.

Additionally, most pure-play alternative energy firms are too small for traditional investors, and many remain private. However, the publicly traded universe is growing. As of 2007, the 140 highest-valued publicly traded renewable energy firms were estimated to each have a market cap greater than $40 million and yielded a combined market capitalization of over $100 billion.[27]

While there are countless firms engaged in many types of alternative energy businesses, the investment universe is mainly concentrated among firms engaged in power generation—solar, wind, nuclear, and hydroelectric—and biofuels production.

Table 6.1. shows examples of some firms generally considered to be pure-play alternative energy. While this list is by no means comprehensive, it encompasses some of the largest players within the category.

Table 6.1   Pure-Play Alternative Energy Companies

Name	Market Cap (Billions)	Sector	Country	Alternative Energy
Iberdrola Renovables S.A.	$35.1	Utilities	Spain	Wind, solar, electric
Renewable Energy Corp. ASA	$25.1	Industrials	Norway	Solar
First Solar, Inc.	$20.8	Industrials	US	Solar
Vestas Wind Systems A/S	$20.0	Industrials	Denmark	Wind
Suzlon Energy LTD	$14.1	Industrials	India	Wind
Cameco	$13.7	Energy	Canada	Uranium/ nuclear
Suntech Power Holdings Co., Ltd.	$12.7	Industrials	US	Solar
Q-Cells AG	$11.5	Industrials	Germany	Solar
Gamesa Corporación Tecnológica S.A.	$11.4	Industrials	Spain	Wind
SolarWorld AG	$6.8	Industrials	Germany	Solar
SunPower Corporation	$5.1	Industrials	US	Solar
LDK Solar Company Ltd.	$5.0	Information Technology	China	Solar

Source: Standard & Poor's Research Insight ®[28] as of 12/31/07.

There are many more examples of firms with alternative energy divisions, but they generate the vast majority of sales through other business lines. When researching these types of firms, it is especially important to determine to what extent the company's earnings are driven by the alternative energy divisions. Table 6.2 shows examples of firms with alternative energy divisions.

Table 6.2   Companies With Alternative Energy Divisions

Name	Market Cap (Billions)	Sector	Country	Alternative Energy
General Electric	$370.2	Industrials	US	Wind
Siemens	$147.2	Industrials	Germany	Wind
DuPont	$39.6	Materials	US	Solar
Schneider Electric SA	$30.3	Industrials	France	Electric
Archer Daniels Midland Company	$29.9	Consumer Staples	US	Ethanol
Praxair Inc	$28.0	Materials	US	Fuel cells & hydrogen
Applied Materials	$24.6	Information Technology	US	Solar
Johnson Controls, Inc.	$21.4	Consumer Discretionary	US	Fuel cells
Air Products & Chemicals	$21.2	Materials	US	Fuel cells & hydrogen
MEMC Electronic Materials Inc.	$20.3	Information Technology	US	Solar
Acciona S.A.	$20.1	Industrials	Spain	Wind, hydro, solar, & biomass
Orkla-Borregaard AS, Inc.	$19.9	Industrials	Norway	Solar
Sharp Corp.	$19.6	Consumer Discretionary	Japan	Solar

Source: Standard & Poor's Research Insight [®29] as of 12/31/07.

As shown in Tables 6.1 and 6.2 firms providing products and services related to alternative energy are highly diversified among several sectors and countries. While categorized as alternative or clean energy, almost all these firms fall outside the Energy sector.

A separate way to gain exposure to the alternative energy theme is to invest in firms specializing in energy efficiency. These would be firms providing products and services to help businesses and consumers reduce their energy use. That, however, is another topic entirely.

Chapter Recap

Alternative energy has garnered much media attention, sparked new legislation in several countries, and attracted billions of investor dollars, but it remains a highly risky, uncertain investment class. In any budding industry, there are few big winners and many, many losers, making it difficult to forecast which alternative energy source will lead in the future. While some alternative energy sources hold promise, it is clear the world's energy needs will continue to be met predominantly by traditional energy sources of oil, coal, nuclear, and natural gas for a long time.

- A common investor trap is flocking to the new, hot investment class, consisting of firms with uncertain fundamentals. Be cautious when exploring firms engaged in alternative energy businesses.
- The vast majority of renewable energy is for power generation. Hydropower makes up the majority of power generation from renewable energy sources.
- Biofuels like ethanol currently make up a very small percentage of transportation fuels. Increasing the use of such fuels will require overcoming numerous challenges.
- Nuclear power, while not a renewable fuel, is the most efficient, abundant, clean, and economical form of energy available in the world today.
- Firms with alternative energy business operations are also affected by high-level drivers. Among them are commodity prices, government policies, and technological advancements.
- There is no well-defined alternative energy investment universe. Instead, there are firms with varying proportions of revenues tied to alternative energy, and almost all fall outside of the Energy sector.

III

THINKING LIKE A PORTFOLIO MANAGER

THE TOP-DOWN METHOD

So if you're bullish on Energy, how much of your portfolio should you put in Energy stocks? Twenty-five percent? Fifty percent? One hundred percent? This question concerns portfolio management. Most investors concern themselves only with individual companies ("I like Exxon, so I'll buy some) without considering how it fits into their overall portfolios. But this is no way to manage your money.

In Part 3 of this book, we show you how to analyze Energy companies like a top-down portfolio manager. This includes a full description of the top-down method, how to use benchmarks, and how the top-down method applies to the Energy sector. We then delve into security analysis, where we provide a framework for analyzing any company, and then discuss many of the important questions to ask when analyzing Energy companies. In the last chapter, we give a few examples of specific investing strategies for the Energy sector.

INVESTING IS A SCIENCE

Too many investors today think investing has "rules"—that all one must do to succeed in investing for the long run is find the right set of investing rules. But that simply doesn't work. Why? All well-known and widely discussed information is already reflected in stock prices. This is a basic tenet of market theory and commonly referred to as *market efficiency*. So if you see a headline about a stock you follow, there's no use trading on that information—it's already priced in. You missed the move.

If everything known is already discounted in prices, the only way to beat the market is by knowing something others don't. Think about it: There are many intelligent investors and long-time professionals who fail to beat the market year after year, most with the same access to information as anyone, if not more. Why?

Most view investing as a craft. They think, "If I learn the craft of value investing and all its rules, then I can be a successful investor using that method." But that simply can't work because by definition all the conventional ways of thinking about value investing will already be widely known and thus priced in. In fact, most investment styles are very well known and already widely practiced. There are undoubtedly millions of investors out there much like you, looking at the same metrics and information you are. So there isn't much power in that information. Even the investing techniques themselves are widely known—taught to millions in universities and practiced by hundreds of thousands of professionals globally. There's no edge.

Moreover, it's been demonstrated that investment styles move in and out of favor over time—no one style or category is inherently better than another in the long run. You may think *value* investing works wonders to beat markets, but the fact is growth stocks will trounce value at times.

The key to beating stock markets lies in being dynamic—never adhering for all time to a single investment idea—and gleaning information the market hasn't yet priced in. In other words, you cannot adhere to a single set of "rules" and hope to outperform markets over time.

So how can you beat the markets? By thinking of investing as a science.

EINSTEIN'S BRAIN AND THE STOCK MARKET

If he weren't so busy becoming the most renowned scientist of the 20th century, Albert Einstein would have made a killing on Wall Street—but not because he had such a high IQ. Granted, he was immensely intelligent, but a high IQ alone does not a market guru make. (If it did, MIT professors would be making millions managing money instead of teaching.) Instead, it's the style of his thought and the method of his work that matter.

Based on the little we know about Einstein's investment track record, he didn't do very well. He lost most of his Nobel Prize money in bad bond ventures.[1] Heck, Sir Isaac Newton may have given us the three laws of motion, but even his talents didn't extend to investing. He lost his shirt in the South Sea Bubble of the early 1700s, explaining later, "I can calculate the movement of the stars, but not the madness of men."

So why believe Einstein would have been a great portfolio manager if he put his mind to it? In short, Einstein was a true and highly creative scientist. He didn't take the acknowledged rules of physics as such—he used prior knowledge, logic, and creativity combined with the rigors of a verifiable, testable scientific method to create an entirely new view of the cosmos. In other words, he was dynamic and gleaned knowledge others didn't have. Investors must do the same. (Not to worry though, you won't need advanced calculus to do it.)

Einstein's unique character gave him an edge—he truly had a mind made to beat markets. Scientists have perused his work, his speeches, his letters—even his brain (literally)—to find the secret of his intellect. In all, his approach to information processing and idea generation, his willingness to go against the grain of the establishment, and his relentless pursuit of answers to questions no one else was asking during his time ultimately made him a genius.

Most biographers and his contemporaries agree one of Einstein's foremost gifts was his ability to discern "the big picture." Unlike many scientists who could easily drown themselves in data minutiae, Einstein had an ability to see above the fray. Another way to say this is he could take the same information everyone else at his time was looking at and interpret it differently, yet correctly. He accomplished this using his talent for extracting the most important data from what he studied and linking them together in innovative ways no one else could.

Einstein called this *combinatory play*. Similar to a child experimenting with a new Lego set, Einstein would combine and recombine seemingly unrelated ideas, concepts, and images to produce new, original discoveries. In the end, almost all new ideas are merely the combination of existing ones in one form or another. Take $E = mc^2$: Einstein was not the first to discover the concepts of energy, mass, or the speed of light; rather, he combined these concepts in a novel way and, in the process, altered the way in which we view the universe.[2]

Einstein's combinatory play is a terrific metaphor for stock investing. To be a successful market strategist, you must be able to extract the most important data from all of the *noise* permeating today's markets and generate conclusions the market hasn't yet appreciated. Central to this task is your ability to link data together in unique ways and produce new insights and themes for your portfolio in the process.

Einstein learned science basics just like his peers. But once he had those mastered, he directed his brain to challenging prior assumptions and inventing entirely different lenses to look through.

This is why this book isn't intended to give you a "silver bullet" for picking the right energy stocks. The fact is the "right" Energy stocks will be different in different times and situations. You don't have to be Einstein; you just have to think differently, and like a scientist, if you want to beat markets.

THE TOP-DOWN METHOD

Overwhelmingly, investment professionals today do what can broadly be labeled as *bottom-up* investing. Their emphasis is stock selection. A typical bottom-up investor researches an assortment of companies and attempts to pick those which, based on individual merits, have the greatest likelihood of outperforming the market. The selected securities are cobbled together to form a portfolio, and factors like country and economic sector exposures are purely residuals of security selection, not planned decisions.

Top-down investing reverses the order. A top-down investor first analyzes big-picture factors like economics, politics, and sentiment to forecast which investment categories are most likely to outperform the market. Only then, within those categories, does a top-down investor begin looking at individual securities. Top-down investing is inevitably more concerned with a portfolio's aggregate exposure to investment categories and factors than with any individual security. Thus, top-down is an inherently *dynamic* mode of investment because investment strategies are based upon the prevailing market and economic environment (which changes often).

There's significant debate in the investment community as to which approach is superior. This book's goal is not to reject bottom-up investing—there are indeed investors who've successfully utilized bottom-up approaches. Rather, the goal is to introduce a comprehensive and flexible methodology that any investor could use to build a portfolio designed to beat the global stock market in any investment environment. It's a framework for gleaning new insights and making good on information not already reflected in stock prices.

Before we describe the method, let's explore several key reasons why a top-down approach is advantageous:

- **Scalability:** A bottom-up process is akin to looking for needles in a haystack. A top-down process is akin to seeking the haystacks with the highest concentration of needles. Globally, there are nearly 25,000 publicly traded stocks. Even the largest institutions with the greatest research resources cannot hope to adequately examine all these companies. Smaller institutions and individual investors must prioritize where to focus their limited resources. Unlike a bottom-up process, a top-down process makes this gargantuan task manageable by determining, up front, what slices of the market to examine at the security level.
- **Enhanced stock selection:** Well-designed top-down processes generate insights that can greatly enhance stock selection. Macroeconomic or political analysis, for instance, can help determine what types of strategic attributes will face head or tailwinds (see Chapter 8 for a full explanation).
- **Risk control:** Bottom-up processes are highly subject to unintended risk concentrations. Top-down processes are inherently better suited to manage risk exposures throughout the investment process.
- **Macro overview:** Top-down processes are more conducive to avoiding macro-driven calamities like the bursting of the Japan

bubble in the 1990s, the Technology bubble in 2000, and the bear market of 2000 to 2002. No matter how good an individual company may be, it is still beholden to sector, regional, and broader market factors. In fact, there is evidence *macro* factors can largely determine a stock's performance, regardless of individual merit.

Top-Down Means Thinking 70-20-10

A top-down investment process also helps focus on what is most important to investment results: asset allocation and sub-asset allocation decisions. Many investors focus most of their attention on security-level portfolio decisions, like picking individual stocks they think will perform well. However, studies have shown that over 90 percent of return variability is derived from asset allocation decisions, not market timing or stock selection.[3]

Our own research shows about 70 percent of return variability is derived from asset allocation, 20 percent from sub-asset allocation (such as country, sector, size, and style), and 10 percent from security selection. While security selection can make a significant difference over time, higher-level portfolio decisions dominate investment results more often than not.

The balance of this chapter defines the various steps in the top-down method, specifically as they relate to making sub-asset allocation decisions (i.e., country, sector, and style decisions). This same basic framework can be applied to portfolios to make allocations within sectors. At the end of the chapter, we detail how this framework can be applied to the Energy sector. Chapter 8 deals with security selection.

Benchmarks

A key part of the top-down model is using benchmarks. A benchmark is typically a broad-based index of securities such as the S&P 500, MSCI World, or Russell 2000. Benchmarks are indispensable roadmaps for structuring a portfolio, monitoring risk, and judging performance over time.

Tactically, a portfolio should be structured to maximize the probability of consistently beating the benchmark. This is inherently different than maximizing returns. Unlike aiming to achieve some fixed rate of return each year, which will cause disappointment when capital markets are very strong and is potentially unrealistic when the capital markets are very weak, a properly benchmarked portfolio provides a realistic guide for dealing with uncertain market conditions.

Portfolio construction begins by evaluating the characteristics of the chosen benchmark: sector weights, country weights, and market cap and valuations. Then an expected risk and return is assigned to each of these segments (based on portfolio drivers), and the areas most attractive are overweighted, while the least attractive are underweighted. Table 7.1 shows MSCI World benchmark sector characteristics as of December 31, 2007, as an example, while Table 7.2 shows country characteristics and Table 7.3 shows market cap and valuations.

Based on benchmark characteristics, portfolio drivers are then used to determine country, sector, and style decisions for the portfolio. For example, the Financials sector weight in the MSCI World Index is about 23 percent. Therefore, a portfolio managed against this benchmark would consider a 23 percent weight in Financials *neutral*, or market-weighted. If you believe Financials will perform better than the market in the foreseeable future, then you would *overweight* the sector, or carry a percentage of stocks in your portfolio greater than 23 percent. The reverse is true for an *underweight*—you'd hold less

Table 7.1   MSCI World Characteristics—Sectors

Sector	Weight
Financials	22.6%
Industrials	11.4%
Information Technology	11.0%
Energy	10.9%
Consumer Discretionary	9.8%
Consumer Staples	8.8%
Health Care	8.7%
Materials	7.2%
Telecommunication	4.9%
Utilities	4.7%

Source: Thomson Datastream, MSCI, Inc[4] as of 12/31/07.

Table 7.2   MSCI World Characteristics—Countries

Country	Weight
US	47.1%
United Kingdom	10.8%
Japan	9.7%
France	5.2%
Germany	4.6%
Canada	4.1%
Switzerland	3.3%
Australia	3.2%
Spain	2.1%
Italy	1.9%
Netherlands	1.4%
Hong Kong	1.2%
Sweden	1.1%
Finland	0.9%
Belgium	0.6%
Singapore	0.5%
Norway	0.5%
Denmark	0.5%
Greece	0.4%
Ireland	0.3%
Austria	0.3%
Portugal	0.2%
New Zealand	0.1%
Emerging Markets	0.0%

Source: Thomson Datastream, MSCI, Inc[5] as of 12/31/07.

than 23 percent in Financials if you were pessimistic on the sector looking ahead.

Note that being pessimistic on Financials *doesn't necessarily mean holding zero stocks*. It might only mean holding a lesser percentage of stocks in your portfolio than the benchmark. This is an important feature of benchmarking—it allows an investor to make strategic

Table 7.3   MSCI World Characteristics—Market Cap and Valuations

	Valuations
Median Market Cap	$7,291 Million
Weighted Average Market Cap	$80,908 Million
P/E	15.5
P/B	2.6
Div Yield	2.3
P/CF	12.7
P/S	2.4
Number of Holdings	1,959

Source: Thomson Datastream, MSCI, Inc[6] as of 12/31/07.

decisions on sectors and countries, but maintains diversification, thus managing risk more appropriately.

For the Energy sector, we can use Energy-specific benchmarks like the S&P 500 Energy, MSCI World Energy, and Russell 2000 Energy indexes. The components of these benchmarks can then be evaluated at a more detailed level such as industry and sub-industry weights. (For a breakdown of sub-industry benchmark characteristics, see Chapter 3.)

TOP-DOWN DECONSTRUCTED

The top-down method begins by first analyzing the macro environment. It asks the "big" questions like: Do you think stocks will go up or down in the next 12 months? If so, which countries or sectors should benefit most? Once you have decided on these high-level portfolio *drivers* (sometimes called *themes*), you can examine various macro portfolio drivers to make general overweight and underweight decisions for countries, sectors, industries, and sub-industries versus your benchmark.

For instance, let's say we've determined a macroeconomic driver that goes something like this: "In the next 12 months, I believe global oil demand will be greater than most expect." That's a very high-level statement with important implications for your portfolio. It means you'd want to search for stocks that would benefit most from increased oil demand.

The second step in top-down is applying quantitative screening criteria to narrow the choice set of stocks. Since, in our hypothetical example, we believe oil demand will be high, it likely means we're bullish on Energy stocks. But which ones? Are you are bullish on, say, refiners? Drillers? Do you want small-cap Energy companies or large cap? And what about valuations? Are you looking for growth or value? (Size and growth/value categories are often referred to as *style* decisions.) These criteria and more can help you narrow the list of stocks you might buy.

The third and final step is performing fundamental analysis on individual stocks. Notice that a great deal of thinking, analysis, and work is done before you ever think about individual stocks. That's the key to the top-down approach: It emphasizes high-level themes and funnels its way down to individual stocks, as is illustrated below.

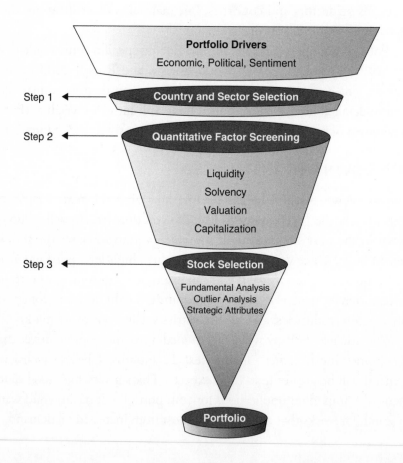

Step 1: Analyze Portfolio Drivers and Country and Sector Selection

Let's examine the first step in the top-down method more closely. In order to make top-down decisions, we develop and analyze what we call *portfolio drivers* (as mentioned previously). We segment these portfolio drivers into three general categories: *economic, political,* and *sentiment.*

Portfolio drivers are what drive the performance of a broad category of stocks. Accurately identifying current and future drivers will help you find areas of the market most likely to outperform or underperform your benchmark (i.e., the broader stock market).

Table 7.4 shows examples of each type of portfolio driver. It's important to note these drivers are by no means comprehensive nor are they valid for all time periods. In fact, correctly identifying new portfolio drivers is essential to beating the market in the long term.

Economic Drivers   An economic driver is anything related to the macroeconomic environment. This could include monetary policy, interest rates, lending activity, yield curve analysis, relative GDP growth analysis, and myriad others. What economic forces are likely to drive GDP growth throughout countries in the world? What is the outlook

Table 7.4   Portfolio Drivers

Economic	Political	Sentiment
Yield curve spread	Taxation	Mutual fund flows
Relative GDP growth	Property rights	Relative style and asset class valuations
Monetary base/growth	Structural reform	Media coverage
Currency strength	Privatization	Institutional searches
Relative interest rates	Trade/capital barriers	Consumer confidence
Inflation	Current account	Foreign investment
Debt level (sovereign, corporate, consumer)	Government stability	Professional investor forecasts
Infrastructure spending	Political turnover	Momentum cycle analysis
M&A, issuance, and repurchase activity	Wars/conflicts	Risk aversion

for interest rates and how would that impact sectors? What is the outlook for technology and infrastructure spending among countries?

Economic drivers pertain not only to the fundamental outlook of the economy (GDP growth, interest rates, inflation), but also to the stock market (valuations, M&A activity, share buybacks). As an investor, it's your job to identify these drivers and determine how they'll impact your overall portfolio and each of its segments.

The following is an example list of economic drivers that could impact portfolio performance:

- US economic growth will be higher than consensus expectations.
- European Union interest rates will remain benign.
- Mergers, acquisitions, and share buybacks will remain strong.
- Emerging market growth will drive commodity demand.

Political Drivers   Political drivers can be country specific, pertain to regions (European Union, OECD), or affect interaction between countries or regions (such as trade policies). These drivers are more concerned with categories such as taxation, government stability, fiscal policy, and political turnover. Which countries are experiencing a change in government that could have a meaningful impact on their economies? Which sectors could be at risk from new taxation or legislation? Which countries are undergoing pro-growth reforms?

Political drivers will help determine the relative attractiveness of market segments and countries based on the outlook for the political environment. Be warned: Most investors suffer from *home country bias*, where they ascribe too much emphasis on the politics of their own country. Always keep in mind it's a big, interconnected world out there, and geopolitical developments everywhere can have implications.

What are possible political drivers you can find? The following is a list of examples that can drive stocks up or down:

- Political party change in Japan driving pro-growth reforms.
- New tax policies in Germany stalling economic growth.

- Protests, government coups, and conflict driving political instability in Thailand.

Sentiment Drivers Sentiment drivers attempt to measure consensus thinking about investment categories. Ideally, drivers identify market opportunities where sentiment is different than reality. For example, let's say you observe broad market sentiment currently expects a US recession in the next year. But you disagree and believe GDP growth will be strong. This presents an excellent opportunity for excess returns. You can load up on stocks that will benefit from an economic boom and watch the prices rise as the rest of the market realizes it much later.

Since the market is a discounter of all known information, it's important to try and identify what the market is pricing in. The interpretation of such investor drivers is typically counterintuitive (avoid what is overly popular and seek what is largely unpopular). Looking forward, which sectors are investors most bullish about and why? What countries or sectors are widely discussed in the media? What market segments have been bid up recently based on something other than fundamentals? If the market's perception is different than fundamentals in the short term, stocks will eventually correct themselves to reflect reality in the long term.

A note of caution: Gauging market sentiment does not mean being a *contrarian*. Contrarians are investors who simply do the opposite of what most believe will happen. Instead, find places where sentiment (people's beliefs) doesn't match what you believe is reality and position your portfolio accordingly. Examples of potentially actionable sentiment drivers include:

- Investors remain pessimistic about Technology despite improving fundamentals.
- Sentiment for the Chinese stock market is approaching euphoria, stretching valuations.
- Professional investors universally forecast US small-cap stocks to outperform.

How to Create Your Own Investment Drivers

In order to form your own investment drivers, the first step is accessing a wide array of data from multiple sources. For country drivers, this could range from globally focused publications like the *Wall Street Journal* or *Financial Times* to regional newspapers or government data. For sector drivers, this could include reading trade publications or following major company announcements.

Remember, however, that markets are efficient—they reflect all widely known information. Most pertinent information about public companies is, well, *public*. Which means the market already knows. News travels fast, and markets absorb the knowledge and expectations very quickly. Those seeking to profit on a bit of news, rumor, or speculation must acknowledge the market will probably move faster than they can. Therefore, in order to consistently generate excess returns, you must either know something others don't or interpret widely known information differently and correctly from the crowd. (For a detailed discussion on these factors and more, read *The Only Three Questions That Count* by Ken Fisher.)

Step 2: Quantitative Factor Screening

Step two in the top-down method is screening for quantitative factors. With your portfolio drivers in place, this allows you to narrow the potential list of stocks.

There are thousands and thousands of stocks out there, so it's vital to use a series of factors like market capitalization and valuations to narrow the field a bit. Securities passing this screen are then subjected to further quantitative analysis that eliminates companies with excessive risk profiles relative to their peer group, such as companies with excessive leverage or balance sheet risk and securities lacking sufficient liquidity for investment.

The rigidity of the quantitative screens is entirely up to you and will determine the number of companies on your prospect list. The more rigid the criteria, the fewer the companies that make the list. Broader criteria will increase the number of companies.

How can you perform such a screen? We show two examples of quantitative factor screenings to show how broad or specific you can be.

You might want to apply very strict criteria, or you may prefer to be very broad.

Strict Criteria

- First, you decide you want to search for Energy firms only. By definition, that excludes all companies from the other nine sectors. You've already narrowed the field a lot!
- Now, let's say you want European Energy stocks only. By excluding all other regions besides Europe, you've narrowed the field even more.
- Next, let's decide to search only for Exploration & Production firms in the Energy sector.
- Perhaps you don't believe very small stocks are preferable, so you limit market capitalization to $5 billion and above.
- Last, let's set some parameters for valuation:
  P/E (price to earnings) less than 12
  P/B (price to book) less than 8
  P/CF (price to cash flow) less than 10
  P/S (price to sales) less than 10

This rigorous process of selecting parameters will yield a small number of stocks to research, all based on your higher-level themes. But maybe you have reason to be less specific and want to do a broader screen because you think Energy in general is a good place to be. (Note: Professionals can subscribe to databases with screening tools. Individual investors can access simplified versions online, like Google Finance—http://finance.google.com/finance/stockscreener.)

Broad Criteria

- Energy sector
- Global (no country or region restrictions)
- Market caps above $10 billion

This selection process is much broader and obviously gives you a much longer list of stocks to choose from. Doing either a strict or broad screen isn't inherently better. It just depends on how well formed and specific your higher-level themes are. Obviously, a stricter screen means less work for you in step three—actual stock selection.

Step 3: Stock Selection

After narrowing the prospect list, your final step is identifying individual securities possessing strategic attributes consistent with higher-level portfolio themes. (We'll cover the stock selection process specifically in more detail in Chapter 8.) Your stock selection process should attempt to accomplish two goals:

1. Seek firms possessing strategic attributes consistent with higher-level portfolio themes, derived from the drivers that give those firms a competitive advantage versus their peers. For example, if you believe owning firms with dominant market shares in consolidating industries is a favorable characteristic, you would search for firms with that profile.

2. Seek to maximize the likelihood of beating the category of stocks you are analyzing. For example, if you want a certain portfolio weight of Integrated Oil & Gas companies and need 4 stocks out of 12 meeting the quantitative criteria, you then pick the 4 that, as a group, maximize the likelihood of beating all 12 as a whole. This is different than trying to pick "the best four." By avoiding stocks likely to be extreme or "weird" outliers versus the group, you can reduce portfolio risk while adding value at the security selection level.

In lieu of picking individual securities, there are other ways to exploit high-level themes in the top-down process. For instance, if you feel strongly about a particular sub-industry, but don't think you can add value through individual security analysis, it may be more prudent to buy a group of companies in the sub-industry or via a category product like an exchange traded fund (ETF). There are a growing variety of ETFs that track the domestic and global energy sector, industries, and even specific commodity prices. This way, you can be sure to gain broad Energy exposure without much stock-specific risk. (For more information on ETFs, visit www.ishares.com, www.sectorspdr. com, or www.unitedstatesoilfund.com.)

MANAGING AGAINST AN ENERGY BENCHMARK

Now we can practice translating this specifically to your Energy allocation. Just as you analyze the components of your benchmark to determine country and sector components in a top-down strategy, you must analyze each sector's components, as we did in Chapter 3. To demonstrate how, we'll use the MSCI World Energy Sector index as the benchmark. Table 7.5 shows the MSCI World Energy sub-industry weights as of December 31, 2007. We don't know what the sample portfolio weights should be, but we know it should add up to 100 percent of the energy allocation.

Keeping the sub-industry weights in mind will help mitigate benchmark risk. If you have a portfolio of stocks with the same sub-industry weights as the MSCI World Energy Index, you're *neutral*—taking no benchmark risk. However, if you feel strongly about a sub-industry, like Coal & Consumable Fuels, and decide to only purchase those firms

Table 7.5   MSCI World Energy Sub-Industry Weights vs. Sample Portfolio

Sub-Industry	MSCI World	Sample Portfolio
Coal & Consumable Fuels	1.8%	?
Integrated Oil & Gas	63.4%	?
Oil & Gas Drilling	3.5%	?
Oil & Gas Equipment & Services	10.9%	?
Oil & Gas Exploration & Production	14.8%	?
Oil & Gas Refining & Marketing	2.8%	?
Oil & Gas Storage & Transportation	2.8%	?
Total	100.0%	100.0%

Source: Thomson Datastream, MSCI, Inc.[7] as of 12/31/07.

(the smallest weight in the sector), you're taking a huge benchmark risk. The same is true if you significantly *underweight* a sub-industry. All the same rules apply as when you do this from a broader portfolio perspective, as we did earlier this chapter.

The benchmarks, sub-industry weights provide a jumping-off point in making further portfolio decisions. Once you make higher-level decisions on the sub-industries, you can make choices versus the benchmark by overweighting the sub-industries you feel likeliest to perform best and underweighting those likeliest to perform worst. Table 7.6 shows how you can make different portfolio bets against the benchmark by over- and underweighting sub-industries.

Note: Portfolio A might be a portfolio of all-Energy stocks, or it can simply represent the Energy allocation in a larger portfolio.

The "Difference" column shows the relative difference between the benchmark and Portfolio A. In this example, Portfolio A is most overweight to Oil & Gas Drilling and Equipment & Services and most underweight to Integrated Oil & Gas and Exploration & Production.

In other words, for this example, we expect Oil & Gas Drilling and Equipment & Services to outperform the sector and Integrated Oil & Gas and Exploration & Production to underperform the sector.

Table 7.6   Portfolio A

Sub-Industry	MSCI World	Portfolio A	Difference
Coal & Consumable Fuels	1.8%	0.0%	−1.8%
Integrated Oil & Gas	63.4%	50.0%	−13.4%
Oil & Gas Drilling	3.5%	10.0%	6.5%
Oil & Gas Equipment & Services	10.9%	20.0%	9.1%
Oil & Gas Exploration & Production	14.8%	10.0%	−4.8%
Oil & Gas Refining & Marketing	2.8%	5.0%	2.2%
Oil & Gas Storage & Transportation	2.8%	5.0%	2.2%
Total	100.0%	100.0%	100.0%

Source: Thomson Datastream, MSCI, Inc.[8] as of 12/31/07.

But in terms of benchmark risk, we remain fairly close to the benchmark weights, so our relative risk is quite modest. This is extremely important: By managing against a benchmark, we have made strategic choices to beat the index, but we haven't concentrated too heavily in a specific area and are well diversified within the sector.

Table 7.7 is another example of relative portfolio weighting versus the benchmark. Portfolio B is significantly underweight to Integrated Oil & Gas and most overweight to Refining & Marketing, Drilling, and Equipment & Services. Because the sub-industry weights are so different from the benchmark, we are taking on substantially more relative risk in Portfolio B versus A.

Regardless of how your portfolio is positioned relative to the benchmark, it's important to use benchmarks to identify where your relative risks are before investing. Knowing the benchmark weights and having opinions on the future performance of each sub-industry is a crucial step in building a portfolio designed to beat the benchmark. Should you make the correct overweight and underweight decisions, you're likelier to beat the benchmark regardless of the individual securities held within. But even if you're wrong, you'll have diversified enough not to lose your shirt.

Which again brings us to picking individual stocks, and Chapter 8.

Table 7.7   Portfolio B

Sub-Industry	MSCI World	Portfolio B	Difference
Coal & Consumable Fuels	1.8%	5.0%	3.2%
Integrated Oil & Gas	63.4%	20.0%	−43.4%
Oil & Gas Drilling	3.5%	15.0%	11.5%
Oil & Gas Equipment & Services	10.9%	30.0%	19.1%
Oil & Gas Exploration & Production	14.8%	5.0%	−9.8%
Oil & Gas Refining & Marketing	2.8%	25.0%	22.2%
Oil & Gas Storage & Transportation	2.8%	5.0%	2.2%
Total	100.0%	100.0%	100.0%

Source: Thomson Datastream, MSCI, Inc.[9] as of 12/31/07.

Chapter Recap

A more effective approach to sector analysis is *top-down*. A top-down investment methodology analyzes big picture factors such as economics, politics, and sentiment to forecast which investment categories are likely to outperform the market. A key part of the process is the use of benchmarks (such as the MSCI World Energy or S&P 500 Energy indexes) as guides for building portfolios, monitoring performance, and managing risk. By analyzing portfolio drivers, we can identify which Energy industries and sub-industries are most attractive and unattractive, ultimately filtering down to stock selection.

- The top-down investment methodology first identifies and analyzes high-level portfolio drivers affecting broad categories of stocks. These drivers help determine portfolio country, sector, and style weights. The same methodology can be applied to a specific sector to determine industry and sub-industry weights.
- Quantitative factor screening helps narrow the list of potential portfolio holdings based on characteristics such as valuations, liquidity, and solvency.
- Stock selection is the last step in the top-down process. Stock selection attempts to find companies possessing strategic attributes consistent with higher-level portfolio drivers.
- Stock selection also attempts to find companies with the greatest probability of outperforming its peers.
- It's helpful to use an Energy benchmark as a guide when constructing a portfolio to determine your sub-industry overweights and underweights.

SECURITY ANALYSIS

Now that we've covered the top-down method, let's pick some stocks, shall we? This chapter walks you through analyzing individual Energy firms using the top-down method presented in Chapter 7. Specifically, we'll demonstrate a five-step process to analyzing firms relative to peers.

Every firm and every stock is different, but viewing them through the right lens is vital. You need a functional, consistent, and reusable framework for analyzing Energy securities and asking the most important questions when researching a stock. While by no means comprehensive, the framework provided and the questions at this chapter's end should serve as good starting points to help identify strategic attributes and company-specific risks.

While volumes have been written about individual security analysis, a top-down investment approach de-emphasizes the importance of stock selection in a portfolio. As such, we'll talk about the basics of stock analysis for the beginning to intermediate investor. For a more thorough understanding of financial statement analysis, valuations, modeling, and other tools of security analysis, additional reading is suggested.

Top-Down Recap

As covered in Chapter 7, you can use the top-down method to make your biggest, most important portfolio decisions first. However, the same decision process applies when picking stocks, and those high-level portfolio decisions ultimately filter down to individual securities.

Step one is analyzing the broader global economy and identifying various macro *drivers* affecting the entire sector or industry. Using the drivers, you can make general allocation decisions for countries, sectors, industries, and sub-industries versus the given benchmark. Step two is applying quantitative screening criteria to narrow the choice set of stocks. It's not until all those decisions are made that we get to analyze individual stocks. Security analysis is the third and final step.

For the rest of the chapter, we assume you have already established a benchmark, solidified portfolio themes, made sub-industry overweight and underweight decisions, and are ready to analyze firms within a peer group. (A *peer group* is a group of stocks you'd generally expect to perform similarly because they operate in the same industry, possibly share the same geography, and have similar quantitative attributes.)

MAKE YOUR SELECTION

Security analysis is nowhere near as complicated as it may seem. You've got one basic task: spot opportunities not currently discounted into prices. Or put differently, know something others don't. Investors should analyze firms by taking consensus expectations for a company's estimated financial results and then assessing whether it will perform below, in line, or above those baseline expectations. Profit opportunities arise when your expectations are different and more accurate than consensus expectations. Trading on widely known information or consensus expectations adds little to no value to the stock selection process. Doing so is little different than trading on a coin flip.

The top-down method offers two ways to spot such opportunities. First, accurately predict high-level, macro themes affecting an industry or group of companies—these are your portfolio drivers. Second, find firms that will benefit *most* if those high-level themes and drivers play out. This is done by finding firms with *competitive advantages* (we'll explain this concept more in a bit).

Since the majority of excess return is added in higher-level decisions during the top-down process, it's not vital to pick the "best" stocks in the universe. Rather, you want to pick stocks with a good probability of outperforming their peers. Doing so can enhance returns without jeopardizing good top-down decisions by picking risky, go-big-or-go-home stocks. Being right more often than not should create outperformance relative to the benchmark over time.

A FIVE-STEP PROCESS

Analyzing a stock against its peer group can be summarized in a five-step process:

1. Understand business and earnings drivers.
2. Identify strategic attributes.
3. Analyze fundamental and stock price performance.
4. Identify risks.
5. Analyze valuations and consensus expectations.

These five steps provide a consistent framework for analyzing firms in their peer groups. While these steps are far from a full stock analysis, they provide the basics necessary to begin making better stock selections.

Step 1: Understand Business and Earnings Drivers

The first step is understanding what the business does, how it generates its earnings, and what drives those earnings. Here are a few tips to help in the process.

- **Industry overview.** Begin any analysis with a basic understanding of the firm's industry, including its drivers and risks. You should be familiar with how current economic trends affect the industry.
- **Company description.** Obtain a business description of the company, including an understanding of the products and services within each business segment. It's generally best to go directly to a

company's financial statements for this. (Almost every public firm makes their financial statements readily accessible online these days.) Browse the firm's website and financial statements/reports to gain an overview of the company and how it presents itself.

- **Corporate history.** Read the firm's history since its inception and over the last several years. An understanding of firm history may reveal its growth strategy or consistency with success and failure. This also will provide clues on what its true core competencies are. Ask questions like: Has the firm been an industry leader for decades, or is it a relative newcomer? Has it switched strategies or businesses often in the past?

- **Business segments.** Break down company revenues and earnings by business segment and geography to determine how and where they make their money. Find out what drives results in each business and geographic segment. Begin thinking about how each of these business segments fits into your high-level themes.

- **Recent news/press releases.** Read all recently released news about the stock, including press releases. Do a Google search and see what comes up. Look for any significant announcements regarding company operations. What is the media's opinion of the firm? Is it a bellwether to the industry or a minor player?

- **Markets and customers.** Identify main customers and the markets it operates in. Determine if the firm has any particularly large, single customer or a concentrated customer base.

- **Competition.** Find the main competitors and how market share compares with other industry players. Is it highly segmented? Assess the industry's competitive landscape. Keep in mind the biggest competitors can sometimes lurk in different industries—sometimes even in different sectors! Get a feel for how they stack up—are they industry leaders or minor players? Does market share matter in that industry?

Step 2: Identify Strategic Attributes

After gaining a firm grasp of firm operations, the next step is identifying strategic attributes consistent with higher-level portfolio themes. Also known as *competitive* or *comparative advantages*, strategic attributes are unique features allowing firms to outperform their industry or sector. As industry peers are generally affected by the same high-level drivers, strong strategic attributes provide the edge in creating superior outperformance. Examples of strategic attributes include:

- High relative market share
- Low-cost producer
- Sales relationships/distribution
- Economic sensitivity
- Vertical integration
- Management/business strategy
- Geographic diversity or advantage
- Consolidator
- Strong balance sheet
- Niche markets
- Pure play
- Potential takeover target
- Proprietary technologies
- Strong brand name
- First mover advantage

Strategic Attributes: Making Lemonade

How do strategic attributes help you analyze individual stocks? Consider a simple example: Five lemonade stands of similar size, product, and quality within a city block. A scorching heat wave envelops the city, sending a rush of customers in search of lemonade. Which stand benefits most from the industry-wide surge in business? This likely depends on each stand's strategic attributes. Maybe one is a cost leader and has cheapest access to homegrown lemons. Maybe one has a geographic advantage and is located next to a basketball court full of thirsty players. Or maybe one has a superior business strategy with a "buy two, get one free" initiative that drives higher sales volume and a bigger customer base. Any of these are core strategic advantages.

Portfolio drivers help determine which kind of strategic attributes are likely to face head- or tailwinds. After all, not all strategic attributes will benefit a firm in all environments. For example, while higher operating leverage might help a firm boost earnings in the booming part of an industry, it would have the opposite effect in a down cycle. A pertinent example to Energy is access to oil and gas reserves—currently a huge strategic attribute in today's environment due to the industry's difficulty increasing production. During the 2001 recession, reserves were less important since there was ample excess production capacity in the world. Thus, it's essential to pick strategic attributes consistent with higher-level portfolio themes and analyze which ones hold more importance in the current environment.

A strategic attribute is also only effective to the extent management recognizes and takes advantage of it. Execution is key. For example, if a firm's strategic attribute is technological expertise, it should focus its effort on research and development to maintain that edge. If their strategic attribute is its position as a low-cost producer in its peer group, it should capitalize by potentially lowering prices to gain market share.

Identifying strategic attributes may require thorough research of the firm's financial statements, website, news stories, history, and discussions with customers, suppliers, competitors, or management. Don't skimp on this step—be diligent and thorough in finding strategic attributes. It may feel like an arduous task at times, but it's also among the most important in security selection.

Step 3: Analyze Fundamental and Stock Price Performance

Once you've gained a thorough understanding of the business, earnings drivers, and strategic attributes, the next step is analyzing firm performance both fundamentally and in the stock market.

Using the latest earnings releases and annual report, determine how well the company has performed in recent quarters and why. Ask the following:

- What's the recent trend of its sales, earnings, and margins?
- Which business segments are seeing rising or falling revenues?

- Is the firm growing its business organically or because of acquisitions?
- How sustainable is either strategy?
- Are earnings growing because of strong demand or because of cost cutting?
- Is it using tax loopholes and one-time items?
- What is management's strategy to grow the business for the future?
- What is the financial health of the company?

Not all earnings results are created equal. Understanding what drives results will give clues to what drives future performance.

Check the company's stock chart for the last few years and try to determine what has driven performance. Explain any big up or down moves and identify any significant news events. If the stock price has trended steadily downward despite consistently beating earnings estimates, there may be a force driving the whole industry downward, like expectations for lower natural gas prices. Likewise, if the company's stock soared despite reporting tepid earnings growth or prospects, there may be some force driving the industry higher, like takeover speculation. Or stocks can simply move in sympathy with the broader market. Whatever it is, make sure you know.

After reading the earnings calls of a firm and its peers (these are typically posted on the investor relations section of a firm's website every quarter), you will begin to notice similar trends and events affecting the industry. Take note of these so you can distinguish between issues that are company specific or industry-wide. For instance, cost inflation in the Energy sector tends to affect most firms universally. Other issues like large discoveries or reserve write downs are company specific.

Step 4: Identify Risks

There are two main types of risks in security analysis: stock-specific risk and systematic risk (also known as non-stock-specific risk). Both can be equally important to performance.

Stock-specific risks, as the name suggests, are issues affecting the company in isolation. These are mainly risks affecting a firm's business operations or future operations. Some company-specific risks are discussed in detail in the 10-K for US firms and the 20-F for foreign filers. These can be found at www.sec.gov. But one can't rely solely on firms self-identifying their risk factors. You've got to see what analysts and investors are saying about them and identify all risks for yourself. Some examples include:

- Stock ownership concentration (insider or institutional)
- Customer concentration
- Sole suppliers
- Excessive leverage or lack of access to financing
- Obsolete products
- Poor operational track record
- High cost of products versus competitors
- Late SEC filings
- Qualified audit opinions
- Hedging activities
- Pension or benefit underfunding risk
- Regulatory or legal—outstanding litigation
- Pending corporate actions
- Executive departures
- Regional, political/government risk

Systematic risks include macroeconomic or geopolitical events out of a company's control. While the risks may affect a broad set of firms, they will have varying effects on each. Some examples include:

- Commodity prices
- Industry cost inflation
- Economic activity
- Labor scarcity
- Strained supply chain
- Legislation affecting taxes, royalties, or subsidies

- Geopolitical risks
- Capital expenditures
- Interest rates
- Currency
- Weather

Identifying stock-specific risks helps an investor evaluate the relative risk and reward potential of firms within a peer group. Identifying systematic risks helps you make informed decisions about which sub-industries and countries to overweight or underweight.

If you don't feel strongly about any company in a peer group within a sub-industry you wish to overweight, you could pick the company with the least stock-specific risk. This would help to achieve the goal of picking firms with the greatest probability of outperforming its peer group and still performing in line with your higher-level themes and drivers.

Step 5: Analyze Valuations and Consensus Expectations

Valuations can be tricky. They *are* tools used to evaluate market sentiment and expectations for firms. They *are not* foolproof to see if a stock is "cheap" or "expensive." Valuations are primarily used to compare firms against their peer group (or peer average) or a company's valuation relative to its own history. As mentioned earlier, stocks move not on the expected, but the unexpected. We aim to try and gauge what the consensus expects for a company's future performance and then assess whether that company will perform below, in line, or above expectations.

Valuations provide little value by themselves in predicting future stock performance. Just because one company's P/E is 20 while another is 10 does not mean you should buy the one at 10 because it's cheap and the other expensive. There's likely a reason why one company has a different valuation than another, including such things as strategic attributes, earnings expectations, sentiment, stock-specific risks, and management's reputation. The main usefulness of valuations is explaining why a company's valuation differs from its peers and determining if it's justified.

There are many different valuation metrics investors use in security analysis. Some of the most popular include:

- P/E—price to earnings
- P/FE—price to forward earnings
- P/B—price to book
- DY—dividend yield
- EV/EBITDA—enterprise value to earnings before interest, taxes, depreciation, and amortization

Once you've compiled the valuations for a peer group, hypothesize why there are relative differences and if they're justified. Is a company's relatively low valuation due to stock-specific risk or low confidence from investors? Is the company's forward P/E relatively high because consensus is wildly optimistic about the stock? A firm's higher valuation may be entirely justified, for example, if it has a growth rate greater than its peers. A lower valuation may be warranted for a company facing a challenging operating environment in which it was losing market share. Seeing valuations in this way will help to differentiate firms and spot potential opportunities or risks.

Valuations should be used in combination with previous analysis of a company's fundamentals, strategic attributes, and risks. For example, the grid below shows how an investor could combine an analysis of strategic attributions and valuations to help pick firms. Stocks with relatively low valuations but attractive strategic attributes may be underappreciated by the market. Stocks with relatively high valuations but no discernible strategic attributes may be overvalued by the market. Either way, use valuations appropriately and in the context of a larger investment opinion about a stock, not as a panacea for true value.

		Valuation Low	Valuation High
Strategic Attributes	Relatively Attractive	Best	
	Relatively Unattractive		Worst

IMPORTANT QUESTIONS TO ASK

While this chapter's framework can be used to analyze any firm, there are additional factors specific to each Energy sub-industry that must be considered. The following section provides some of the most important factors and questions to consider when researching Energy firms, broken down by sub-industry. Answers to these questions should help distinguish between Energy firms within a peer group and help identify strategic attributes and stock-specific risks. While there are countless other questions and factors that could and should be asked when researching Energy firms, these should serve as a good starting point.

Integrated Oil & Gas, Exploration & Production, and Refining & Marketing Sub-Industries

Revenues and Earnings Breakdown. How is the firm's revenue and earnings divided between exploration and production, refining and marketing, or other divisions like petrochemicals? This will reveal the firm's relative sensitivity to commodity prices and petroleum products.

Production and Reserve Breakdown. How are the firm's production and reserves split between oil, natural gas, or some other mix? This mix between oil, natural gas, and other hydrocarbons will show which commodity has a greater effect on the firm's operations. This mix can explain significant differences in performance among firms, as oil and natural gas prices can diverge widely.

Oil and Gas Production Growth. Is the firm consistently growing oil and gas production or experiencing declines? What is its production growth relative to peers? Is growth organic or due to acquisitions? What is the firm's strategy to grow oil and gas reserves?

Hedging. To what degree does the firm use hedging in its operations? How exposed are the firm's operations to oil and natural gas prices? Firms' hedging strategies tend to show which ones have the most upside and downside relative to where commodity prices end up.

Reserve Replacement. What is the firm's history of reserve replacement? How many years can it sustain production with current reserves? Firms with relatively long life reserves may not need to take major risks to grow production in the future. This could be a distinct competitive advantage.

Exploration and Production Costs. How do the firm's finding and development costs compare with peers? How do operating costs and exploration expenses compare? Is the firm a particularly low-cost producer or is it engaged in high-cost operations like the oil sands, oil shale, or other unconventional resources? Typically, firms with particularly high-cost operations are more negatively affected by falling commodity prices as they have lower profit margins.

Geopolitical Risk. What is the firm's geopolitical risk profile? Where are most of the firm's current and future planned production sites and refining assets? Are the sites in politically stable or unstable countries? What percentage of production comes from politically unstable regions? Does the firm have a solid history of operating in foreign territories? Has it ever had disruptions due to a geopolitical squabble?

While a firm with relatively high exposure to a geopolitically unstable region may face higher risks of government intervention or production disruption, the potential additions to production growth may warrant these risks.

Government Ownership. Are the firm's shares owned or controlled by a government, and if so, to what degree? Especially in emerging market countries, governments and powerful families can play a huge role in the Energy sector. Often, government-controlled Energy firms are subject to unique taxes, royalties, subsidies, and price controls. Such inhibitors can spring up unexpectedly—at the whim of the controlling government.

Cash Flow Use. How is the firm spending its cash flow? To what degree is it buying back shares, paying dividends, spending on capital expenditures, or paying down debt? Depending on industry conditions, investors may prefer a firm that rewards shareholders with dividends and share buybacks over taking on risky and aggressive new drilling plans.

Refining Complexity. How complex are the firm's refineries? Does it do just one kind of refining, or many? How diversified are the firm's sources and types of crude oil? Is it dependent on one supplier or many? Firms capable of processing heavier crudes or a more diverse complexity may have a competitive advantage depending on the differences between light and heavy crude oil.

Petroleum Product Mix. A firm's production mix between transportation fuels versus chemicals or other products will determine to what extent factors like economic growth, driving trends, and weather will affect product demand. What is the firm's mix of petroleum products (gasoline/diesel/heating oil/chemicals)?

Oil & Gas Storage & Transportation Sub-Industry

Revenues and Earnings Breakdown. Firms in the storage and transportation sub-industry can have incredibly diverse and complex business operations, making it important to understand what drives overall results. What percentage of the firm's revenues and earnings are regulated or unregulated? Does the firm have production or trading assets? Which of the two is more important to the bottom line?

Competition. What is the competitive landscape of the firm's peers? Does the firm operate in a region with significant barriers to entry? Pipeline operators generally face less competition than firms in the shipping business. This is because, in general, regulatory approval is needed to build new pipelines.

Balance Sheet. Many firms in this sub-industry tend to carry heavy debt loads, so financial health can vary widely. Those with greater financial resources could be more capable of funding future growth opportunities. Does the firm have the financial ability to make large acquisitions to fuel growth? Does the firm's balance sheet allow it to take on additional leverage? Debt isn't necessarily a bad thing—many firms generate an excellent return on borrowed funds. In either case, it's vital to understand the capital structure of a firm.

Regulation. How are the firm's operations affected by regulation? Does the firm operate in a favorable regulatory environment currently? How might that change? What is the firm's history with gaining regulatory approval for its projects? Firms with more regulated assets are exposed to regulatory risks, but they may also have more stable returns.

Interest Rates. How sensitive are the firm's operations to interest rates? Are rising or falling rates good or bad for the firm's operations and share price? Firms with greater leverage tend to be affected by interest rate movements due to changes in interest expense. Firms with more regulated assets also tend to be more interest rate sensitive because their stable cash flows make them akin to bond proxies (since bond prices move inversely to interest rates).

Distributions. Does the firm have a reliable history of paying and growing distributions to shareholders? Because high cash flow distributions are one of the unique and most attractive characteristics of many pipeline master limited partnerships (MLPs), a stable history of distributions is an important attribute.

Tax Implications. Are there any tax implications for investing in the firm? Owning an MLP, for instance, can have unique tax implications, so it's a good idea to consult a tax adviser before investing.

Coal & Consumable Fuel Sub-Industry

Coal Supply/Demand Environment. What is the supply-demand environment for coal within the firm's countries of operation? How have prices been affected? Both supply and demand factors will have a great influence on prices, which can be volatile.

Production Growth. What is the firm's production growth history? What is its strategy for increasing coal production? Is it organic or through acquisitions? As we previously mentioned, there are pros and cons to organic and acquisition strategies for oil and gas production growth. However, because coal is not in short supply, it may not always be the best financial strategy to increase coal volumes simply for volume's sake. Instead, firms may find share buybacks or dividends as better means of increasing shareholder value.

Geographic Breakdown. Prices can vary dramatically between home and export markets, thus diversification can mitigate risks of big price changes in any one market. In which regions does the firm generate its sales? Is the firm an exporter or does it supply mainly to its own country? Is the firm beholden to trade problems with other regions?

Production Costs. Firms can have highly different cost profiles due to their ability to take advantage of economies of scale. What are the firm's production costs relative to its peers? What factors are driving its production costs?

Vertical Integration. Does the firm benefit from vertical integration? (i.e., does it have the ability to handle all stages of the energy process by itself, or is it reliant upon outside vendors for parts of the process?) To what degree is it reliant on other firms in its operations? Firms with more vertical integration may be able to mitigate cost increases in times of industry cost inflation.

Transportation. Since transportation costs of coal make up a large percentage of overall costs, a firm's strategy for transportation can have a major effect. How does the firm deliver its coal to end users? Are there any transportation bottlenecks, and if so, how has the firm responded in the past?

Legislative Risks. Are there any legislative risks regarding CO^2 emissions in the firm's countries of operation that could materially affect operations? Environmental concerns surrounding coal use will need to be watched closely given ongoing debates about global warming.

Government Control. Does the firm secure free market pricing for its coal or are prices set by the government? Governments in emerging markets will likely play a bigger role in their country's coal industry than those in developed markets. Often, controlled prices play havoc with a firm's profitability.

Oil & Gas Drilling Sub-Industry

Rig Types. Knowing the firm's rig mix will help determine which commodities and regions have the greatest effect on results. What's the breakdown of the firm's rig fleet (land or offshore, shallow or deepwater, etc.)? Do these rigs drill primarily for natural gas or oil?

Contract Types. Which type(s) of contracts does the firm use to contract its rigs (daywork, footage, or turnkey)? What percentages of its fleet use each? Generally, daywork contracts are viewed more favorably because they provide stable revenues, but this isn't always the case. Take a keen look at a firm's contract structure to determine its prospects for profitability.

Dayrates. What has been the trend of the firm's dayrates? What is the potential for dayrate expansion once its rig contracts expire? Dayrates can vary somewhat between rig operators but tend to follow industry trends.

Contract Length. When do the firm's current rig contracts expire? How many of the firm's rigs are due to come off contract in the short or long term? Depending on industry conditions, a short or long contract can be beneficial or harmful.

Rig Quality. Are the firm's rigs more technologically advanced than competitors? Do oil and gas firms pay a premium for the firm's rigs? The drilling industry is highly competitive, so having technologically advanced rigs can help in pricing negotiations.

Rig Location. Where are the rigs located? What are the supply–demand dynamics in each region? Is it the firm's strategy to stick to a specific region or expand geographically? How easily can it move its rigs to more attractive locations? Rig demand varies considerably by region, thus firms able to adapt quickly to changing supply and demand dynamics have the ability to reap rewards.

Rig Utilization. What percentage of the firm's rigs is in service? Is utilization growing, stable, or falling? This should help to gauge demand of the firm's rigs and whether it has the capacity to take on more business.

Rig Growth Strategy. What is the firm's strategy to grow its asset base? Does it plan to build new rigs or acquire a competitor? At what pace can it build new rigs?

Rig Fleet Age. What is the average age of the firm's fleet? Is it expanding its rig fleet or retiring old rigs? To what extent will the firm need to take rigs out of service for upgrades or maintenance?

Operating and Maintenance Costs. How do the firm's operating and maintenance costs compare with peers? What is the firm's strategy to mitigate industry cost inflation? Because rig firms often secure steady cash flows through contracts, their ability to control cost inflation will have a big impact on margins.

Oil & Gas Equipment & Services Sub-Industry

Revenues and Earnings Breakdown. Firms in this sub-industry can be very concentrated in one type of business or highly diversified among many products and services. What is the breakdown of the firm's revenue and earnings between products and services? Do the firm's businesses rely on the spot market, long-term contracts, or both? Are the firm's revenues coming mainly from new products or older, more mature products?

Supply/Demand Dynamics of Products and Services. Depending on industry conditions, certain products and services will be in higher demand than others (for example, services for exploration might be in higher demand at a given time than production-related services). What drives demand for the firm's products and services? What is the competitive landscape for these products and services?

Technology and Innovation. New technology and innovation is incredibly important in this sub-industry of largely commoditized products and services. Does the firm possess any proprietary technologies or patents giving it a competitive edge? Does the firm continually release new products or does it specialize in more mature markets?

Geographic Breakdown. What is the firm's geographic mix? Does the firm plan to focus on one region or expand geographically? Do its core competencies jibe with that strategy? Product and services demand can vary considerably by region due in part to varying exposure to oil and natural gas. For example, firms with more revenues from North America will generally be more affected by the natural gas market than oil due to the region's relatively higher natural gas reserves.

Market Share and Pricing Power. What is the firm's market share in each of its business segments? Does the firm have pricing power for its products and services? Since this sub-industry is fiercely competitive with many industry players, a firm's ability to maintain market share and pricing will vary considerably depending on industry conditions.

Project Execution. For firms operating on long-term contracts, project execution and cost control will make or break results. Does the firm execute its projects on time and on budget? Does the firm put cost contingencies in its contracts? Have projects ever been disrupted in the past due to unforeseen problems?

Product Backlog. A strong backlog of business increases earnings visibility and is a sign of strong industry demand. How healthy is the firm's product backlog? Is it rising or falling? Do its competitors have a bigger or smaller backlog?

Chapter Recap

Security analysis is not nearly as difficult as it seems. In the top-down investment process, stocks are essentially tools we use to take advantage of opportunities we identify in higher-level themes. Once we identify an attractive segment of the market, we attempt to find firms most likely to outperform their peers by identifying firms with strategic attributes. While the five-step security selection process is just one of many ways to research firms, it is an effective framework for selecting securities within the top-down process. Last, do not limit yourself to the questions provided in this chapter when researching energy firms—they are just some tools to help you distinguish between firms. The more questions you ask, the better your analysis will be.

- Stock selection, the third and final step in the top-down investment process, attempts to identify securities that will benefit from our high-level portfolio themes.
- Ultimately, stock selection attempts to spot opportunities not currently discounted into prices.
- To identify firms most likely to outperform their peer group, we must find firms that possess competitive advantages (a.k.a. strategic attributes).
- A five-step security selection process can be used as a framework to research firms.
- Firms within each Energy sub-industry have specific characteristics and strategies separating potential winners from losers. Asking the right questions can help identify them.

ENERGIZE YOUR PORTFOLIO

Now it's time to transfer our Energy sector knowledge and analysis into strategy. In this chapter, we discuss various Energy investment strategies, including examples of when to overweight and underweight industries and sub-industries throughout a market cycle.

As covered so far, fundamentals can differ widely by sub-industry, so overweight and underweight decisions in each area are vital for success. Remember, we're investing within the context of a top-down model (if you need a refresher, revisit Chapter 7). So we'll be talking less about specific stocks and more about overweighting industries and sub-industries that should benefit if higher-level themes play out as we expect them to.

While investment strategies presented here are by no means comprehensive, they provide a good starting point to help construct a portfolio that can increase your likelihood of outperforming Energy benchmarks. They should also help spur some investment strategy ideas of your own. After all, investing is all about using this framework to discover information few are looking at.

STRATEGY 1: COMMODITIZE

One of the simplest ways to invest in Energy is commodity speculation. Why mess with pesky stocks when you're most interested in oil price movements? Investing directly in oil, natural gas, or numerous other Energy commodities is the most direct way to gain exposure to changes in commodity prices. Just because oil or natural gas prices rise or fall doesn't necessarily mean Energy stocks will do the same. Commodity investing gets right to the heart of the matter.

But caution: Commodity investing is not for everyone. Oil and natural gas prices can be extremely volatile, moving on entirely unpredictable events. Fortunes have been made and lost speculating on commodities. Thus, investors planning to invest in commodities should be prepared to stomach extreme volatility and have a high risk tolerance. That's the dark side of commodity investing.

Commodities can also be used as a hedge. For example, if you expect commodities to decline significantly in the short to medium term but still want to hold your Energy stocks for the long term, you could short commodities in the futures market or use options to bet against prices. This too entails higher risk if not structured properly and should only be attempted by sophisticated investors.

There are numerous ways to invest in crude oil and natural gas. The most direct way is to call your custodian and set up a futures account, allowing you to invest directly in oil and natural gas futures. Additionally, there are several ways to buy securities tied to the price of oil and natural gas without a futures account through other investment vehicles like ETFs or mutual funds. For example, the US Oil Fund (ticker: USO) and MACROshares Oil Up Tradeable (ticker: UCR) both track the price of crude oil. The MACROshares Oil Down Tradeable Trust (ticker: DCR) does the opposite, tracking the inverse performance of crude oil prices. For US natural gas, the ETF US Natural Gas Fund (ticker: UNG) attempts to track prices of natural gas delivered at the Henry Hub in Louisiana. (Note: These are just a few examples of securities linked to the price of oil and natural gas. Further research should be done for more investment options.)

Because commodity investing is not the focus of this book, we won't go into further detail, but there are plenty of publications available for more information on investing directly in commodities.

STRATEGY 2: PLAYING SUB-INDUSTRIES

Another strategy is to overweight and underweight Energy sub-industries based on your market outlook and analysis. Within the Energy sector, each sub-industry falls in and out of favor frequently—no one sub-industry outperforms consistently over the long term. Each will lead or lag depending on drivers like the direction of oil prices, natural gas prices, refining margins, and capital expenditures.

A look at the historical performance of the main S&P 500 Energy sub-industries since 1995 (Table 9.1) illustrates the variability of returns throughout time. (Note: Coal & Consumable Fuels and Oil & Gas Storage & Transportation have been omitted due to lack of historical sub-industry return data.) Calendar year sub-industry index total returns are compared to changes in crude oil prices as measured by West Texas Intermediate (WTI). Shaded regions highlight when sub-industries outperformed the sector as a whole.

In the last 13 years, there are several observations worth noting about each sub-industry:

1. Integrated Oil & Gas returns have the least amount of volatility and outperform the other sub-industries in down markets.
2. Oil & Gas Drilling and Energy Equipment & Services perform very similarly, generally outperforming in up markets and underperforming in down markets. These have much greater volatility than Integrated Oil & Gas.
3. Oil & Gas Exploration & Production is also quite volatile, typically performing best in up markets and worst in down, but has years when it acts differently than the rest of the sector.
4. Refining & Marketing acts the least like the others and is highly volatile, but has some of the highest absolute returns.

Table 9.1   S&P Energy Sub-Industry Index Returns

	Energy Sector	Integrated Oil & Gas	Oil & Gas Drilling	Oil & Gas Equip & Serv	Oil & Gas Explor & Prod	Oil & Gas Refing & Mark	Crude Oil WTI Spot $/bbl
1995	31.0%	30.6%	37.7%	38.6%	17.5%	N/A	12.2%
1996	25.9%	24.3%	105.0%	39.4%	32.5%	N/A	32.4%
1997	25.3%	23.6%	33.4%	55.2%	−8.4%	44.0%	−32.0%
1998	0.6%	8.9%	−57.4%	−42.0%	−31.8%	−10.5%	−31.7%
1999	18.7%	17.7%	60.2%	36.0%	19.4%	−24.4%	112.4%
2000	15.7%	10.4%	51.6%	34.0%	59.1%	29.8%	4.8%
2001	−10.4%	−5.7%	−29.4%	−33.4%	−21.0%	35.5%	−26.3%
2002	−11.1%	−12.2%	−12.5%	−11.5%	−1.5%	−23.0%	57.9%
2003	25.6%	26.7%	6.7%	24.7%	23.6%	59.0%	4.2%
2004	31.5%	28.8%	45.1%	31.9%	34.9%	64.2%	33.5%
2005	31.4%	17.6%	53.2%	48.6%	66.4%	79.2%	40.5%
2006	24.2%	34.8%	3.3%	15.5%	4.7%	−5.1%	0.0%
2007	34.4%	29.9%	41.0%	47.9%	44.4%	33.0%	57.2%
Average Annualized Return	17.6%	17.2%	17.7%	17.1%	14.8%	20.5%	
Standard deviation	15.7%	14.3%	42.8%	31.4%	29.6%	36.2%	

Source: Thomson Datastream.

After analyzing returns of the past several years and knowing the market fundamentals driving those returns, some general conclusions can be made about which sub-industries will perform best in different market environments. Note: *Always remember past performance is no guarantee of future performance.* All you can hope to gain from studying past performance is to increase your chances of outperforming should the future resemble the past. The past is about understanding context and precedent for investing—it's not a roadmap for the future.

Here are a few examples of sub-industries outperforming and underperforming based on industry fundamentals.

Oil & Energy Equipment & Services Relative Performance

The Energy Equipment & Services (EES) industry is sometimes referred to as the *high beta* industry within Energy because it tends to outperform the Oil & Gas (O&G) industry during periods of rapidly rising oil prices and underperform during periods of stagnant or declining prices.

The O&G and EES industries contain firms with very different characteristics, thus their performances differ greatly. While the O&G industry is dominated by huge, internationally diverse integrated oil and gas firms, the EES industry is mostly smaller, US-based energy services providers. EES firms also tend to have high operating leverages and can see earnings skyrocket during up cycles or plummet during down cycles. These firms live and die on the capital expenditure budgets of the O&G industry, which fluctuate over time. Characterized by boom and bust cycles, these firms see some of the most dramatic swings in stock prices.

Investors may choose to own higher quality firms like those in the O&G industry—and specifically, the Integrated Oil & Gas sub-industry—during periods of falling oil prices. Worried about deteriorating fundamentals within the sector, investors may demand firms able to withstand falling oil and gas prices without a high probability of going bankrupt. Thus, Integrated Oil & Gas firms are sometimes viewed as a defensive play and tend to outperform in periods of stagnant or falling oil prices.

Figure 9.1 shows how changes in oil prices affect the spread between O&G and EES industries. The black line is the annual performance spread between the MSCI World EES industry and MSCI World O&G industry, rolling monthly. The gray line is the year-over-year change in oil prices. When the black line rises above

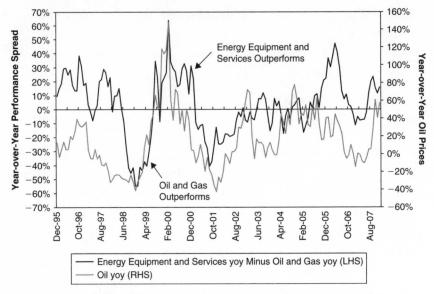

Figure 9.1   Oil and Energy Equipment & Services Relative Performance
Source: Thomson Datastream, MSCI, Inc.[1]

zero percent, it signifies EES outperformed O&G over the previous years. When the black line falls below zero percent, O&G outperforms.

The graph shows a distinct positive correlation between changes in oil prices and the performance spread between EES and O&G. Thus, when a large year-over-year increase in oil prices is expected, overweighting the EES industry can add significantly to returns. Consequently, it may be a good time to overweight the integrated oil firms and reduce or abandon EES altogether if you expect flattish or declining oil prices.

Though this relationship generally holds, there are also several instances in history when the EES industry did not outperform the O&G industry during periods of rising oil prices. This is just one of several reasons, or drivers, behind an industry overweight or underweight decision. Whenever making investment judgments, it's vital to assemble myriad drivers, not just rest your laurels on one.

World Rig Count and Energy Equipment & Services Relative Performance

Besides rising oil prices, world rig count growth is also a coincident indicator of EES outperformance over O&G through history.

Figure 9.2 shows how world rig count affects the relative perform-ance of EES versus O&G. The black line is the annual performance spread between the MSCI World EES industry and MSCI World O&G industry, rolling monthly. The gray line is the year-over-year percentage change in the world rig count. When the black line rises above zero percent, it signifies EES outperformed O&G over the previous years. When the black line falls below zero percent, O&G outperformed.

As Figure 9.2 shows, EES tends to outperform O&G during periods of rising worldwide rig count growth. Additionally, the industry gener-ally underperforms when worldwide rig count growth slows or falls.

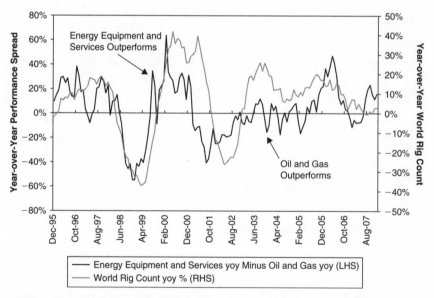

Figure 9.2   World Rig Count vs. Energy Equipment & Services Performance

Source: Thomson Datastream, MSCI, Inc.,[2] Baker Hughes.

Rising worldwide rig count growth typically benefits EES because it is an indicator of a healthy drilling market. As rig demand increases, drillers are able to increase rig dayrates since more equipment and services are needed for new rigs.

Because this indicator is coincident (i.e., does not predict the future), it in itself holds little value to forecast the future relative performance of EES versus O&G. It's more important to study the supply and demand dynamics of the worldwide rig market to forecast whether rig growth is poised to accelerate or decelerate. And it may be a good time to overweight EES if you believe worldwide rig count growth is set to accelerate.

Upstream Capital Expenditures & Energy Services Performance

The level and rate of change of upstream capital expenditures by the O&G industry will be the main driver of performance of the EES industry. Periods of rapidly rising spending for oil and gas exploration and production typically leads to a boom in Energy Services performance, while falling spending typically leads to the reverse. Unfortunately, most capital expenditure data reported by firms will be backward looking, though many firms do provide guidance about their expected levels of capital expenditures over the next year.

Because of this, investors and analysts seek out surveys of planned capital expenditures by the O&G industry (the *Oil & Gas Journal* typically provides these) to forecast the performance of the EES industry. These surveys provide clues into how the operating environment will be for the Energy Services industry and may help in the decision to overweight or underweight the industry relative to the benchmark.

US Exploration & Production and Natural Gas Prices

Exploration & Production (E&P) firms are directly affected by oil and gas prices, but depending on the company, one commodity will have a greater impact on overall results than the other. In the US, where most publicly traded independent E&P firms are located, most firms tend to concentrate on natural gas in North American basins. As a

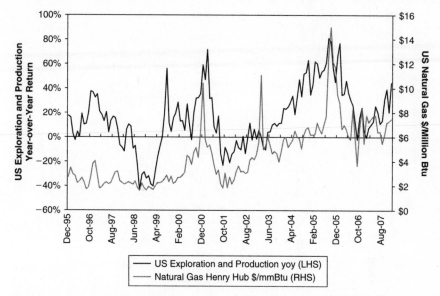

Figure 9.3   US E&P Performance & US Natural Gas Prices
Source: Thomson Datastream.

result, the S&P 500 Oil & Gas E&P sub-industry tends to be more responsive to changes in US natural gas prices than oil.

Figure 9.3 shows the year-over-year performance of the S&P 500 Oil & Gas E&P sub-industry index versus the absolute performance of US natural gas prices over the last several years.

Because US natural gas prices vary widely from oil prices, so too does the performance of the US E&P sub-industry vary from the other Energy sub-industries. While US E&P firms tend to perform well during periods of rising oil prices, it's best to overweight the sub-industry when you feel strongly about US natural gas prices. For the global E&P sub-industry, it's difficult to make broad generalizations about performance due to the differences between firms and the regional differences of natural gas prices.

US Refining & Marketing Margins

The US Refining & Marketing (R&M) sub-industry acts the least like other sub-industries in the S&P 500 Energy index. This sub-industry

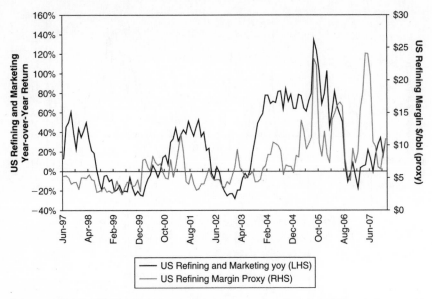

Figure 9.4   US Refining & Marketing Performance and US Refining Margins

Source: Thomson Datastream, Bloomberg Finance L.P.

reacts more to changes in refining margins than oil or natural gas prices alone.

Figure 9.4 shows the year-over-year performance of the S&P 500 R&M sub-industry index versus the absolute performance of US refining margins over the last several years. The sub-industry's returns tend to rise and fall alongside refining margins.

Figure 9.4 shows it's best to overweight this sub-industry when you expect rising refining margins and underweight when you expect the opposite. However, because of the difficulty of accurately predicting the direction of refining margins—especially given their volatility—take caution when making any significant bets and be prepared to stomach big swings in performance.

Like the E&P sub-industry, it is difficult to make broad generalizations about global R&M performance due to the vast differences between firms and regions.

Energy Sector Downturn?

As of December 2007, the Energy sector has been on an incredible multiyear run, producing strong double-digit returns in each of the last five years. But sooner or later, the tide will change. Why? Because no one sector can outperform forever. The stock market will eventually sniff out all opportunities to make excess returns and sector leadership will change. So it's important to continually review all the drivers and question your high-level portfolio themes regularly.

A downturn in the Energy sector could refer to either a period of falling Energy company stock prices if oil or natural gas prices fall, sinking refining margins, some combination of these two, or some other factor entirely. While there are countless reasons why any of these could fall, here are a few possible examples.

Potential Causes of Falling Oil or Natural Gas Prices

- Falling demand
  - Recession or economic slowdown—regional or global; perceived or real
  - Increasing use of substitute fuels
  - Weather-related
  - High prices reducing consumption
  - New technology or alternatives reducing oil or natural gas consumption
- Increasing supply
  - New fields beginning production
  - New discoveries
  - Increasing OPEC output
  - Increasing global inventories
  - Increasing LNG imports (liquefied natural gas)
- Easing geopolitical uncertainty
- Legislation positively affecting supplies or reducing demand
- Overly bullish sentiment causing speculative bubble

Should your analysis lead you to believe the next 12 months will be a bad time for Energy stocks—due to the above reasons or something else—then it may be appropriate to either reduce or eliminate your weight in Energy firms or adopt a defensive position in the portfolio. Or the more sophisticated investor could use short sales or options strategies to profit from the downside.

STRATEGY 3: COMPANY BETS

A more advanced strategy entails making bets against firms within a sub-industry based on its business lines. This strategy could be based on different opinions about oil, natural gas, refining margins, capital expenditures, or some combination of all. For example, if you are of the opinion oil prices will accelerate while US natural gas will fall in the near future, you could:

- Short natural gas-focused E&Ps and go long oil-focused E&Ps
- Overweight E&P firms with little to no hedging on oil production relative to peers
- Overweight E&P firms with relatively greater natural gas hedging than peers
- Short EES firms with operations focused on North American natural gas markets and go long EES firms focused on foreign oil operations
- Short North American land drillers and go long offshore drillers

These are just a few examples, but countless other strategies could be employed within sub-industries. As you become more familiar with specific energy firms and their industries, you can eventually develop your own strategies. Always be vigilant for company-specific issues that could cause a stock to act differently than you would expect in the context of your broader strategy.

MORE SUB-INDUSTRY TIPS

Ultimately, your decision to overweight or underweight a sub-industry relative to the benchmark should tie in to your high-level portfolio drivers. While we showed a few examples of when it's best to favor one sub-industry over another, there are a few additional tips that can help. Here are a few pointers as they relate to each sub-industry.

Integrated Oil & Gas

- The Integrated Oil & Gas sub-industry makes up a large weight in most major equity Energy indexes, so it's a good idea to hold at least a small allocation of them in any energy portfolio to reduce benchmark risk.

- This sub-industry tends to perform relatively better than others in periods of falling energy prices due to their diversified business lines and size. Hence, some investors overweight the sub-industry to take a defensive stance.

Oil & Gas Exploration & Production

- As the most directly leveraged to oil and natural gas prices, these firms typically can hold the most upside and downside through an energy cycle.
- Be sure to understand which commodity (oil or natural gas) the company is more leveraged to, as prices can vary greatly.

Oil & Gas Refining & Marketing

- Refining margins can be incredibly volatile and unpredictable. A large overweight to this sub-industry carries a high risk/reward profile.
- This is one sub-industry where rising oil prices can actually be bad for earnings (since oil represents a cost).

Oil & Gas Storage & Transportation

- Because many of these firms are indirectly affected by commodity prices, they may be a good holding for a defensive play within Energy.
- Many firms within this sub-industry—notably MLPs—carry high leverage and issue large dividends. As a result, they can be relatively more interest rate sensitive than other firms in the Energy sector.

Oil & Gas Drilling

- This is historically a boom/bust industry. It's generally best to overweight the drillers when you expect commodity prices to rise significantly and underweight (or even short) when you expect the opposite.

- Land drillers and offshore drillers can perform very differently, as some land drillers focus primarily on natural gas, while offshore drillers focus primarily on oil.

Oil & Gas Equipment & Services

- Like Oil & Gas Drillers, this sub-industry is generally best to overweight during periods of high and rising commodity prices as they are fueled by upstream capital expenditures.
- Equipment & Services is a very diverse sub-industry in which the complexity of constituent firms can see big performance divergence.

Coal & Consumable Fuels

- This small sub-industry is in many ways more like the Materials sector than Energy and thus has very different drivers.
- Most Energy benchmarks have very little, if any, weight in coal firms. Thus, overweighting this sub-industry carries high benchmark risk.

With that, you should now have a great head start to investing in Energy. We've covered a lot in these pages—Energy's basics, its drivers, the investment universe, and all the commonly followed industry fundamentals. But remember: Like all sectors, Energy is dynamic. The drivers and fundamentals that are vital today may not be tomorrow. But with the top-down method, you can apply a consistent framework to analyze the sector regardless of the current environment.

Chapter Recap

We couldn't possibly list every investment strategy out there for this dynamic sector. Different strategies will work best at different times. Some will become obsolete. New ones will be discovered. Whatever strategies you choose, *always know you could be wrong!* Decisions to significantly overweight or underweight a sub-industry relative to the benchmark, using shorting or options strategies, or speculating on commodity prices should be based on a multitude of factors, including an assessment of risk. The point of benchmarking is to properly diversify, so make sure you always have counterstrategies built into your portfolio.

- There are numerous ways to invest in the Energy sector. These include investing directly in commodities, utilizing indexes or mutual funds, or buying the stocks themselves.
- Trading the commodities directly offers the best way to speculate on oil and natural gas prices. However, commodities can be highly volatile.
- Investors can enhance returns by overweighting and underweighting Energy sub-industries based on a variety of high-level drivers. For example, EES tends to outperform O&G during periods of rising oil prices.
- An advanced strategy involves making bets on firms with different business lines within sub-industries like buying an E&P company producing natural gas and shorting another that produces oil.

Appendix
Energy Sector Resources

The resources available for analyzing the Energy sector are numerous. Statistics on oil and natural gas supply and demand are widely available, the vast majority of which are free. This appendix lists a variety of publications and websites providing nearly all the data you need for comprehensive sector analysis.

Two widely used sources for worldwide oil industry statistics are the International Energy Agency (IEA) and the Energy Information Administration (EIA). Both organizations provide free, detailed statistics for all things Energy, including comprehensive reports with analyses and forecasts. The EIA is the statistical arm of the US Department of Energy, and thus provides the most up-to-date information available pertaining to the US Energy sector. The EIA publishes weekly inventory data for both oil and natural gas and monthly data on demand. Both organizations provide detailed statistics for the oil markets, but the EIA is generally more helpful when analyzing the US natural gas market and US refining and marketing sub-industry.

For the Energy Equipment & Services industry, data is less widely available for free but can be obtained through subscription services like those offered by ODS-Petrodata Group or Rig Zone. Baker Hughes Inc. and Smith International provide free data on rig counts.

As for industry publications, one of the most helpful is the *Oil and Gas Journal* (OGJ). The OGJ is the most widely read petroleum industry publication with the latest international oil and gas news, analysis of issues and events, and important statistics on international markets and activity. The *Oil and Gas Financial Journal*, published by the same group, relates more to the sector's most important financial developments and can sometimes be even more helpful for analysts and investors.

Last, while not specifically focused on the Energy sector, you can find Fisher Investments' up-to-date views on broader markets and the economy on www.marketminder.com.

INDUSTRY PUBLICATIONS

The following publications provide relevant information to the Energy sector, primarily the Oil and Gas industry:

- *Oil and Gas Journal* (www.OGJ.com)
  - *Oil and Gas Financial Journal*
  - *Offshore*
  - *Oil, Gas and Petrochem Equipment*
- *Platts* (www.platts.com)
  - *Platts Oilgram News*
  - *Platts Oilgram Price Report*
- *Energy Intelligence* (www.energyintel.com)
  - *Petroleum Intelligence Weekly*
  - *Natural Gas Week*
- *Oil and Gas Investor* (www.oilandgasinvestor.com)
- *National Petroleum News* (www.npnweb.com)

The following are monthly publications provided by government agencies:

- Energy Information Association (www.eia.doe.gov)
  - *Monthly Energy Review*
- International Energy Agency (www.iea.org)
  - *Oil Market Report*
- American Petroleum Institute (www.api.org)
  - *Monthly Statistical Report*

The following publications provide relevant information primarily to the Energy Equipment & Services industry:

- *World Oil Magazine* (www.worldoil.com)
- *Drilling Contractor* (www.iadc.org)
- *The Land Rig Newsletter* (www.landrig.com)

HELPFUL WEBSITES

The following websites provide industry statistics:

- Energy Information Administration (www.eia.doe.gov)
- International Energy Agency (www.iea.org)
- American Petroleum Institute (www.api.org)
- Organization of Petroleum Exporting Countries (OPEC) (www.opec.org)
- BP Statistical Review of World Energy (www.bp.com)
- Platts (www.platts.com)

These websites provide statistics for the Energy Equipment & Services industry:

- Baker Hughes (www.bakerhughes.com)
- Smith International (www.smith-intl.com)
- ODS-Petrodata (www.ods-petrodata.com)
- Rig Zone (www.rigzone.com)

These websites provide information relevant to the US Refining & Marketing sub-industry:

- Environmental Protection Agency (www.epa.gov)
- National Petrochemicals and Refiners Association (www.npra.org)

This website provides information relevant to the US Oil & Gas Drilling sub-industry:

- Minerals Management Service (www.mms.gov)

Notes

CHAPTER 1: ENERGY BASICS

1. US Department of Energy, Energy Information Administration, "World Proved Reserves of Oil and Natural Gas, Most Recent Estimates" (January 9, 2007), http://www.eia.doe.gov/emeu/international/reserves.html (accessed April 9, 2008).
2. Drake Well Organization, "About Us Homepage," http://www.drakewell.org/aboutUs.php (accessed April 9, 2008).
3. US Department of Energy, Energy Information Administration, "Supply," http://www.eia.doe.gov/pub/oil_gas/petroleum/analysis_publications/oil_market_basics/supply_text.htm (accessed April 9, 2008).
4. Canadian Association of Petroleum Producers, "Oil Sands," http://www.capp.ca/default.asp?V_DOC_ID=688 (accessed April 9, 2008).
5. Robert Simpson, "A Roadmap to North American Oil Self-Sufficiency: Lessons Learned from Alberta,"*Alberta Chamber of Resources Directory 2007*, 34, http://www.acr-alberta.com/features/roadmap.pdf (accessed April 9, 2008).
6. US Department of Energy, Energy Information Administration, "International Energy Glossary: Definition of API Gravity" (June–October 2007), http://www.eia.doe.gov/emeu/iea/glossary.html (accessed April 9, 2008).

CHAPTER 2: WHAT MAKES ENERGY BURN: KEY DRIVERS OF THE ENERGY SECTOR

1. US Department of Energy, Energy Information Administration, "Table 1.7 OECD Countries and World Petroleum (Oil) Demand, 1997–Present," *March 2008 International Petroleum Monthly* (April 11, 2008), http://www.eia.doe.gov/emeu/ipsr/t17.xls (accessed May 5, 2008).
2. US Department of Energy, Energy Information Administration, "World Petroleum Consumption, Most Recent Annual Estimates, 1980–2007" (March 28, 2008), http://www.eia.doe.gov/emeu/international/RecentPetroleumConsumptionBarrelsperDay.xls (accessed May 5, 2008).
3. US Department of Energy, Energy Information Administration, "US Primary Energy Consumption by Source and Sector, 2006" (June 27, 2007), http://www.eia.doe.gov/emeu/aer/pecss_diagram.html (accessed May 8, 2008).

4. US Department of Energy, Energy Information Administration, "Petroleum 2006," *Energy Infocard-United States* http://www.eia.doe.gov/kids/infocardnew.html (accessed April 10, 2008).

5. US Department of Energy, Energy Information Administration, "World Proved Crude Oil Reserves, January, 1, 1980–January 1, 2008 Estimates" (January 14, 2008), http://www.eia.doe.gov/pub/international/iealf/crudeoilreserves.xls (accessed May 8, 2008).

6. US Department of Energy, Energy Information Administration, "World Oil Supply, 1997–Present" (April 11, 2008), http://www.eia.doe.gov/emeu/ipsr/t14.xls (accessed May 8, 2008).

7. Canadian Association of Petroleum Producers, "Industry Facts and Information: Oil Sands," http://www.capp.ca/default.asp?V_DOC_ID=688 (accessed May 8, 2008).

8. See note 2.

9. Ibid.

10. See note 4. "Natural Gas 2006."

11. US Department of Energy, Energy Information Administration, "World Electricity Generation by Fuel, 2004–2030" (May 2007), http://www.eia.doe.gov/oiaf/ieo/excel/figure_63data.xls (accessed May 5, 2008).

12. "Policymakers to Affect North American Gas Security," *Oil & Gas Journal* (January 29, 2008).

13. US Department of Energy, Energy Information Administration, "How Natural Gas Was Formed" (April 2007), http://www.eia.doe.gov/kids/energyfacts/sources/non-renewable/naturalgas.html#naturalgasformation (accessed April 10, 2008).

14. US Department of Energy, Energy Information Administration, "World Dry Natural Gas Production, Most Recent Estimates, 1980–2006" (April 15, 2008), http://www.eia.doe.gov/emeu/international/RecentNaturalGasProductionTCF.xls (accessed May 5, 2008).

15. US Department of Energy, Energy Information Administration, "US Natural Gas Imports by Country" (April 30, 2008), http://tonto.eia.doe.gov/dnav/ng/ng_move_impc_s1_a.htm (accessed May 8, 2008).

16. US Department of Energy, Energy Information Administration, "Natural Gas Consumption by End Use" (April 30, 2008), http://tonto.eia.doe.gov/dnav/ng/ng_cons_sum_dcu_nus_a.htm (accessed May 8, 2008).

17. US Department of Energy, Energy Information Administration, "World LNG Imports by Origin, 2006" (November 20, 2007), http://www.eia.doe.gov/emeu/international/LNGimp2006.html (accessed April 10, 2008).

18. Source: MSCI. The MSCI information may only be used for your internal use, may not be reproduced or redisseminated in any form and may not be used to create any financial instruments or products or any indices. The MSCI information is provided on an "as is" basis and the user of this information assumes the entire risk of any use made of this information. MSCI, each of its affiliates and each other person involved in or related to compiling, computing or creating any MSCI information (collectively, the "MSCI Parties") expressly disclaims all warranties (including, without limitation, any warranties of originality, accuracy, completeness, timeliness, non-infringement, merchantability and fitness for a particular purpose) with respect to this information. Without limiting any of the foregoing, in no event shall any MSCI Party have any liability for any direct, indirect, special, incidental, punitive, consequential (including, without limitation, lost profits) or any other damages.

19. Exxon Company Filings, 2007 10-K.

20. "Offshore Rig Review: US vs UK," Rigzone.com (January 25, 2007) http://www.rigzone.com/analysis/rigs/insight.asp?i_id=258 (accessed August 12, 2008).

CHAPTER 3: ENERGY-SECTOR BREAKDOWN

1. MSCI Barra, "Global Industry Classification Standard," http://www.mscibarra.com/products/gics/index.jsp (accessed April 10, 2008).
2. Source: MSCI. The MSCI information may only be used for your internal use, may not be reproduced or redisseminated in any form and may not be used to create any financial instruments or products or any indices. The MSCI information is provided on an "as is" basis and the user of this information assumes the entire risk of any use made of this information. MSCI, each of its affiliates and each other person involved in or related to compiling, computing or creating any MSCI information (collectively, the "MSCI Parties") expressly disclaims all warranties (including, without limitation, any warranties of originality, accuracy, completeness, timeliness, non-infringement, merchantability and fitness for a particular purpose) with respect to this information. Without limiting any of the foregoing, in no event shall any MSCI Party have any liability for any direct, indirect, special, incidental, punitive, consequential (including, without limitation, lost profits) or any other damages.
3. Ibid.
4. See note 2.
5. Ibid.
6. Rice University, The Baker Institute Energy Forum, "The Role of National Oil Companies in International Energy Markets," http://www.rice.edu/energy/research/nationaloil/index.html (accessed April 10, 2008).
7. See note 2.
8. Ibid.
9. Marathon Petroleum Company LLC, "Louisiana Refining Division" (April 9, 2007), http://www.bloomberg.com/apps/news?pid=10000087&sid=ai2PoL0XZ1zY&refer=to_world_news (accessed April 10, 2008).
10. See note 2.
11. Ibid.
12. US Department of Energy, Energy Information Administration, "International Energy Outlook 2007" (May 2007), http://www.eia.doe.gov/oiaf/ieo/coal.html (accessed May 8, 2008).
13. US Department of Energy, Energy Information Administration, "US Coal Consumption by End-Use Sector," http://www.eia.doe.gov/cneaf/coal/quarterly/html/t25p01p1.html (accessed May 8, 2008).
14. US Department of Energy, Energy Information Administration, "Basic Electricity Statistics" (November 2007), http://www.eia.doe.gov/basics/quickelectric.html (accessed May 8, 2008).
15. US Department of Energy, Energy Information Administration, "Coal Consumption in China by Sector, 2004, 2015, and 2030" (May 2007), http://www.eia.doe.gov/oiaf/ieo/excel/figure_58data.xls (accessed April 10, 2008).
16. See note 12.
17. See note 2.
18. Baker Hughes Investor Relations, "US Rig Report—Current and Historical Data" (May 1, 2008), http://investor.shareholder.com/bhi/rig_counts/rc_index.cfm (accessed May 8, 2008).

19. Baker Hughes Investor Relations, "International Rig Count Spreadsheet (monthly)" (May 6, 2008), http://investor.shareholder.com/bhi/rig_counts/rc_index.cfm (accessed May 9, 2008).
20. See note 18.
21. See note 2.
22. Ibid.
23. See note 18.

CHAPTER 4: WHY WE'LL NEVER RUN DRY

1. US Department of Energy, Energy Information Administration, "World Proved Crude Oil Reserves, January 1, 1980–January 1, 2008 Estimates" (January 14, 2008), http://www.eia.doe.gov/pub/international/iealf/crudeoilreserves.xls (accessed April 10, 2008).
2. Exxon company balance sheet as of December 31, 2007.
3. World Nuclear Association, "French Nuclear Power Program" (April 2007), http://www.world-nuclear.org/info/inf40.htm (accessed April 10, 2008).
4. US Department of Energy, Energy Information Administration, "OECD Countries and World Petroleum (Oil) Demand, 1970–2006" (March 7, 2008), http://www.eia.doe.gov/emeu/ipsr/t46.xls (accessed April 10, 2008).
5. International Energy Agency, "Key World Energy Statistics 2007," p. 42, http://www.iea.org/textbase/nppdf/free/2007/key_stats_2007.pdf?bcsi_scan_34E336E4D93AA9DD=0&bcsi_scan_filename=key_stats_2007.pdf (accessed April 10, 2008).
6. "How Long Will It Last," *Popular Mechanics*, April 2008.
7. The White House, Office of the Press Secretary, Press Release, "Fact Sheet: Energy Independence and Security Act of 2007" (December 19, 2007), http://www.white-house.gov/news/releases/2007/12/20071219-1.html (accessed May 7, 2008).
8. US Department of Energy, Energy Information Administration, "US Crude Oil Field Production" (March 25, 2008), http://tonto.eia.doe.gov/dnav/pet/hist/mcrfpus2M.htm (accessed April 10, 2008).
9. Will You Join Us, "Introduction Homepage," Chevron Corporation, http://www.willyoujoinus.com/energy-issues/supply/default.aspx (accessed April 10, 2008).
10. Brad Reagan, "America @ $100/Barrel: How Long Will the Oil Last?" *Popular Mechanics* (April 2008), http://www.popularmechanics.com/science/earth/4254875.html?page=2 (accessed May 8, 2008).
11. US Department of Energy, Energy Information Administration, "Table 4.6: OECD Countries and World Petroleum (Oil) Demand, 1970–2007" (April 11, 2008), http://www.eia.doe.gov/emeu/ipsr/t46.xls (accessed May 8, 2008).
12. Russell Gold and Ann Davis, "Oil Officials See Limit Looming on Production," *Wall Street Journal* (November 19, 2007).
13. CERA, Press Release, "No Evidence of Precipitous Fall on Horizon for World Oil Production: Global 4.5% Decline Rate Means No Near-Term Peak: CERA/HIS Study" (January 17, 2008), http://www.cera.com/aspx/cda/public1/news/pressReleases/pressReleaseDetails.aspx?CID=9203 (accessed May 8, 2008).
14. Albert Energy, "Alberta's Oil Sands," http://www.energy.gov.ab.ca/OurBusiness/oilsands.asp (accessed August 29, 2008).
15. Canada's Oil Sands, "Overview," http://www.canadasoilsands.ca/en/overview/ (accessed August 29, 2008).
16. See note 1.

17. US Geological Survey, "Arctic National Wildlife Refuge, 1002 Area, Petroleum Assessment, 1998, Including Economic Analysis" (August 24, 2005), http://pubs.usgs.gov/fs/fs-0028-01/fs-0028-01.htm (accessed April 10, 2008).

18. See note 1.

19. Nansen Saleri, "The World Has Plenty of Oil," *Wall Street Journal* (March 4, 2008), p. A17, http://online.wsj.com/article/SB120459389654809159.html?mod=opinion_main_commentaries (accessed April 9, 2008).

20. See note 19.

21. Ibid.

22. Cambridge Energy Research Associates, Press Releases, "No Evidence of Precipitous Fall on Horizon for World Oil Production" (January 17, 2008), http://www.cera.com/aspx/cda/public1/news/pressReleases/pressReleaseDetails.aspx?CID=9203 (accessed April 10, 2008).

CHAPTER 5: STAYING CURRENT: TRACKING INDUSTRY FUNDAMENTALS

1. US Department of Energy, Energy Information Administration, "World Petroleum (Oil) Demand, 2003–2007" (April 11, 2008), http://www.eia.doe.gov/emeu/ipsr/t24.xls (accessed May 8, 2008).

2. Ibid.

3. US Department of Energy, Energy Information Administration, "World Oil Supply, 2003–2007" (April 11, 2008), http://www.eia.doe.gov/emeu/international/oilproduction.html (accessed April 28, 2008).

4. Source: MSCI. The MSCI information may only be used for your internal use, may not be reproduced or redisseminated in any form and may not be used to create any financial instruments or products or any indices. The MSCI information is provided on an "as is" basis and the user of this information assumes the entire risk of any use made of this information. MSCI, each of its affiliates and each other person involved in or related to compiling, computing or creating any MSCI information (collectively, the "MSCI Parties") expressly disclaims all warranties (including, without limitation, any warranties of originality, accuracy, completeness, timeliness, non-infringement, merchantability and fitness for a particular purpose) with respect to this information. Without limiting any of the foregoing, in no event shall any MSCI Party have any liability for any direct, indirect, special, incidental, punitive, consequential (including, without limitation, lost profits) or any other damages.

CHAPTER 6: ALTERNATIVE ENERGY

1. Renewable Energy Policy Network for the 21st Century, "Renewables 2007 Global Status Report 2007," p. 2, http://www.ren21.net/pdf/RE2007_Global_Status_Report.pdf (accessed April 10, 2008).

2. US Department of Energy, Energy Information Administration, "World Consumption of Primary Energy by Energy Type and Selected Country Groups," http://www.eia.doe.gov/pub/international/iealf/table18.xls (accessed April 10, 2008).

3. US Department of Energy, Energy Information Administration, "International Energy Outlook 2007," p.4, http://www.eia.doe.gov/oiaf/ieo/pdf/0484(2007).pdf (accessed April 10, 2008).

4. US Department of Energy, Energy Information Administration, "Renewable Energy Sources: A Consumer's Guide," http://www.eia.doe.gov/neic/brochure/renew05/renewable.html (accessed April 10, 2008).

5. US Department of Energy, Energy Information Administration, "World Consumption of Primary Energy by Energy Type and Selected Country Groups, 1980–2005" (October 2, 2007), http://www.eia.doe.gov/pub/international/iealf/table18.xls (accessed April 10, 2008).

6. "Biofuel Costs Hurt Effort to Curb Oil Price," *Wall Street Journal* (November 5, 2007).

7. See note 5.

8. US Department of Energy, Energy Information Administration, "Biomass—Energy From Plant and Animal Matter," http://www.eia.doe.gov/kids/energyfacts/sources/renewable/biomass.html (accessed April 10, 2008).

9. Renewable Energy Policy Network for the 21st Century, "Renewables 2007 Global Status Report," p. 13, http://www.ren21.net/pdf/RE2007_Global_Status_Report.pdf (accessed April 10, 2008).

10. US Department of Energy, Energy Information Administration, "Ethanol Made from Corn and Other Crops" (October 2007), http://www.eia.doe.gov/kids/energyfacts/sources/renewable/ethanol.html (accessed May 8, 2008).

11. US Department of State, "Twenty in Ten: Strengthening America's Energy Security" (January 23, 2007), http://www.state.gov/g/oes/rls/fs/2007/79330.htm (accessed May 8, 2008).

12. US Government, The White House, "Fact Sheet: Energy Independence and Security Act of 2007" (December 19, 2007), http://www.whitehouse.gov/news/releases/2007/12/20071219-1.html (accessed May 8, 2008).

13. Lauren Etter, "Ethanol Craze Cools As Doubts Multiply," *Wall Street Journal* (November 28, 2007).

14. Joel K. Bourne, Jr., "Green Dreams," *National Geographic* (October 2007), http://ngm.nationalgeographic.com/2007/10/biofuels/biofuels-text (accessed April 10, 2008).

15. See note 13.

16. See note 4.

17. World Wind Energy Association, "Wind Turbines Generate More Than 1% of the Global Electricity," (February 21, 2008), http://www.wwindea.org/home/index.php?option=com_content&task=view&id=198&Itemid=43 (accessed April 10, 2008).

18. Ibid.

19. See note 4.

20. Ibid.

21. US Department of Energy, Energy Information Administration, "Types of Solar Thermal Power Plants," http://www.eia.doe.gov/kids/energyfacts/sources/renewable/solar_plants.html#Parabolic%20Troughs (accessed April 10, 2008).

22. US Department of Energy, Energy Information Administration, "Geothermal Energy—Energy from the Earth's Core" (July 2007), http://www.eia.doe.gov/kids/energyfacts/sources/renewable/geothermal.html (accessed May 8, 2008).

23. World Nuclear Association, "Plans for New Reactors Worldwide" (March 2008), http://www.world-nuclear.org/info/inf17.html (accessed April 10, 2008).

24. US Department of Energy, Energy Information Administration, "Electricity InfoCard 2006," http://www.eia.doe.gov/bookshelf/brochures/electricityinfocard/elecinfocard2006/elecinfocard.html (accessed April 10, 2008).

25. World Nuclear Association, "World Nuclear Power Reactors 2006–08 and Uranium Requirements" (July 31, 2008), http://www.world-nuclear.org/info/reactors.html (accessed April 10, 2008).

26. Ibid.
27. See note 9, p. 6–7.
28. Copyright © 2009 The McGraw-Hill Companies, Inc. Standard & Poor's including its subsidiary corporations (S&P) is a division of the McGraw-Hill Companies, Inc. Reproduction of this Work in any form is prohibited without S&P's prior written permission.
29. Ibid.

CHAPTER 7: THE TOP-DOWN METHOD

1. Matthew Kalman, "Einstein Letters Reveal a Turmoil Beyond Science," *Boston Globe* (July 11, 2006), http://www.boston.com/news/world/middleeast/articles/2006/07/11/einstein_letters_reveal_a_turmoil_beyond_science/ (accessed May 9, 2008).
2. Michael Michalko, "Combinatory Play," *Creative Thinking*, http://www.creativethinking.net/DT10_CombinatoryPlay.htm?Entry=Good (accessed May 9, 2008).
3. Gary P. Brinson, Brian D. Singer, and Gilbert L. Beebower, "Determinants of Portfolio Performance II: An Update," *The Financial Analysts Journal* 47 (1991) 3.
4. Source: MSCI. The MSCI information may only be used for your internal use, may not be reproduced or redisseminated in any form and may not be used to create any financial instruments or products or any indices. The MSCI information is provided on an "as is" basis and the user of this information assumes the entire risk of any use made of this information. MSCI, each of its affiliates and each other person involved in or related to compiling, computing or creating any MSCI information (collectively, the "MSCI Parties") expressly disclaims all warranties (including, without limitation, any warranties of originality, accuracy, completeness, timeliness, non-infringement, merchantability and fitness for a particular purpose) with respect to this information. Without limiting any of the foregoing, in no event shall any MSCI Party have any liability for any direct, indirect, special, incidental, punitive, consequential (including, without limitation, lost profits) or any other damages.
5. Ibid.
6. See note 4.
7. Ibid.
8. Ibid.
9. Ibid.

CHAPTER 9: ENERGIZE YOUR PORTFOLIO

1. Source: MSCI. The MSCI information may only be used for your internal use, may not be reproduced or redisseminated in any form and may not be used to create any financial instruments or products or any indices. The MSCI information is provided on an "as is" basis and the user of this information assumes the entire risk of any use made of this information. MSCI, each of its affiliates and each other person involved in or related to compiling, computing or creating any MSCI information (collectively, the "MSCI Parties") expressly disclaims all warranties (including, without limitation, any warranties of originality, accuracy, completeness, timeliness, non-infringement, merchantability and fitness for a particular purpose) with respect to this information. Without limiting any of the foregoing, in no event shall any MSCI Party have any liability for any direct, indirect, special, incidental, punitive, consequential (including, without limitation, lost profits) or any other damages.
2. Ibid.

Glossary

Note: The following terms are courtesy of the US Department of Energy's glossary. For more, visit them at www.eia.doe.gov.

API gravity American Petroleum Institute measure of specific gravity of crude oil or condensate in degrees. An arbitrary scale expressing the gravity or density of liquid petroleum products. The measuring scale is calibrated in terms of degrees API; it is calculated as follows: Degrees API = (141.5 / sp.gr.60 deg.F/60 deg.F) – 131.5.

Barrel A unit of volume equal to 42 US gallons.

Bbl The abbreviation for barrel(s).

bbl/d The abbreviation for barrel(s) per day.

bcf The abbreviation for billion cubic feet.

Biodiesel Any liquid biofuel suitable as a diesel fuel substitute or diesel fuel additive or extender. Biodiesel fuels are typically made from oils such as soybeans, rapeseed, or sunflowers, or from animal tallow. Biodiesel can also be made from hydrocarbons derived from agricultural products such as rice hulls.

Biofuels Liquid fuels and blending components produced from biomass (plant) feedstocks, used primarily for transportation.

Biomass Organic nonfossil material of biological origin constituting a renewable energy source.

Bitumen A naturally occurring viscous mixture, mainly of hydrocarbons heavier than pentane, that may contain sulphur compounds and that, in its natural occurring viscous state, is not recoverable at a commercial rate through a well.

BOE The abbreviation for barrels of oil equivalent (used internationally).

Btu The abbreviation for British thermal unit(s).

Christmas tree   The valves and fittings installed at the top of a gas or oil well to control and direct the flow of well fluids.

Coal bed methane   Methane is generated during coal formation and is contained in the coal microstructure. Typical recovery entails pumping water out of the coal to allow the gas to escape. Methane is the principal component of natural gas. Coal bed methane can be added to natural gas pipelines without any special treatment.

Coal gasification   The process of converting coal into gas. The basic process involves crushing coal to a powder, which is then heated in the presence of steam and oxygen to produce a gas. The gas is then refined to reduce sulfur and other impurities. The gas can be used as a fuel or processed further and concentrated into chemical or liquid fuel.

Conventional oil and natural gas production   Crude oil and natural gas that is produced by a well drilled into a geologic formation in which the reservoir and fluid characteristics permit the oil and natural gas to readily flow to the well bore.

Crude oil   A mixture of hydrocarbons that exists in liquid phase in natural underground reservoirs and remains liquid at atmospheric pressure after passing through surface separating facilities.

Crude oil stocks   Stocks of crude oil and lease condensate held at refineries, in pipelines, at pipeline terminals, and on leases.

Cubic foot (cf), natural gas   The amount of natural gas contained at standard temperature and pressure (60 degrees Fahrenheit and 14.73 pounds standard per square inch) in a cube whose edges are one foot long.

Development costs   Costs incurred to obtain access to proved reserves and to provide facilities for extracting, treating, gathering, and storing the oil and gas.

Development drilling   Drilling done to determine more precisely the size, grade, and configuration of an ore deposit subsequent to when the determination is made that the deposit can be commercially developed.

Development well   A well drilled within the proved area of an oil or gas reservoir to the depth of a stratigraphic horizon known to be productive.

Diesel fuel   A fuel composed of distillates obtained in petroleum refining operation or blends of such distillates with residual oil used in motor vehicles. The boiling point and specific gravity are higher for diesel fuels than for gasoline.

Distillate fuel oil   A general classification for one of the petroleum fractions produced in conventional distillation operations. It includes diesel fuels and fuel oils. Products known as No. 1, No. 2, and No. 4 diesel fuel are used in on-highway diesel engines, such as those in trucks and automobiles, as well as off-highway engines, such as those in railroad locomotives and agricultural machinery. Products known as No. 1, No. 2, and No. 4 fuel oils are used primarily for space heating and electric power generation.

DOE   Department of Energy.

Dry hole   An exploratory or development well found to be incapable of producing either oil or gas in sufficient quantities to justify completion as an oil or gas well.

E85   A fuel containing a mixture of 85 percent ethanol and 15 percent gasoline.

EIA   The Energy Information Administration. An independent agency within the US Department of Energy that develops surveys, collects energy data, and analyzes and models energy issues. The Agency must meet the requests of Congress, other elements within the Department of Energy, Federal Energy Regulatory Commission, the Executive Branch, its own independent needs, and assist the general public, or other interest groups without taking a policy position.

Ethanol (CH_3-CH_2OH)   A clear, colorless, flammable oxygenated hydrocarbon. Ethanol is typically produced chemically from ethylene, or biologically from fermentation of various sugars from carbohydrates found in agricultural crops and cellulosic residues from crops or wood. It is used in the US as a gasoline octane enhancer and oxygenate (blended up to 10 percent concentration). Ethanol can also be used in high concentrations (E85) in vehicles designed for its use.

Exploration drilling   Drilling done in search of new mineral deposits, on extensions of known ore deposits, or at the location of a discovery up to the time when the company decides that sufficient ore reserves are present to justify commercial exploration. Assessment drilling is reported as exploration drilling.

Field   An area consisting of a single reservoir or multiple reservoirs all grouped on, or related to, the same individual geological structural feature and/or stratigraphic condition. There may be two or more reservoirs in a field that are separated vertically by intervening impervious strata or laterally by local geologic barriers, or by both.

Fuel cell   A device capable of generating an electrical current by converting the chemical energy of a fuel (e.g., hydrogen) directly into electrical energy. Fuel cells differ from conventional electrical cells in that the active materials such as fuel and oxygen are not contained within the cell but are supplied from outside. It does not contain an intermediate heat cycle, as do most other electrical generation techniques.

Gasoline   A complex mixture of relatively volatile hydrocarbons, with or without small quantities of additives, blended to form a fuel suitable for use in spark-ignition engines. Motor gasoline, as defined in ASTM Specification D 4814 or Federal Specification VV-G-1690C, is characterized as having a boiling range of 122 to 158 degrees Fahrenheit at the 10 percent recovery point to 365 to 374 degrees Fahrenheit at the 90 percent recovery point. Motor gasoline includes conventional gasoline; all types of oxygenated gasoline, including gasohol; and reformulated gasoline; but excludes aviation gasoline. Volumetric data on blending components, such as oxygenates, are not counted in data on finished motor gasoline until the blending components are blended into the gasoline. *Note* E85 is included only in volumetric data on finished motor gasoline production and other components of product supplied.

Geothermal energy   Hot water or steam extracted from geothermal reservoirs in the earth's crust. Water or steam extracted from geothermal reservoirs can be used for geothermal heat pumps, water heating, or electricity generation.

Geothermal plant   A plant in which the prime mover is a steam turbine. The turbine is driven either by steam produced from hot water or by natural steam that derives its energy from heat found in rock.

Heavy oil   The fuel oils remaining after the lighter oils have been distilled off during the refining process. Except for start-up and flame stabilization, virtually all petroleum used in steam plants is heavy oil. Includes fuel oil numbers 4, 5, and 6; crude; and topped crude.

Hydroelectric power   The use of flowing water to produce electrical energy.

IEA   International Energy Agency.

Offshore   That geographic area that lies seaward of the coastline. In general, the coastline is the line of ordinary low water along with that portion of the coast that is in direct contact with the open sea or the line marking the seaward limit of inland water.

Oil reservoir   An underground pool of liquid consisting of hydrocarbons, sulfur, oxygen, and nitrogen trapped within a geological formation and protected from evaporation by the overlying mineral strata.

Oil shale   A sedimentary rock containing kerogen, a solid organic material.

Oil well   A well completed for the production of crude oil from at least one oil zone or reservoir.

OPEC (Organization of the Petroleum Exporting Countries)   An intergovernmental organization whose stated objective is to coordinate and unify petroleum policies among member countries. It was created at the

Baghdad Conference on September 10 to 14, 1960, by Iran, Iraq, Kuwait, Saudi Arabia, and Venezuela. The five founding members were later joined by nine other members Qatar (1961), Indonesia (1962), Libya (1962), United Arab Emirates (1967), Algeria (1969), Nigeria (1971), Ecuador (1973–1992, 2007), Gabon (1975–1994), and Angola (2007).

Petrochemicals   Organic and inorganic compounds and mixtures that include but are not limited to organic chemicals, cyclic intermediates, plastics and resins, synthetic fibers, elastomers, organic dyes, organic pigments, detergents, surface active agents, carbon black, and ammonia.

Petroleum   A broadly defined class of liquid hydrocarbon mixtures. Included are crude oil, lease condensate, unfinished oils, refined products obtained from the processing of crude oil, and natural gas plant liquids. *Note:* Volumes of finished petroleum products include nonhydrocarbon compounds, such as additives and detergents, after they have been blended into the products.

Photovoltaic cell (PVC)   An electronic device consisting of layers of semiconductor materials fabricated to form a junction (adjacent layers of materials with different electronic characteristics) and electrical contacts and being capable of converting incident light directly into electricity (direct current).

Production costs   Costs incurred to operate and maintain wells and related equipment and facilities, including depreciation and applicable operating costs of support equipment and facilities and other costs of operating and maintaining those wells and related equipment and facilities.

Propane (C_3H_8)   A normally gaseous straight-chain hydrocarbon. It is a colorless paraffinic gas that boils at a temperature of –43.67 degrees Fahrenheit. It is extracted from natural gas or refinery gas streams.

Refiner   A firm or the part of a firm that refines products or blends and substantially changes products, or refines liquid hydrocarbons from oil and gas field gases, or recovers liquefied petroleum gases incident to petroleum refining and sells those products to resellers, retailers, reseller/retailers, or ultimate consumers. *Refiner* includes any owner of products that contracts to have those products refined and then sells the refined products to resellers, retailers, or ultimate consumers.

Refinery capacity utilization   Ratio of the total amount of crude oil, unfinished oils, and natural gas plant liquids run through crude oil distillation units to the operable capacity of these units.

Reserve   That portion of the demonstrated reserve base that is estimated to be recoverable at the time of determination. The reserve is derived by applying a recovery factor to that component of the identified coal resource designated as the demonstrated reserve base.

Reserve additions　The estimated original, recoverable, salable, and new proved reserves credited to new fields, new reservoirs, new gas purchase contracts, amendments to old gas purchase contracts, or purchase of gas reserves in place that occurred during the year and had not been previously reported. Reserve additions refer to domestic in-the-ground natural gas reserve additions and do not refer to interstate pipeline purchase agreements; contracts with foreign suppliers; or coal gas, SNG, or LNG purchase arrangements.

Reserve revisions　Changes to prior year-end proved reserves estimates, either positive or negative, resulting from new information other than an increase in proved acreage (extension). Revisions include increases of proved reserves associated with the installation of improved recovery techniques or equipment. They also include correction of prior year arithmetical or clerical errors and adjustments to prior year-end production volumes to the extent that these alter reserves estimates.

Residual fuel oil　A general classification for the heavier oils, known as No. 5 and No. 6 fuel oils, that remain after the distillate fuel oils and lighter hydrocarbons are distilled away in refinery operations.

Royalty　A contractual arrangement providing a mineral interest that gives the owner a right to a fractional share of production or proceeds there from, that does not contain rights and obligations of operating a mineral property, and that is normally free and clear of exploration, developmental, and operating costs, except production taxes.

Shut in　Closed temporarily; wells and mines capable of production may be shut in for repair, cleaning, inaccessibility to a market, and so on.

Solar energy　The radiant energy of the sun, which can be converted into other forms of energy, such as heat or electricity.

Unconventional oil and natural gas production　An umbrella term for oil and natural gas that is produced by means that do not meet the criteria for conventional production.

Well　A hole drilled in the earth for the purpose of (a) finding or producing crude oil or natural gas; or (b) producing services related to the production of crude or natural gas.

Wind energy　Kinetic energy present in wind motion that can be converted to mechanical energy for driving pumps, mills, and electric power generators.

Wind turbine　Wind energy conversion device that produces electricity; typically three blades rotating about a horizontal axis and positioned up-wind of the supporting tower.

About the Authors

Aaron M. Azelton (San Francisco, California) is an equity research analyst covering the Energy sector at Fisher Investments. Aaron graduated from the University of California at Berkeley with a B.A. in Economics. He has been with Fisher Investments since 2002. Aaron grew up in Santa Monica, California and is currently living in San Francisco.

Andrew S. Teufel (San Francisco, California) has been a member of Fisher Investments research staff since 1995 and is currently Co-President and Director of Research. Prior to joining the firm, he worked at Bear Stearns as a corporate finance analyst. He is a graduate of the University of California at Berkeley, and has lectured at the Haas School of Business on topics in investment management. Andrew has conducted hundreds of investment seminars and educational workshops throughout the US and the United Kingdom. He also serves as Editor-in-Chief of MarketMinder.com.

Index